REMAKING EASTERN EUROPE –
ON THE POLITICAL ECONOMY OF TRANSITION

International Studies in Economics and Econometrics

VOLUME 23

The titles published in this series are listed at the end of this volume.

Remaking Eastern Europe – On the Political Economy of Transition

by

Jozef M. van Brabant

KLUWER ACADEMIC PUBLISHERS
DORDRECHT / BOSTON / LONDON

Library of Congress Cataloging-in-Publication Data

Brabant, Jozef M. van.
Remaking eastern Europe : on the political economy of transition / Jozef M. van Brabant.
p. cm. -- (International studies in economics and econometrics ; v. 23)
Includes bibliographical references and index.
ISBN 0-7923-0955-3 (alk. paper)
1. Europe, Eastern--Economic policy. 2. Europe, Eastern--Foreign economic relations. 3. Council for Mutual Economic Assistance.
I. Title. II. Series.
HC244.B72745 1990
338.947--dc20 90-5223

ISBN 0-7923-0955-3

Published by Kluwer Academic Publishers,
P.O. Box 17, 3300 AA Dordrecht, The Netherlands.

Kluwer Academic Publishers incorporates
the publishing programmes of
D. Reidel, Martinus Nijhoff, Dr W. Junk and MTP Press.

Sold and distributed in the U.S.A. and Canada
by Kluwer Academic Publishers,
101 Philip Drive, Norwell, MA 02061, U.S.A.

In all other countries, sold and distributed
by Kluwer Academic Publishers Group,
P.O. Box 322, 3300 AH Dordrecht, The Netherlands.

Printed on acid-free paper

Printed in the Netherlands

To Claus Wittich - for friendship

Preface

This compact volume is meant as a modest contribution to the ongoing debate on how to transform in particular the radically reforming Eastern European economies into more productive sociopolitical organizations. Although my main focus here is on the economics of reform and east-west assistance, I have tried to embed the multiple technical aspects of restructuring such a resource allocation into the context of remaking Eastern Europe. That the volume coincides with the seminal transformations of the communist countries of Eastern Europe is, of course, not fortuitous. But I shall have much less to say about the political transitions from communism to parliamentary democracy, except the ways in which the latter may bolster or hinder the hoped-for economic mutations.

In taking stock of where I stand on the issue of "radical reform" of planned economies in general and the CMEA in particular, both still moving targets, I have benefited greatly from participation in formal and informal conferences on economic reform. The product has also profited from many informal discussions and exchanges of views among friends and colleagues, including those entrusted with and purely interested in efforts on the overall topic of the study launched from within the broad context of the United Nations, my at times reluctant employer.

Although it would be churlish on my part not to acknowledge with gratitude my undeniable debt to the brainstorming and doubts that all these contacts have afforded over the years, I hasten to add that no single individual or institution should be held responsible for any of the opinions expressed here. Finally, although this monograph was written in my "spare" time, while employed by the United Nations, I wish to emphasize most emphatically that the opinions expressed here are mine and do not necessarily reflect those that may be held by the United Nations at large and the United Nations Secretariat in New York in particular.

I would be remiss if I did not explicitly single out the bedrock of discussions, exchanges of views, and other contacts on so many different issues, including Eastern Europe, that I have been privileged to enjoy with Claus Wittich during so many years. Indeed he was present at the gestation of this product. In dedicating this volume to him, I wish to acknowledge my admiration for his fine palate and renaissance mind, both of which have made for so many enjoyable days in spite of it all.

Jozef M. van Brabant
New York, 31 July 1990

Table of contents

Abbreviations

ADB	Asian Development Bank
BTPA	bilateral trade and payments agreement
CEEC	Committee for European Economic Co-operation
CMEA	Council for Mutual Economic Assistance
CoCom	Coordinating Committee for Multilateral Export Controls
CPE	centrally planned economy
CSCE	Conference on Security and Cooperation in Europe
CSFR	Czech and Slovak Federative Republic
DE	developing economy
DME	developed market economy
EBRD	European Bank for Reconstruction and Development
EC	European Communities
ECA	Economic Cooperation Administration
ECCS	European Community for Coal and Steel
ECU	European currency unit
EFTA	European Free Trade Association
EIB	European Investment Bank
EMS	European Monetary System
EPU	European Payments Union
ERP	European Recovery Program
ESOP	employee share-ownership plan
ETN	edinnaya tovarnaya nomenklatura
EWP	east-west price
FDI	foreign direct investment
FRG	Federal Republic of Germany
FTO	foreign trade organization
Fund	International Monetary Fund
GARIOA	Government Aid and Relief in Occupied Areas
GATT	General Agreement on Tariffs and Trade
GDR	German Democratic Republic
GSP	General System of Preferences
IBEC	International Bank for Economic Cooperation
IBRD	International Bank for Reconstruction and Development
IEO	international economic organization
IIB	International Investment Bank
IMF	International Monetary Fund
ME	market economy
MFA	Multi-fibre Arrangement
MFN	most-favored nation
MFT	state monopoly of foreign trade and payments
MIGA	Multilateral Investment Guarantee Agency

MPE	modified planned economy
MSA	Mutual Security Act
NATO	North Atlantic Treaty Organization
NIE	newly industrializing economy
ODA	official development assistance
OECD	Organisation for Economic Co-operation and Development
OEEC	Organisation for European Economic Co-operation
PET	planned economy in transition
PHARE	Pologne/Hongrie: assistance à la restructuration économique
RPE	reformed planned economy
SEI	socialist economic integration
SITC	standard industrial trade nomenclature
SOE	state-owned enterprise
STC	scientific-technological cooperation
TNC	transnational corporation
TR	transferable ruble
TRP	transferable ruble price
UN	United Nations
UNDP	United Nations Development Programme
UNECE	United Nations Economic Commission for Europe
USSR	Union of Soviet Socialist Republics
WMP	world market price
World Bank	International Bank for Reconstruction and Development
WTO	Warsaw Treaty Organization

List of tables

Introduction

Eastern Europe[1] has been in the forefront of international attention since the evolutionary modifications initiated in Hungary and Poland in mid-1989 and the extraordinary revolutionary changes in the political makeup of the entire area, including the Soviet Union, since then. These transitions, one at a time, have been swelling a flood that has rapidly gushed across one of the critical watersheds of postwar economic, political, strategic, and security arrangements in Europe. For the time being, although the foundations of that divide have been severely damaged, it has not yet been replaced by a more robust structure.

It would be very illuminating indeed to place these developments in their appropriate perspective in a comprehensive manner. Unfortunately, this is something that I cannot hope to accomplish in this volume. But the basic building blocks of such a comprehensive analysis will be set forth in brief in Section 1 as the backdrop against which the message that I wish to convey could be more fully assessed by those better versed in those matters. In the next section, I detail the objectives of this study. Then I define the arena into which it should properly be placed. A justification for the terminology embraced here is provided in Section 4. Next I look at the wider ramifications of economic and sociopolitical reforms in Eastern Europe for the global framework. Finally, I guide the reader through the ten chapters of the volume.

1. The new international setting

In more than one respect, the latter half of 1989 was an extraordinary semester for Eastern Europe. Event propelled event in the political sphere throughout the period. It all began with the round-table negotiations between the Communist Government and Party, on the one hand, and the literally just barely legitimized opposition in Poland, on the other. This process had gained some impetus from the parliamentary elections in the Soviet Union in early 1989 which exhibited unexpected briskness and vibrancy. By mid-year, the Soviet Union's political landscape, which had been so stale for so long, was being radically altered under impulse of the remarkably disputatious first session of the newly elected Congress of People's Deputies. Furthermore, the new *Sejm* dominated by the opposition was in session in Poland.

Not only that, the barbed wire had been removed at Hungary's border with Austria. This had perhaps been inspired by the Communist Government's desi-

[1] Eastern Europe here means Bulgaria, Czechoslovakia, the German Democratic Republic (GDR), Hungary, Poland, Rumania, and the Soviet Union. When the context makes it clear, I occasionally exclude the Soviet Union from this concept.

re to extend a symbolic gesture, in the form of a framed part of the "iron curtain," to President George Bush on the occasion of his historic visit in June 1989. This in turn led to a mass exodus of GDR citizens, in the first instance to Hungary and later to Czechoslovakia and Poland as well, who hoped to make it across Austria and into the Federal Republic of Germany (FRG), where they would quickly obtain citizenship and refugee assistance.

Also in Hungary, a new constitution declared the country to be in principle a market economy (ME), although to date this has not quite been carried out in practice. Before the end of the third quarter of 1989, a new Government led by noncommunists was in charge for the first time since postwar stabilization. Before the year was out, Party and/or Government had changed peacefully throughout Eastern Europe, except in Rumania. Most of the Communist Parties had transformed themselves into a political force of more social-democratic leanings. All of these new Governments, at times with Party backing, were committed, albeit to different degrees, to pursuing incisive changes in socioeconomic and political systems.

The dramatic political events themselves, and their subsequent repercussions, owe a good deal to the revocation of the constitutional guarantee of one party's monopoly over sociopolitical life, and often over society as a whole. In most cases, this has since led to the legalization of multiparty systems in the political process. In the economic arena, the essential pillars of an ME are being emplaced by recognizing multiple ownership forms and scarcity indicators as basic guides to resource allocation. In any case, detailed state planning is being forcefully abandoned.

But events have by no means been confined to radical changes in the domestic societal makeup of Eastern Europe. In fact, in consequence of the New Thinking in the Soviet Union and the abrupt assertiveness of the new leaderships throughout Eastern Europe, major changes in international affairs have been crystallizing. When I embarked on this research venture in early February 1990, any lingering doubts about having entered a new phase of postwar evolution was abruptly dispelled by three successive events in Moscow in a matter of less than a week. Arguably foremost was the renunciation on 7 February 1990, after three days of passionate, at times fierce, factional debate, of the constitutional monopoly of the Communist Party's political power by the Plenum of the Central Committee of the Communist Party of the Soviet Union. In purely historical terms, this abdication of the Party's exclusiveness was undoubtedly the most striking development of Soviet *perestroyka* since Mikhail S. Gorbachev first launched his reform campaign in 1985. It also signaled a unique shift in the Soviet Union's revolutionary fervor, including with respect to international economic and political affairs.

Making this constatation is not good enough. Unfortunate as it may be, nobody seems to have the faintest idea as to whether this unexpected reversal of the seminal acquisition of the Bolshevik Revolution will be fast or slow, whether it will be reversible or lead to steady progress toward pluralization and parliamentary democracy or perhaps even to the disintegration of the Soviet Federation. The latter would almost certainly unleash a divisive nationalistic backlash with related revendications, some of whose excesses have painfully come to the fore during the past two years or so.

Toward the end of that week, on 9 February 1990, the United States and the Soviet Union cleared the tables for a series of sweeping arms control agreements, which have since been under intensive negotiations at the fairly technical level; some were signed at the superpower summit in May-June 1990. Not only did this breakthrough provide evidence of a solid rapprochement between the two superpowers and the *de facto* end of the Cold War. It also may mean the gateway to more durable cooperation in many other domains.

To cap it all, on 10 February 1990, in a matter of hours, Chancellor Helmut Kohl and General Secretary Mikhail S. Gorbachev not only recognized the inevitability of German reunification - that long hallowed goal of *Wiedervereinigung* that instills so much fear in so many people. This meeting of minds also settled the principles to govern form, pace, and timing of the fusion of the two Germanies (*Neue Zürcher Zeitung*, 12 February 1990, p. 2), in spite of the very substantial problems of melding two diverse countries, if perhaps not too wholly estranged nations. Furthermore, it left no doubt that unification in the end will entail momentous changes in the balance of Central Europe, in spite of the sovereignty of the Big Four (France, the Soviet Union, the United Kingdom, and the United States) over Berlin and, in the absence of a peace treaty, in spite of their residual responsibilities for Germany as a whole; this issue is now slated to be settled during the next sitting of the Conference on Security and Cooperation in Europe (CSCE), probably in December 1990. Of course, many other countries are wary of the prospect of Germany being unified without there being a firm peace treaty. Lip service was paid to the need for the two Germanies in their negotiations to take into account the interests of the rest of Europe. But this simply amounted to a polite way of not circumventing the allied status in Germany - largely a "courtesy, merely to enable them to wind up their residual limitations on German sovereignty" (Davidson 1990, p. 4). German reunification is by now certain and it will come soon, even before this book sees the light of day; furthermore, it will be clear-cut, a submersion of the GDR into the FRG. This undoubtedly opens a new, rather unexpected, chapter in Europe's postwar evolution. It poses all kinds of dilemmas for east and west alike. If further evidence was needed, this agreement signaled the end of the Cold War. Whether it inaugurated a durable phase of more productive relationships between east, west, south, and north remains to be seen, however.

By anybody's standard, this was an extraordinary sequence of events that would have been unthinkable less than a year earlier. Even so, the key infrastructure that separates east and west remains for now, albeit much weakened. The reinforced concrete necessary to construct a solid buttress for further societal change in east and west is not yet even mixed, let alone paved out. Yet, that is precisely what is required so that the momentum in Eastern Europe will not be prematurely halted for lack of enduring support. Clearly, the irreversible transformations there have the wide support of the population at large. They may also help to strengthen the still ongoing shifts in thinking about the future of Eastern Europe. But the turning toward political democracy and greater marketization of economic affairs has been gathering western applause, even from among the erstwhile most implacable critics of socialism.

Whether these trends can be solidified and Europe as a continent remade in the years to come through further evolutionary change, rather than revolution, is predicated on a wide range of desirable developments, whose emergence is not at all ensured at this juncture. Some can be analyzed at this stage. Others will necessarily leap into the forefront of political attention under impact of mutations in the world at large and Eastern Europe in particular.

One of the critical features that can be examined at this stage is the transition from the Europe divided at Yalta to a continent that, if not quite united, at least assiduously seeks to enhance the depth and breadth of this intercourse. This transformation has many angles, perhaps best symbolized by the notion that there ought to be a "common European home" with open windows and doors for all Europeans. The atmosphere therein should convey all the positive that "Europe" has stood for over the centuries. But it should be shaped in particular by the notions that have been jelling over the last decade or so. This implies greater harmony, certainly fewer recriminations, in strategic affairs, in commerce and finance, in the mobility of individuals, in international economic relations more generally, in cultural exchanges and cross-fertilization, in the political framework of European cooperation, and many other endeavors.

These desirable seminal transformations and their implications will keep scores of researchers, civil servants, and politicians occupied for many years to come. To assemble all of the issues into one coherent volume even at this stage would undoubtedly be well worth the attempt, if only because of the vexing confusion about east-west and European relations that continues to prevail. To contend that I have endeavored to do so here would be unseemly arrogance as I have neither the talents nor the ambition to project my views onto so vast a canvas in this book. My purposes are accordingly far more modest.

2. Objectives of the study

On the strength of my comparative advantage, my contribution to the debate on the economic aspects of European cooperation in support of the ongoing reform in Eastern Europe can be twofold. One is in the area of applying economic techniques in setting the framework within which the economics of transition for the erstwhile centrally planned economies (CPEs) could be analyzed. Also, I hope to place this discourse within the context of how best to solicit and manage regional and international support for such a definitive rupture with traditional central planning. In this respect, I shall, of course, also have to review the options of economic cooperation within the context of the Council for Mutual Economic Assistance (CMEA).

I should like to make it most emphatically clear, however, that I do not wish to confine this study to the pure economics of the transition. The latter is evolving in a convoluted international environment. There is therefore a politics of the transition. This has pronounced short-term causes and effects. It also has longer-term implications for Eastern Europe, relations on the European continent, and the character of the global framework of cooperation, not only in economic matters. To identify correctly this variety of causes and analyze their plausible repercussions, one must first gain a better understanding of what has been happening all over Eastern Europe.

The societal transformations in Eastern Europe since mid-1989, and the promise of more to come in the months ahead, have exhibited their own dynamics. Circumstances of time and place in each country in isolation have been crucial in charting the course and intensity of events since mid-1989. Nevertheless, there is also a considerable degree of commonality in the immediate causalities of the unprecedented sociopolitical transformations. There are furthermore many common aspirations that characterize the economies in transition and their near-term policy goals.

It may be useful to bear in mind five dominant traits of the transition regimes (Wagner 1989). The most obvious force behind the disturbances in Eastern Europe has been widespread popular dissatisfaction with the distribution of consumer goods and services. Many people appear to have become convinced that, after forty years of planning, the central planning system is simply unable to satisfy wants. Second, there has been widespread consternation that a powerful group of state and Party bureaucrats have been shielded from - and in some cases have insulated themselves against - the generally poor economic situation in their respective societies. Their privileges have not only protected them against economic hardships and crises, but have even kept them indifferent to popular feelings, perhaps through their separation from, what should have been, their primary constituency - workers and peasants. An important related factor is the considerable power of this privileged caste to decide a wide range of diverse topics without any public debate at all on the issues; hence, the widespread popular feeling of being powerless, or even disregarded, in the process. Fourth, there is a broadly shared feeling that the socialist system has proved itself to be unable to keep pace with "capitalism." Not only that, socialist systems have been eroding their fiscal base, thus yielding substantial budget deficits and, in some countries, palpable open and repressed inflation in spite of long-standing socialist promises of price and market stability. Furthermore, the ever-increasing obsolescence of the capital stock, the inability of public officials to identify quickly proper areas for capital renewal and to ensure that projects are undertaken efficiently, the flagrant falling behind in the scientific and technological race, and related economic realities have demoralized at least the intelligentsia and professional layers of society. Many other actors have adopted a cynical work ethic and their commitment to participation in society has become perfunctory at best. Finally, there exists a shared perception that the ruling totalitarian communist ideology failed to innovate solutions to even the most urgent problems of the day. It has also forcefully suppressed philosophical and religious dissent, something for which the communist regime lacks legitimacy to an even larger degree than is the case in the economic domains.

These and related factors can all be seen as immediate causes of the Eastern European "refolutions," as Timothy Garton Ash (1989, p. 309) referred to the mutations of the historic choice between reform and revolution in much of Central Europe.[2] This combination of aspiration toward economic reform, so-

[2] I shall be using this notion to denote Czechoslovakia, the GDR, Hungary, and Poland. I am well aware that the concept has a myriad of cultural, historical, political, and other connotations (see Garton 1989, Konrád 1984). These are extremely interesting, but I shall not examine them here.

cial revolution, and political emancipation from rigid, oftentimes mindless, Party control is a very complex sociological phenomenon. As János Kornai (1990a) so passionately emphasizes, the transitional economies of Eastern Europe are societies where public ownership has dominated for over forty years, enabling an almighty bureaucracy with uncounted tentacles to reach throughout society into the life of virtually every citizen. Under the circumstances, sovereignty of the individual; autonomy and private property; business, political, and intellectual freedoms; the institutions of democracy; and the rule of law were suppressed for decades. Small wonder that the revolutions of late 1989 and early 1990 have led to a revendication with a vengeance, for example, as regards privatization of state assets. As a result, political and emotional issues get inextricably intertwined with economic rationality as to the best ways to reach certain objectives.[3] Yet, it would be instructive to distinguish between economic rationality and the more emotional, political, and ideological *obiter dicta* so pervasive in the recent literature on reform. As far as economic management is concerned, a host of questions revolve around the overwhelming influence of the erstwhile political monopoly of the Communist Party, the enormous power of the government bureaucracy over macro- and microeconomic affairs, and the highly monopolized economic structure, particularly in industry. The revolutions in Eastern Europe were essentially determined by a groundswell of opposition to the entrenched political and bureaucratic powers in place. But these rapid changes could not have occurred without the seminal changes in the Soviet Union. This New Thinking has also unleashed a variety of compensatory forces that may help to redesign Europe, if not from the ground up at least through major surgery in key constituent parts.

The rapprochement that has thus become thinkable once again has not remained unanswered in Western Europe. Changes in Europe as a whole have been crystallizing in ways that could not even have been dreamed of a year ago or so. Because there is now more than at any time since 1945 a chance for remaking Europe, various types of assistance from west to east, primarily in Europe, have been coming to the fore.

Assistance can be divided into financial aid and what could be rendered by transmitting knowledge and experience, primarily in the business and economic domains but also in policies and legal systems. Financial assistance is a two-edged sword. By ostensibly providing a breathing space in the need to adjust macroeconomic policies it can delay necessary reform, as was so evident in the cases of Hungary and Poland during most of the 1970s. If policy makers in these countries do not wish, or are unable, to open up their economies to broad competition from world markets, even the most generous amount of western financial assistance will in the end be so much more money down the drain. This imperative should not be lost sight of, not even in the event of emergencies.

[3] This is a factor not limited to privatization in Eastern Europe, however. Indeed, the more general debate has inevitably been influenced more by ideology, political philosophy, and real-life expediency than by the niceties of economic analysis (Vickers and Yarrow 1988, p. 2).

Perhaps most important in this context is whether Europe can bring itself to unite and thus reinforce its position in the world and buffer the smaller and weaker countries on the continent against the crosswinds of national chauvinism and hegemonic behavior on the part of big powers. It will also exert a powerful influence on revitalizing the idea of unifying the continent. In a narrower perspective, European integration should foster more rapid economic development, hence the buildup of wealth, in the weaker countries of the continent and thus perhaps become a magnet for economic progress elsewhere in the global economy.

The type and manner of assistance provided by the west to the east can influence the future *Gestalt* of Europe. Critical here is whether a feeling of European solidarity can take root. This I hold to be even more important than the embracement of political democracy in Eastern Europe. The most immediate repercussions of the transformations in Eastern Europe are in Europe itself, especially the way in which the two halves will succeed in overcoming their long-standing prejudices and real differences. These changes have implications also for the rest of the world community. One such instance is the relationship between individual countries (such as Soviet-Japanese or American-Soviet relations). Another is the role of official development assistance (ODA) from Eastern Europe primarily to a few favored socialist developing economies (DEs). Beyond that, however, one can discern in a more medium perspective the emergence of a new environment for global cooperation in many endeavors, including in managing the global economy through the formal international economic organizations (IEOs) established in the postwar period.

The modifications in Europe are crystallizing at a time that major changes in the global economy are occurring. In and of themselves, they require a reexamination of the postwar global economic framework centered on the General Agreement on Tariffs and Trade (GATT) for commercial policy issues, the International Monetary Fund (IMF or Fund) for global monetary issues, and the International Bank for Reconstruction and Development (IBRD or World Bank[4]) for international finance. Whether the institutions have been as successful as they could have been deserves to be reassessed, certainly against the backdrop of the degree to which they can respond to the rapidly changing international environment in general and attendant seminal shifts in the world economy in particular. I have in mind not only the revolutionary changes of the past months in Eastern Europe. At stake indeed are the transformations in the world economy of the past two decades or so and the radically changed thinking about global economic organization that has come to the fore to some degree under impetus of Soviet *perestroyka*.

In addition, the traditional bifurcation along military security lines, both in the American-Soviet confrontation and the opposing military blocs of the Warsaw Treaty Organization (WTO), or Warsaw Pact, and the North Atlantic Treaty Organization (NATO), has been losing much of its *raison d'être* over the past

[4] There exists a specific nomenclature for describing the World Bank in the strict sense and in conjunction with its various affiliated agencies (Brabant 1990a, p. 254). But this will be ignored here for now as the refinement is immaterial to the argument that I wish to make.

several years. The New Thinking in the Soviet Union and the recognition of the ever-growing interdependence in international affairs more generally have contributed measurably to this renaissance in international affairs. However, there is as yet no consensus on how best to take maximum advantage of this internationalization, while mitigating its adverse aspects. Remaking the postwar global framework is not something that can be left to economics alone or to the discipline's practitioners for that matter.

Aside from security, defense, and political angles, the transformation process in Eastern Europe is also being assisted by a wide variety of national and international, governmental and private, multilateral and bilateral actors. The diverse behaviors of some of these actors individually may be examined from within a pure economic framework. Others properly belong in the ill-defined purview of and discourse on "international relations." Together the behavioral interactions of this multitude of agents involved in the economics of transition can be gauged only from within the context of international relations - economics alone simply will not suffice.

Furthermore, the economics of transition is thus far uncharted territory. The western-trained economist and the western specialist in Eastern European economic affairs may have a fair understanding of how the market works and what was done in the process of turning quasi MEs in the postwar period into CPEs. He or she will also have a fair comprehension of what went awry with administrative management in CPEs and what should be done to correct these negative developments. How to get from here to there, however, is a field wide open to innovative thinking and, in the end, to the hard test of practical validation through experimentation. Rather than construct this program from the ground up, I shall argue that several critical experiences of the postwar period should be carefully reassessed. From them it might be possible not only to get a better grip on the economics of transition, but importantly to say something more positive and concrete about the sequencing of the various policy actions and institutional transformations that together make up the transition phase.

3. Focus of the study

One core point of this book is advocacy of a fairly prominent role for the CMEA in buttressing the economic transition process in Eastern Europe. This will undoubtedly raise eyebrows in east and west alike. I hope to explain my positions cogently in Chapters 1, 2, and 9 in particular. It should be borne in mind, of course, that the CMEA is a regional organization whose behavior is the outcome of complex geopolitical, ideological, security, and economic impulses and motivations. Its study can therefore not be confined solely to fostering economic interaction, but must encompass most notably political and security affairs and indeed the position of the member countries in the global context.

The CMEA is a complex organization that finds itself at this stage in considerable disarray. It is often claimed that it includes countries from four continents - Africa, Asia, Europe, and Latin America. But this assertion must be placed in its proper perspective. As far as its membership is concerned, various tiers can be distinguished. First of all there are eleven full members, including one (Albania) that is inactive. In addition to Eastern Europe as defined here, all of which, except the GDR, are founder members of the CMEA, other active full members are Cuba, Mongolia, and Vietnam. All three have a special developing country status in the CMEA. These countries endorsed the CMEA's charter and thereby expressed their willingness to subscribe to the purposes and means of the CMEA as a regional organization entrusted with the promotion of what has become known as socialist economic integration (SEI). Whether this objective is still a realistic one after the seminal changes in Eastern Europe needs to be carefully weighed.

In addition to full membership, the Council recognizes three other types of involvement with the CMEA. A second type of participation is associate membership. This status means essentially that the associate fully participates in some activities of the CMEA upon which the various partners have mutually agreed. The only country with that status is Yugoslavia.

A third variety of participants have obtained a cooperant status by concluding special bilateral agreements with the CMEA. These usually envisage the creation of special bilateral cooperation commissions that in due course will define areas in which collaboration between the cooperant and the CMEA is to be strengthened and enhanced. This status is presently occupied by Finland and eight noncommunist DEs. The latter are Afghanistan, Angola, Ethiopia, Iraq, Mexico, Mozambique, Nicaragua, and Democratic Yemen.[5] These countries as a rule obtain special facilities that enable them to increase their trade with the full CMEA members more rapidly than would most other DEs. Cooperant status is probably more significant for fostering scientific-technological cooperation (STC) and facilitating the reciprocal flow of pertinent economic, commercial, and other information. These selected countries may also be granted a larger share of the development assistance that the CMEA countries individually and as a group extend (Brabant 1990d).

Finally, the CMEA has a varying number of observers. These are by and large other members of the traditional world socialist system (China, North Korea, and since the late 1970s Laos), a wide range of DEs that do not covet more formal ties, and international organizations that are at times invited to share in the experience of some CMEA deliberations and even more formal conferences.

There should be no doubt, however, that this monograph is devoted to Eastern Europe as defined here and especially to the economies that have already wedded their socioeconomic policies to seeking market-oriented economic reforms. In choosing this focal theme, I have no intention of belittling the potential advantages that non-European countries may derive from some form of association with the CMEA. Neither do I wish to ignore the place of Albania and Yugoslavia. In a number of respects, the latter is also an economy in transition and recognized as such in much of the ongoing east-west discussions. Albania may soon join the group of transitional economies.

[5] Northern and southern Yemen were reunified in May 1990 as Yemen, essentially under the leadership of the Democratic Yemen. The new country has probably assumed all treaty obligations of Democratic Yemen, but I have no solid evidence on this.

More specifically, the central question here revolves around the ways in which the international community at large could facilitate the realization of the commitment of some Eastern European countries to move away decisively, once and for all, from detailed central planning through a wide-ranging bureaucratic apparatus controlled by the Party *apparat* and its associated *nomenklatura*, and what role regional economic cooperation, including in the CMEA context, can play therein. For that reason, I shall have little to say about CMEA members other than the active European ones. Although the Soviet Union has not yet expressed a firm resolve to seek greater market orientation and hence organic integration in the world economy, that country cannot, of course, be excluded from the analysis. Because it unquestionably constitutes the largest market for Eastern Europe and happens to be the major political and military power in the area, it is *the* key player in the international "affairs" of Eastern Europe.

Moreover, whatever may have gone awry in the economic relations between the Soviet Union and Eastern Europe should not deflect attention from the fact that there are comparative advantages to be reaped even within the Eastern European context, some of which have emanated from the many ways in which CMEA cooperation proceeded for more than four decades. To exploit these static comparative advantages and indeed to deepen them into dynamic ones that can emerge from profound structural changes to be pursued with determination over the next few years, it will be necessary to embrace the proper policies, institutions, and policy instruments as seen from within the context of greater market orientation in Eastern Europe.

4. Terminology

With the overt commitment to seeking seminal changes in the traditional management of the Eastern European economies, one faces a major problem of nomenclature. All countries that figure prominently here used to be referred to as CPEs. This designation is becoming less and less appropriate, quite apart from the fact that several of these countries themselves have resolved to dissociate themselves explicitly from the CPE label, or, for that matter, from any grouping that would explicitly acknowledge these economies as differing in aims and substance from MEs. They have recently been quite adamant on ensuring such an "equal" treatment in numerous international fora.

I shall be using the familiar terminology here only as a shorthand. The choice is somewhat arbitrary. Nevertheless, few independent observers will dispute that these countries unquestionably exhibit far more features of traditional central planning than of market orientation. One could, therefore, justify using the traditional CPE terminology. Some CMEA members, including Rumania and the Soviet Union, have thus far remained CPEs for all practical purposes. Using the label as indicated would hence not require a justification.

There is no all-around satisfactory solution, short of identifying these countries by their individual name tags, something that would render the analysis rather cumbersome. In what follows, I shall use the designation CPE to refer to countries that have not yet set in train seminal steps toward market orientation, even though some may already have expressed a firm political commitment to seeking radical economic reform or have already incorporated this into some coherent program for decisive change. The Eastern European countries that have experimented with various forms of decentralization over the past two decades or so and whose economic organization continues to embody key features thereof will be characterized as modified planned economies (MPEs). Finally, the principal focus of the inquiry is on those countries that have already embarked on market orientation. For want of a better name, I shall call them planned economies in transition or PETs - no pun intended. These economies aim at radically transforming themselves and doing away with virtually the entire wherewithal of traditional central planning, including its macro- and microeconomic approaches and the institutions and instruments associated with them. The overriding features that these countries are aiming at resemble those of a, possibly mildly, socialist welfare state. The eventual status sought by these economies, given the combination of their specific social preferences superimposed upon a curtailed market framework (Lamb 1990), I shall designate as reformed planned economies (RPEs). The crucial distinguishing features of CPEs, MPEs, PETs, and RPEs are detailed in Chapters 3 and 4.

5. Remaking the global economic framework?

Although this study concentrates on the reform processes in Eastern Europe and the outside support they are mustering particularly in Western Europe, there are several ramifications that need to be addressed, however incompletely. One is how these countries could best be supported by the western democracies. Also, the precise role of the CMEA in the evolving mutations needs to be spelled out. Furthermore, the ongoing events in Eastern Europe and how the many problems bound to crop up in the process will be resolved in the international context have important repercussions on international relations more generally. They do indeed affect essential premises and precepts of the postwar global framework. The issue is not only whether or not these countries should be admitted into the multilateral IEOs in place and, if so, what their role there could or should be. I have dwelt at length elsewhere (Brabant 1990a) on how reforming CPEs and MPEs could be gradually accommodated in IEOs without infringing too much on the regimes that the IEOs have been called upon to serve. Although what I had to say there has not been completely overhauled by the political events since that manuscript was completed, the entire character of the reform intentions and the drift of the associated debates have been shifting beyond the linkage between reform and participation in IEOs that I could discern in mid-1989.

The avalanche of changes in Eastern Europe, especially in the PETs, present a new set of circumstances that may exert wider implications for global cooperation. This includes economic matters. But the discourse certainly cannot be confined to one side of the unprecedented historical developments. Any substantial realignment of the forces on the European continent will have fundamental economic, strategic, security, and political implications for the Atlantic alliance. It will also affect the dialogue with the south and how the developed countries perceive their obligations *vis-à-vis* the less fortunate in this world - hence the future of the global economic framework.

As far as economics is concerned, a drastic shift in the relative power of Europe raises many questions. Is there now more room for improving the management of the global economy to ensure that national policies take at least cognizance of the potentially adverse consequences for other countries? Should the latter's emergence or effects be mitigated through some form of global economic advisory service? Could one now conceive of a partnership becoming the driving force behind the north-south dialogue, which in any case will need to be revived in some form? What role should be allotted to social equity precepts as opposed to technical economic efficiency considerations in the global allocation of resources? There is, of course, a myriad of other questions that could be raised. I have no intention of broaching these wider issues here, except insofar as key aspects of global economic security are concerned.

6. A guide through the volume

This monograph starts off with the review of the state of affairs in Eastern Europe in general and CMEA cooperation in particular at this particular juncture. Rather than advocating "radical reform" by doing without the CMEA, Chapter 1 takes off from the constatation that the Eastern European economies are highly interdependent. This suggests that a solution to the region's problem must be found against that backdrop as well as that of the revolutionary changes in its political landscape since about mid-1989. It also examines the new opportunities created in the process for fostering a new growth path for these countries individually.

The recent changes in Eastern Europe, I believe, offer a fresh opportunity for revamping the regional framework of economic cooperation. Chapter 2 looks at the painful way in which the CMEA went through a protracted soul-searching as to how best to reform itself since about 1980. It simply summarizes the cautious suggestions on reform in and of the CMEA that I have formulated at much greater length on earlier occasions (such as Brabant 1989a, pp. 394-418) seen against the agony of accepting the political necessity of reforming the CMEA even in the absence of domestic reforms in Eastern Europe.

Chapter 3 briefly recapitulates the key features of the CPE as backdrop to a more in-depth examination of the legacies that confront the reforming countries at this stage. The chapter also examines the treadmill of economic reforms walked from the late 1950s through the beginning of the current ferment for genuine and comprehensive economic transformation in key CMEA members. Rather than look at individual country experiences, the chapter is concerned essentially with the generic characteristics of CPEs and MPEs.

This sets the stage for an examination in Chapter 4 of the economics of transition of CPEs and MPEs into PETs and ultimately into RPEs. It takes for granted that these countries desire to move toward a more market-oriented economic environment within the parameters demarcated by a democratically elected pluralistic parliamentary system. The latter sets priorities and ensures that actions are taken in accordance with a social contract. This must result explicitly or implicitly from the social arrangements that the majority of the country can subscribe to. Only then can support be found for resource allocation that in the short run may impose considerable adjustment costs, but promises in time to yield steady economic expansion and ultimately measurable improvements in levels of living. How to get to this stage given the starting conditions of a disarrayed, if perhaps not completely derailed, central planning system and the multiple legacies of over four decades of administrative regulation of resource allocation as a whole, forms the core of the discussion of the political economy of transition.

The economies that form the object of this inquiry are in "Europe." The political commitment to remaking these societies into more democratic entities that fit more readily within "Europe" has been taken as a signal that the western democracies ought to support the transitions in Eastern Europe. This assistance has multiple facets. Those belonging properly in the political economy of transition are recounted in Chapter 5.

The example of the Marshall Plan, as the European Recovery Program (ERP) in the late 1940s and early 1950s was known, has recently been invoked as providing a model of how the assistance to Eastern European PETs could best be imagined and organized. The foundations of the Marshall Plan, in which instances it contributed most to the postwar socioeconomic and political developments in Western Europe, and what its weaknesses were are reviewed in Chapter 6. The drift of the argument is that the situation in Eastern Europe is very different from the tasks faced by Western Europe after World War II and that thus an alternative to the Marshall Plan needs to be designed.

Property relations have been one of the key distinguishing features of socialist and capitalist societies, the former relying on state or societal ownership and the latter primarily on private ownership. The transition to democratic societies whose productive resources are allocated through market relations poses the question of whether it is desirable to privatize state assets and what the role of property relations in the PETs should be. Chapter 7 examines key aspects of property rights, the formation of alternative types of property, and the desirability of privatizing state assets to bolster the transition to functioning markets.

The analyses of Chapters 5 and 6 suggest that there are many technical aspects of facilitating the transitions in economic systems in Eastern Europe. I shall concentrate on the "international economics" of aiding the transitions in Eastern Europe in Chapter 8 from the point of view of "four freedoms" - the movement of goods, services, capital, and labor. The political economy of the transition is here seen as addressing both the goals and the means. With respect to the goals, primacy ought to be accorded to what these societies themselves hope to accomplish. The means are by and large determined by the volume and forms of assistance that third countries are willing to provide and the ways in which it can be distributed.

Although the CMEA itself forms part and parcel of the transformation of Eastern Europe, there is also a component that emanates from the "international economics" of the transition. Chapter 9 argues the case for renewing economic integration in particular among the transforming economies. It also posits that this should be seen as an essential ingredient of the east-west assistance effort. It should maximize the benefits that the PETs can obtain. At the same time, it should offer profitable opportunities to the donor countries, at least in the medium to long run.

Chapter 10 rounds off the study. It looks into the ramifications of the remaking of Europe for the continent and beyond. What has been happening in Eastern Europe cannot but have far-reaching implications for the global framework of cooperation. This has already come to the fore in security affairs. Its salutary effect is bound to be even greater in economics, not necessarily the purely materialistic domains. A renaissance of artistic and intellectual life, such as the revival of the manifold issues associated with *Mitteleuropa* at this juncture, in my view, merits a lot of attention in this context. But that interesting discussion cannot be documented and analyzed here at any length, though it must be broached. Even when linked to the more immediate aspects of international interaction, there is a need to examine the consequences of the transformations in Eastern Europe and the remaking of Europe as a whole for the postwar global economic framework and its principal institutions.

The four principal points emphasized throughout this study are briefly summarized in the conclusion.

1

Eastern Europe in transition

In the wake of the astounding avalanche of political transitions in Eastern Europe since about mid-1989, the question of the CMEA's demise or the need to scrap it soon, has been raised many times. Such a transformation would leave Eastern Europe without even a moderately cohesive framework for economic cooperation. Certainly, the CMEA regime since postwar stabilization has been largely *ad hoc*. It nonetheless permitted a growing volume of trade to emerge. There is therefore good reason to inquire into how these countries can be weaned of their overwhelming intragroup dependence, particularly imports of fuels and critical raw materials in exchange for manufactures that are on the whole below world standards.

Any of the premises of postwar global arrangements in general and the way in which the "world socialist economic system" was to function have been shattered with the ongoing realignments in Eastern Europe. Since postwar stabilization and the decisive shift toward central planning as the pivotal organizing principle of socioeconomic life under the overpowering role of the Communist Party, close economic, political, cultural, social, and other types of interactions among the "fraternal" countries have been quintessential to the welfare of these countries. In this, an important role was carved out for economic cooperation, including through the policies, institutions, and instruments available within the context of the CMEA; at least, what it should have ideally stood for. In that sense, it will be instructive not to confine the discussion to the strict features of the CMEA as a regional economic organization.

To clarify matters, it must be recalled that the notion "CMEA" has frequently been used in varying contexts. Those advocating its demise do not always make it crystal clear what particular incarnation of the CMEA they would like to see obliterated or, in their view, has already been superseded by recent events. Clarification of this point is very instructive in pondering the transition phase, even of the most liberal PETs. Section 1 examines five cloaks of CMEA economic relations sketched against the backdrop of recent CMEA debates. These developments in CMEA trade and payments relations are summarized next. Section 3 illustrates empirically the importance of the CMEA.

1. On the meanings of the CMEA

Judging by its hobbling evolution during the last decade or so, as sketched in Chapter 2, the CMEA has been incapable of transforming itself into an effective buttress for market-oriented reforms in its component economies. Neither has it provided an environment conducive to formulating constructive suggestions for changing the complex political and economic interrelations among its members, including in trade and payments regimes. All this has lent strength to the contention that this peculiar IEO is dead for all practical purposes. But to ascertain the CMEA's *raison d'être* at this juncture solely against the recent political backdrop would be shortsighted, possibly a highly misleading way of assessing recent developments and their longer-term implications.

For all practical purposes, the CMEA as a regional organization has been in considerable disarray at least since the late 1970s. In some respects, one may even go back to the failure to act upon the more hopeful strands of promises made at the time the document entitled *Comprehensive program for the further extension and improvement of cooperation and the development of economic integration by the CMEA member countries* (see Tokareva 1972, pp. 29-103) was launched in the late 1960s (Brabant 1980, pp. 229-37; 1989a, pp. 82-91). Hopes for its slow but steady convalescence have repeatedly been dashed under impulse of weak commitment toward reforming the organization; they may by now have faded altogether. I see little reason to pronounce the CMEA dead or to disconnect its remaining life-support system, for that matter, without carefully weighing the alternatives available to the various actors most directly affected in the process.

Is the CMEA dead? Can it survive? Is it bound to be obliterated soon? These are but a sample of rhetorical questions posed in particular in the more journalistic treatments of the CMEA during the past several months. In light of the stagnation in CMEA relations since about the mid-1970s, the answer might at first sight be unambiguously affirmative. Although I subscribe wholeheartedly to the notion that already far too much time has been wasted in trying to infuse new life into the CMEA, a reasoned answer to the key issue at hand - whether the organization could perform a useful role at all - can be formulated only by clarifying the concept of the CMEA as unambiguously as possible. Such a rounded approach is all the more warranted if questions such as the above-cited are placed against the backdrop of the rapid political changes in the European members of the CMEA since mid-1989 and the far-reaching economic reforms currently on the agenda of many of the new leaders of these countries. Because the nuts and bolts of these coveted alternatives are as yet to be designed and machined into fairly polished pieces that fit into a coherent, functioning whole, it seems all the more instructive to carefully scrutinize the multiple issues involved.

I see at least five useful ways of debating what is at stake. From its inception, CMEA has been the regional economic organization entrusted with monitoring and recommending improvements in trade and payments regimes, especially of the European member countries; until it was felt politic to admit Mongolia in 1962, the CMEA was indeed constitutionally intended exclusively for the European socialist countries. In that respect, debates on how best to reform the CMEA have been evolving for a long time, at least since the late 1970s. Those that are currently still on the policy agenda find their origin in the difficulties encountered in trying to maintain reasonable levels of domestic economic growth and buoyant intragroup trade expansion since the early 1980s (Brabant 1987c).

After protracted debates, the CMEA economic summits of June 1984 and November 1986 identified five areas in which major changes would have to be undertaken (Brabant 1989a, pp. 110-17 and 132-4): (1) rebuilding the institutional features of the regional organization in its own right; (2) the role of relations with the three developing country members (Cuba, Mongolia, and Vietnam) in SEI, including the commitment of the European members to lending economic, financial, and technical development assistance to these countries and how best to capitalize on the limited resources available; (3) the strategy at which SEI should be aimed; (4) the means to promote the breadth and depth of SEI as exemplified by the corresponding economic mechanism, which envelops macroeconomic policies, institutions, and policy instruments to ensure profitable economic interaction among the component economies; and (5) the desirability of aiming at a unified or common market in Eastern Europe and how this can be brought about, possibly through some kind of regional planning.

Excepting the first two items, nothing much has been achieved since these topics were debated in depth at the highest political level in November 1986 (see Chapter 2). If only because of the inability to redefine itself as far as the strategy and mechanism of SEI are concerned, the CMEA is barely alive, but only barely. With the seesaw changes in political regimes since mid-1989, one may well question whether the reform aspects debated and negotiated in some detail during 1987-1989 are still pertinent to the current policy agenda. I for one believe that the discourse on all of these issues could benefit substantially from factoring into the debate recent economic and political changes, and indeed a good deal of economic realism. At the same time, I am convinced that the drift of the arguments as perceived at this stage will be very different from the directions taken in 1987-1989.

In its second cloak, the CMEA has frequently been described as an alliance with strong political overtones, seen essentially as an extension of the WTO into the security aspects of international economic dependence. The CMEA in that framework simply provides the group's economic underpinnings for enhanced military strength, with pertinent economic interactions among the members being geared primarily by Soviet hegemony. There have undoubtedly been periods in postwar intragroup relations when hegemony held sway even over elementary considerations inspired by economic rationality. In that respect, many changes both in the Soviet role in Eastern Europe as well as in the merits of the Warsaw Pact have been taking place. The prime moving force has been the "New Thinking" under Gorbachev's leadership. But other factors should be taken into account too.

I am not sure whether it is appropriate to characterize the CMEA as being dead in this second connotation. After all, the geography of Soviet-Eastern European relations has not changed and the Warsaw Pact is still a fact of life. Nonetheless, the seminal changes in security and defense thinking in the Soviet Union since 1986 have considerably weakened the usefulness of the CMEA as an instrument for reinforcing the WTO, whose military linkages have been sharply crimped. In that respect, the CMEA is certainly not much alive and will probably not need to be resurrected any time soon.

A third possible meaning of the CMEA is that of being the simple collection of bilateral trade and payments agreements (BTPAs). From its inception, the CMEA as a regional organization has been somewhat separate from the way in which the member countries have arranged their reciprocal trade and payments. The heartland of trading in the postwar period, as briefly summarized in Chapter 2, has been bilateralism, with detailed trade contracts negotiated at the intergovernmental level or institutions, such as foreign trade organizations (FTOs), that are directly subordinated to one ministry or another within the context of the state monopoly of foreign trade and payments (MFT). External economic relations have traditionally been divorced from domestic economic magnitudes through price equalization (see Chapter 3).

With the reforms under way, after the experiences of the early 1980s, I firmly believe that the CMEA in that respect is dangling at the end of a tightening rope. There is no doubt about its imminent demise in this sense at least for the members that are currently engaged in or envisaging the creation of greater market-orientation centered around considerable autonomy of economic agents. These include MPEs as well as the PETs. These countries advocate not only genuine decentralization in economic affairs, but also the dismantling of the traditional bilateralism, anchoring trade to world market prices (WMPs), and effecting settlement in convertible currency. Such seminal shifts in intragroup relations could not but mandate major changes in this particular configuration of the CMEA.

As a counterpart of the preceding meaning, the CMEA has also its own intragroup arrangements for trade and payments. That particular notion of the CMEA is closely related to the former concept. But some nontrivial differences must be noted. Viewing the CMEA in light of its own arrangements for smoothing intragroup trade and payments flows imparts a different meaning to the organization than if it is understood as the simple aggregate of BTPAs, inasmuch as, over the years, distinct groupwide trade and payments regimes have emerged. Thus, the traditional bilateralism has been anchored to detailed BTPAs negotiated at peculiar prices that can be characterized as the transferable ruble price (TRP) regime; clearing arranged through the transferable ruble (TR) at the International Bank for Economic Cooperation (IBEC), which is also the emittor of the TR; purely formalistic regional multilateralism; and some measure of intragroup capital flows supervised by the International Investment Bank (IIB). In addition, these instruments have been linked through the mechanisms of plan coordination to national economic planning with the goal of fostering integration through production specialization rather than market interaction.

Especially in this area, major changes are bound to occur in the near term. The traditional CMEA arrangements for conducting intragroup transactions have become archaic and in many respects dysfunctional in the context of efforts to promote market-oriented economic decisions, including concerning foreign trade and payments. Although these old arrangements are not yet dead for practical reasons, they clearly no longer satisfy key CMEA participants, even those that by and large are still overwhelmingly CPEs.

Finally, the CMEA can be viewed against the backdrop of the regional dependence in trade and payments that has emerged over nearly half a century of economic collaboration. Although there have recently been serious obstacles to maintaining the trade volumes gradually built up over the years, there is little doubt that all countries continue to depend on each other a substantial share, perhaps 40 and 80 percent, of their overall trade (see Section 3). Moreover, substantial components of that trade are funneled through a unique transportation infrastructure. This consists of oil and gas pipelines, standardized barges, ocean-going vessels, railroad cars, a uniform power grid, interlinked highways, and others. Furthermore, there continues to be a need to service a machine park that has been constituted overwhelmingly with equipment manufactured in the CMEA to produce machinery and other manufactures for CMEA demand.

If only for the above-cited very pragmatic reasons, the CMEA context is certainly not yet a dead issue. Forgoing such trade ties would require massive diversion of trade to MEs and very incisive structural changes in the CMEA economies. The cost of the required adaptations to accommodate trade switching and related adjustments on a broad front would be so massive that in the process the sociopolitical fabric of these countries might be stretched beyond its already taut limit. But there is another factor to be reckoned with: Although a rational allocation of resources within the region would certainly lead to a very different level, geographical direction, and commodity composition of trade than has prevailed over the past decades, such a reanchoring of the trading relationships on positive economic grounds would not altogether suppress trade. In other words, there are significant comparative advantages embodied in resource endowments in the region as a whole. With positive growth anticipated from economic reform policies, also considerable dynamic comparative advantages are bound to come to the fore. True, proper institutions, instruments, and policies are required to exploit these static and dynamic comparative advantages more fully and thus to enhance welfare levels in the region and perhaps those of third countries as well (see Chapter 9).

Whatever the angle one wishes to choose for the discourse on the present and future of the CMEA, it is necessary to specify effects against alternative time horizons. Regardless of the systemic changes that may be in the offing, the short-term effects of the adjustment burden are likely to result in a contraction of the real volume of trade and payments. Inasmuch as trade with most MEs is already conducted in convertible currency, the short-term contraction may be largest for those flows unless CMEA economic relations were to collapse altogether. But that can only be a transitory phenomenon. The realignment of economic structures at home and in CMEA relations under impulse of the more rigorous application of the economic calculus is bound to affect the level, geographical direction, and commodity composition of trade. These changes cannot but benefit global welfare and trade simply because the current trade allocation is by no means Pareto-optimal.

Whereas the medium- to long-term effects of marketizing the CMEA will undoubtedly exert a beneficial impact on global trade and welfare, neither the difficulties of this transition nor the negative short-term implications for trading partners, in the CMEA as elsewhere, should be understated or ignored. This follows in part from worrisome developments since mid-1989 and the intrinsic interdependence of the CMEA countries, as examined in the next two sections, respectively.

2. Recent developments in CMEA relations

Not all of the recent events in Eastern Europe can be detailed here. Even a brief examination of their most critical economic aspects helps to highlight the situation in which these countries find themselves. Only some of them stem from the recent political transitions themselves. Most find their origin in more fundamental problems, some of which I address later in a balanced and comprehensive manner. Many of these topics need to be placed within the delicate context of ongoing political revolutions in these countries, without attempting to do so in any comprehensive framework. While the latter may be a drawback, the former is an absolute necessity for otherwise my positioning of the issues would necessarily blunt the scope of even a balanced economic assessment. *In fine*, these set the boundaries for the framework within which policies may be formulated to assist the desirable transitions in the CMEA in general and the PETs in particular.

The very depth, speed, and sweep of the changes that have been taking place in Eastern Europe during the past several months exhibit several angles. It is simply impossible to generalize about the economic implications of these changes for the region as a whole or even for any one country in particular, except perhaps when the purview is the very short run. A useful perspective on the economic consequences of ongoing events may be distilled under four broad headings: (1) the forms of regional economic cooperation, placing the accent on their ramifications for commercial and financial relations with the main groups of partner countries and repercussions for development assistance efforts; (2) the national economic reform movements, including the problems of the transition from the centrally planned environment to a much more market-oriented economic system; (3) miscellaneous sociopolitical events that affect at least short-term economic performances of some countries; and (4) implications for east-west economic, political, military, and other forms of desirable cooperation, especially in a European perspective.

1. Intragroup economic relations

Perhaps the greatest common denominator of events over the past months has been the *de facto* disintegration of the CMEA as the regional economic organization entrusted with enhancing intragroup economic integration and ensuring stable trade and payments flows. This has been in marked contrast to what should have emerged, particularly in the course of 1989.

1989 should have provided an opportunity for celebration for at least two reasons. One is that the organization marked its fortieth anniversary (see Brabant 1989a, pp. 3-42). Perhaps more important, seminal steps should have been set on the road to further refining and gradually implementing major changes in SEI strategy and mechanisms. Both should have been crowned at the third economic summit of the 1980s (earlier ones having been held in June 1984 and November 1986), which was first slated to be convened in March 1989 in Prague; after several false restarts in April and May 1989, it was postponed indefinitely, although the members were still deliberating about the usefulness and agenda of such a meeting through late 1989. They should also have been the main focus of the regular, 45th Council Session, first slated to be held in June 1989 in Sofia, as per the CMEA's statutes. It would have placed the official imprimatur on the seminal changes that had been expected to be endorsed at the summit and indeed put in train concrete actions. The Council Session of 1989 was repeatedly deferred from June to October and every month later in the year. It was finally held in Sofia from 9 to 10 January 1990, in spite - perhaps because - of very unusual circumstances for seminal deliberations about revitalizing intragroup economic cooperation. In the event, the Session took note of the so-called "comprehensive reform" report prepared by the Bogomolov commission since 1987, on which more in Chapter 2, and immediately decided to shelve it. It was generally agreed that the measures that had earlier been thought of as revolutionary were no longer that at all. The Session aired fundamental issues and decided once again to defer any incisive decision. Instead, a new reform commission was entrusted with elaborating ambitious changes in the foundations of CMEA trade and payments by mid-1990.

Instead of commemorating forty years of cooperation, the year was marked by indecision, vacillation, and recrimination. Friction in CMEA economic relations has been mounting now for several years. It has led to two kinds of actions that are detrimental to within-group cooperation, even when its discourse is confined to strictly economic parameters. One has taken the form of placing additional constraints on trade and payments to prevent private arbitrage from clearing consumer markets with relatively open national frontiers for "tourist" and "border" traffic. Such measures have been imposed since the second half of 1988 by a growing number of countries in an effort to prevent the exploitation of substantial relative price differentials and different consumer market imbalances in neighboring CMEA countries from aggravating already strained domestic supplies. Even the Soviet Union has found it necessary to impose stringent export controls on a wide range of mostly durable consumer manufactures, but also some foodstuffs, to limit private arbitrage and to restrict even commercial transactions.

The other one has been the imposition of tightening constraints on regular commercial transactions. These have become more acute since 1989 for two reasons. One stems essentially from the inability - and partly unwillingness - of the Soviet Union to ensure larger export volumes of fuels and raw materials at the traditional TRPs cleared within the context of the regular TR mechanism supervised by the IBEC. This supply constraint is due to domestic output difficulties, which has been limiting the USSR's capacity, but also its willingness, to offset the losses in CMEA terms of trade that it has had to sustain over the past several years, basically because of weak global oil and gas prices. The other one derives from reluctance on the part of the Eastern European countries to honor agreed-upon export volumes of chiefly investment goods and durable consumer manufactures, as stipulated in the applicable medium-term trade agreements. Without such outright export denial, these countries would record substantial current account surpluses in TRs. These are essentially inconvertible at any given moment of time and even hard to mobilize over time, that is, in the next trade and payments agreement. The result has been a gradual contraction of within-group trade values at a time of already strained import possibilities from convertible currency partners.

However, the malaise in the CMEA runs much deeper than these events at first sight might suggest. That is not to deny the latter's debilitating implications for maintaining the pace of intragroup exchanges and hence buttressing domestic economic stability. The probability of any major change being enacted in the very near future so as to foster more buoyant CMEA economic relations for the group as a whole has become very slim at this juncture.

Support for seeking a solution through CMEA economic reforms has been rapidly evaporating since early 1989. For one thing, the Soviet Union has become so enmeshed in its own domestic economic crises, not to mention the various political and other mutations that have been taking place there, that the matter of revitalizing the CMEA appears to have been relegated to the distant background. Not only that, several of the reforming countries are, in fact, seriously questioning the very *raison d'être* of the CMEA. This is not just frivolous posturing emerging from the current environment in which virtually any issue can be publicly raised and openly debated at great length. Rather, it is a recognition of the fact that the CMEA as such really does not matter much, as already noted in Section 1. Furthermore, it illustrates that the traditional trade and payments regimes made up of BTPAs are antiquated, really unsuitable to help promote the kind of economic reform that the most ambitious CMEA members, including the Soviet Union, are currently envisaging.

This reconceptualization of intra-CMEA economic relations has at least three dimensions. One concerns the clearing of regular trade and financial flows. Key CMEA members are presently exploring the possibility of shifting their trade accounting to current WMPs and convertible currency clearing in lieu of orthodox TRPs and the nominally multilateral TR clearing mechanism. Pairs of agreements or understandings have been signed among Czechoslovakia, Hungary, Poland, and the Soviet Union (a more limited one also with Bulgaria) to transit quickly to such a regime; also the GDR had signed some such agreements, but with economic union its trade obligations will henceforth be conducted in deutschmarks (see Chapter 9). Whereas Hungary and Poland had intended to do so beginning in 1990, and Czechoslovakia joined that resolve in early 1990, the other agreements are to take effect one year later; in fact, only the Polish-Soviet agreement for 1990 is moving ahead with partial convertible currency accounting on an experimental basis as 15 percent of their agreed trade value for 1990 evaluated at the habitual TRPs has been set aside for clearing in convertible currency and at current WMPs. Furthermore, the bulk of transactions among these countries are to be conducted directly among enterprises rather than through the medium of detailed BTPAs negotiated at the ministerial level. The weak state of wholesale trading in these countries, especially in the Soviet Union, now and in the foreseeable future may sharply complicate maintaining prevailing trade levels and indeed placing that trade on a much more flexible footing, including the selection of WMPs and the ultimate settlement of imbalances in convertible currency.

Once direct interfirm relations determine trade chiefly on the basis of the firms' own profitability calculations, major changes in the level, commodity composition, and geographical orientation of within-group trade are bound to ensue. Simulations of what may eventually transpire have already given rise to tensions that may in the end be more harmful to within-group goodwill than the undoubtedly beneficial medium-run effects emanating from "marketizing the CMEA."[1] These in turn cannot but impact on the sustainable economic structures of the affected countries, thereby compounding the adjustment problems faced by moving toward a more market-oriented economic arena.

The second revolves around the implications of CMEA trade and payments reforms for the non-European members, all of which have in the past benefited from substantial economic assistance embedded in, and transmitted through, the peculiar trade and payments regimes typical of the CMEA. Indeed, the bulk of aid is channeled through price concessions and tariff discounts for goods and services for Eastern European and Soviet exports or price supplements for imports from the developing members (see Chapter 10). There is little doubt that with the commercialization of economic decisions in the European CMEA members, the real cost of providing development assistance to the non-European members is henceforth going to be carefully scrutinized. At a time of palpable internal and external economic imbalances, chances of holding assistance levels at present levels, let alone of raising them, are not at all promising; some countries have in fact already announced their intention to cut back sharply on their ODA to these countries.[2] Particularly Cuba and Vietnam will in the end have to come to grips with sharply lower real levels of development assistance from the European CMEA members.

The third reverberation of the *de facto* demise of the CMEA is the redrawing of east-west economic cooperation, particularly in Europe. Because of the nature of "Europe," this is bound to have major political and strategic consequences. Aside from autonomous structural adjustments that would have been undertaken in any case by this or that CMEA member, the organization's fragmentation cannot but bring additional external pressure to bear on these countries. They will thus have to carve out for themselves some competitive niche in world markets. This process will necessarily evolve in competition with DEs. This is not perforce an undesirable outcome, provided such competition is waged essentially on the basis of underlying economic strengths. With the CMEA economies undergoing protracted structural adjustments from the central planning environment to a situation in which economic scarcities get increasingly reflected in macro- and microeconomic policies, however, during the transition phase there is every likelihood that pressure to export, largely for balance-of-payments reasons, will gain ascendancy for some time over the eventual recognition of the need to export profitably. For those countries under the

[1] According to interviews in Budapest and Prague in late 1989 and in Warsaw in early 1990, such calculations are based on repricing actual TRP trade at comparable WMPs, however assessed, and estimating the change in the trade balance. For Hungarian-Soviet trade, the imbalance has been estimated to swing from roughly $0.5 surplus in favor of Hungary to a deficit of between $1 and $2 billion. Likewise for Poland: Instead of obtaining a surplus with the Soviet Union - some $1.5 million in 1989 - it would have been in deficit to between $0.5 and 1.5 billion. Neither country feels that such a deficit can be financed at this stage, hence their reluctance to implement these reforms soon for purely pragmatic reasons.

[2] Thus, instead of receiving about $1.5 to 2 billion (at the official exchange rates) per year from the European CMEA, Vietnam is now counting on obtaining perhaps half that amount. Several Eastern European donors have decided to cut out all aid during their adjustment phase.

largest external payments pressures, whether or not they are in the vanguard of moving toward full marketization, this drive to export almost regardless of cost may in the end be more intense than for others that still enjoy somewhat greater policy leeway.

2. Domestic economic reforms

Well before the recent events in Eastern Europe, the drift toward enacting measures that would in time bring about an indirect economic coordination mechanism - a more market-oriented environment, if you wish - was unmistakable. These efforts initially took almost exclusively the form of administrative streamlining, including the decentralization of microeconomic decisions and the enhancement of the managerial and financial autonomy of firms. Price reform and creating room for genuine wholesale trade were avoided for fear of inflation, price gouging as a result of the highly monopolistic structure of production, and the potential loss of control over consumer markets as well as other levers of highly centralized administrative structures. This predominantly technocratic approach to economic reform has recently given way to much more incisive changes.

The entire atmosphere for economic reforms has been sharply modified by efforts to institutionalize multiparty systems and parliamentary democracy. Together, they should exert a determining influence over the formulation and implementation of macroeconomic policy within a revamped institutional framework. The social compact that in principle can thus be attained is expected in time to enhance policy formulation because it will lead to greater consensus over the magnitude of the adjustment cost to be borne as well as its timing and distribution over the various layers of society. For now, however, the polical leaderships of the weak parliamentary democracies in place or soon to emerge exhibit a great deal of uncertainty and hesitancy that are weakening economic stability throughout the group. These countries are by and large inexperienced in parliamentary democracy. Moreover, the political alliances that have slowly been crystallizing around what can reasonably be accomplished, given the prevailing resources and forces competing for attention and power in their societies, exhibit considerable fluidity. As a result, the degree of uncertainty lingering over much of Eastern Europe is likely to intensify rather than to abate in the short to medium run. Failure to defuse social tensions may destabilize the situation well beyond its current precarious balance.

Yet, even in such an uncertain situation and in spite of the manifold pitfalls of transforming economies with large state assets and a substantial "nonmaterial sphere" that is centrally financed, critical reform steps are moving forward through experience "on the go." Though there is no shortage of economic missions and self-appointed blue-ribbon committees confusing policy makers, and in some cases indeed becoming the pawns of political interest groups, I have yet to see some consistent blueprint of the transition phase being put together principally around the perceived interests of one or another Eastern European society in mind. The confusion over the desirability of privatization and how to carry it out in the context of marketization has been particularly vexing, as examined at length in Chapter 7.

Although the political transformation in the Soviet Union in many respects lags behind the recent changes in most of Eastern Europe, the degree of uncertainty there is no less acute. This stems in part from the failure of *perestroyka* thus far to deliver the kind of economic response that its architects had forecast when they embarked on the grandiose remaking of the Soviet economy and society. There are many reasons for this state of affairs. Perhaps the most important is that policy makers of economies in transition invariably understate the dimensions and critical adjustment problems ahead, in part because the desirable shape of macro- and microeconomic policies is inadequately understood. There are moreover powerful forces of resistance built into the coexistence of remnants of the central planning system and the incipient manifestations of a more market-oriented environment. Confusion among economic actors is legion.

The uncertainty involved in the technical design of the transition phase is common to all reforming economies, even without the superimposition of many other vexing aspects of the ongoing sociopolitical revolutions. It is no exaggeration to characterize all of these economies as being in search of anchors for policy making, guidelines to regaining economic stability, and sources of extraneous assistance that might ease the strain of wholesale adjustment for society as a whole and the consumer in particular.

3. Miscellaneous sociopolitical events

In the short run, the economic costs of the sharp population exodus from Bulgaria (about 300,000 net in 1989), the GDR (about 340,000), and the Soviet Union (about 228,600 according to *Pravda*, 14 January 1990, p. 3) and strikes or work stoppages in Poland and the Soviet Union have seriously compounded the search for more rewarding economic management in all economies that seek to remove the Party from economic affairs and implant the conditions for market orientation. The dislocation caused by the emigration, particularly from the GDR, of sizable numbers of relatively young and skilled workers looking for a better livelihood is palpable. Strikes and work stoppages elsewhere, especially in key fuel and transportation sectors of the Soviet Union, have been inhibiting capacity utilization at a tolerable level and maintaining existing export commitments.

If these economic and political events did not already by themselves amount to a sufficiently demanding task, the current situation in Eastern Europe, especially the Soviet Union, is being compounded by a sharp polarization of society and a breakdown of the postwar commitment to socialist solidarity in and among these economies. This may be desirable in the longer run, if only to rid the countries from abuses of power and the resentments caused by heavy-handed policies under the aegis of the erstwhile all-dominant Communist Party in power. In the short to medium run, however, these revendications are divisive. They thus compound the uncertainty in the economic and sociopolitical arenas and may further destabilize these societies.

This uncertainty is being markedly aggravated by the as yet unresolved problems of property right assignments in their broad sense and privatization of state assets that some countries, especially Hungary and Poland, have wedded themselves to. Social tensions have risen as a result of widespread instances of mismanagement and the resulting feeling that "society" at large is pulling at the short end of the stick. In addition, changes in property rights, a more democratic government based on a social consensus, and resolute movement toward marketization require major shifts in managerial styles. Under the central planning system, management was essentially entrusted to the *nomenklatura*, which gained considerable skills in state-owned enterprises (SOEs) under the administrative system of economic decision making. These managerial cadres are unlikely to be acceptable to the remade societies and may not be able to survive in an environment geared by market decision making.

I do not wish to underestimate the innate abilities of these fairly educated societies to grasp hold of their own destiny. But any changeover to private property or a form of detachment of state ownership from the *usufructus* thereof (for example, through management contracts or leasing) in enterprise structures will call for managerial skills that differ very markedly from those wielded during most of the past fifty years. At the very least, time for adjustment is required, which provides another instance of near- to medium-term uncertainty. This is likely to manifest itself in bankruptcies, unemployment, foreign takeovers, sociopolitical revendications, and other dislocations that may be quite disconcerting to societies accustomed to intrinsic stability for so long.

4. Transforming the European scene

Until about the middle of 1989, the most pivotal concerns of policy makers in Western Europe focused nearly exclusively on the creation of the Single Market by the end of 1992 and where to move from there in terms of monetary, fiscal, and eventually political union. With the dramatic events in Hungary and Poland, and especially the more recent emotion-laden transformations in the GDR, the immense task of reaching "1992" is being exacerbated by the perceived need to assist Eastern Europe. This applies in particular to the countries that have committed themselves to the gradual creation of more democratic and market-oriented societies. Assistance takes the form of trade-related concessions, capital flows in the form of loans and foreign direct investment (FDI) in favor of Eastern Europe, giving technical and more general development assistance to the boldest reforming countries and exploring ways of ushering these countries more closely into the "1992 concert" through some form of association with either the European Free Trade Association (EFTA) or the European Communities (EC).

Whereas these measures may ease the adjustment strain of the countries in transition, and thus make the transformations more bearable for the populations at large, there are several economic dangers. The most obvious have been the concerns expressed by DEs of having earmarked ODA and financial flows below-market costs diverted to Eastern Europe. Especially the more competitive of the DEs have emphasized that they are apprehensive about Eastern Europe being granted discriminatory trade preferences. These have already been started in some forms, especially for Hungary and Poland, if only through the removal of discriminatory quantitative restrictions traditionally maintained by the EC against most of Eastern Europe. Little does it matter in the debate that these restrictions had already earlier been slated for normalization by the mid-1990s, a deadline that has now been moved forward by about five years.

But there are also revendications among the candidates for economic assistance. Thus the societal crisis in the GDR is being perceived, certainly by Czechoslovak, Hungarian, and Polish observers, as jeopardizing the assistance from the west that is so desperately needed to ease the implementation of their own democratization and marketization programs. These aspirations go well beyond purely financial or economic assistance. Concerns have been mounting that preoccupation with the German question is deflecting attention from the desire of especially the Central European countries soon to become full-fledged members of the EC or, if that were not to materialize, the EFTA.

Whereas several developed market economies (DMEs), particulary in Western Europe, have generously committed financial and other resources to assist Eastern Europe as a group, or individually targeted countries, there is as yet little by way of genuine coordination of this stage and seeing to it that the earmarked assistance is provided in such as way that it maximizes the benefits accruing to the reforming economies themselves. I firmly believe that it would be useful to come forth with a constructive initiative in that respect.

3. CMEA economic relations

As intimated in Section 1, the CMEA has been the subject of numerous deliberations on how best it could be reformed and thus impart a new impetus to economic integration mainly in Eastern Europe. The key forces leading up to this protracted examination, roughly since 1981, have been many. The most crucial will be highlighted in Chapter 2. By looking at a few trade indicators seen against the backdrop of their overall trade linkages, I shall try to clarify the importance of the CMEA and thus to explain why the reforming members have not so far sought to disengage themselves from their CMEA dependence.

Roughly half of the overall trade of the European CMEA is conducted by the Soviet Union and Eastern Europe. There has been some change in this ratio over time, especially for imports in the case of the Soviet Union mainly on account of sudden jumps in terms of trade. If the increase in trade values in 1980-1989 is deflated, there has hardly been any growth at all for imports by Eastern Europe (perhaps 12 percent), in contrast to the 37 percent recorded by the USSR; export growth there (29 percent) as well as that of the Soviet Union (28 percent) has been more positive, though quite uneven and by no means spectacular. In any case, Eastern Europe's export and import expansion with CMEA partners has been more buoyant than these countries' trade with the MEs; the same holds for Soviet imports. These differential volume changes need to be seen in the context of the broad geographical distribution of trade.

Table 1.1 shows each country's trade shares with Eastern Europe, the Soviet Union, and DMEs for selected years. The Soviet Union evidently plays a paramount role in the trade of all countries, even in the case of Rumania since it started to procure sizable volumes of petroleum there in the late 1970s. Taking all of Eastern Europe, evaluated at the old exchange rates, the share varies between 40 to 80 percent, the highest being for Bulgaria and Czechoslovakia.

Table 1.1. Geographical distribution of CMEA trade (in percent).

EXPORTS	1980			1985			1988 (old)			1988 (new)			1989		
	EE5	SU	DME	EE5	SU	DME	EE5	SU	DME	EE5	SU	DME	EE5	SU	DME
Bulgaria	16.5	49.9	15.8	17.2	56.7	8.5	18.0	62.5	6.4				17.3	65.8	7.3
CSFR	27.8	35.6	21.8	26.6	43.6	15.8	32.3	40.3	18.6	23.6	33.6	27.3	23.1	30.5	31.2
GDR	26.2	33.3	29.3	22.4	37.2	31.5	28.0	37.0	26.6	18.9	24.8	46.2	18.1	23.8	48.5
Hungary	21.0	29.3	34.0	18.7	33.6	30.2	17.0	27.6	39.5				14.8	24.4	48.6
Poland	21.1	31.2	34.4	19.7	28.4	34.7	16.2	24.5	43.5				14.1	21.0	49.3
Rumania	17.7	19.6	34.8	14.5	21.4	33.9	16.9	23.2	33.5				16.5	23.5	36.7
USSR	42.2	n.a.	32.0	52.6	n.a.	19.2	48.9	n.a.	21.9				46.2	n.a.	23.9

IMPORTS	1980			1985			1988 (old)			1988 (new)			1989		
	EE5	SU	DME	EE5	SU	DME	EE5	SU	DME	EE5	SU	DME	EE5	SU	DME
Bulgaria	18.1	57.3	17.2	17.5	56.2	15.2	20.2	53.5	15.4				18.9	53.6	17.0
CSFR	28.7	36.0	24.4	28.6	46.0	15.3	30.1	43.1	16.3	25.2	31.2	30.9	25.1	29.7	31.1
GDR	22.4	33.2	34.6	22.9	38.8	30.2	26.1	38.0	28.6	16.1	24.3	50.8	16.1	22.0	53.1
Hungary	19.2	27.7	39.5	19.3	30.0	38.4	18.7	25.0	43.3				17.3	22.0	49.8
Poland	19.6	33.2	35.1	19.8	34.4	32.3	17.1	23.3	45.9				14.1	18.2	52.8
Rumania	15.1	15.6	31.2	20.4	22.4	17.3	24.3	32.9	11.5				22.3	32.3	10.1
USSR	42.9	n.a.	35.4	47.6	n.a.	27.8	54.1	n.a.	25.1				49.6	n.a.	28.4

n.a.: not applicable.
Source: based on official statistical yearbooks and other releases of the reporting countries. CSFR is Czech and Slovak Federative Republic, EE5 is Eastern Europe, and SU is Soviet Union. New data for Czechoslovakia have been calculated at new exchange rates and contain some revisions from data released earlier.

Table 1.2. Commodity composition of trade of CMEA countries, 1987 (in percent).

		Export				Import			
		Food & Agricult.	Raw materials	Fuels	Manufactures	Food & Agricul.	Raw materials	Fuels	Manufactures
Bulgaria*	EE6	15.7	7.5	0.4	76.4	5.2	8.1	39.9	46.8
	ROW	17.9	18.2	16.0	47.9	20.5	30.1	13.8	35.6
CSFR	EE6	1.3	2.2	2.0	94.5	4.2	6.1	34.6	55.1
	ROW	7.6	6.1	9.4	76.9	12.1	12.6	2.9	72.4
GDR*	EE6	3.5	18.8	0.6	77.1	9.2	17.5	29.3	44.0
	ROW	14.0	30.7	20.1	35.2	21.8	27.5	20.4	30.3
Hungary	EE6	16.6	2.8	0.7	79.9	3.5	7.0	29.8	59.7
	ROW	18.8	8.0	8.5	64.7	10.8	6.6	3.0	79.6
Poland	EE6	3.4	3.0	7.8	85.8	5.2	6.5	28.4	59.9
	ROW	17.3	9.4	14.7	58.6	17.9	14.0	4.3	63.8
Rumania*	EE6	10.4	16.0	4.3	69.3	7.9	37.4	10.9	43.8
	ROW	12.8	26.2	19.9	41.1	8.4	29.2	42.0	14.4

Source: estimated on the basis of partial official statistical releases. An asterisk indices that the regrouping proceeded from the estimated breakdown of trade according to the CMEA nomenclature, the so-called *Edinnaya tovarnaya nomenklatura* or ETN (ETN 5-8, ETN 2b-4, ETN2a, and ETN 1+9, respectively). For the others, the regrouping is derived from the estimated disaggregation according to the Standard International Trade Classification or SITC (SITC 0+1, SITC 2+4, SITC 3, and SITC 5-9, respectively). The correspondence is, of course, very approximate especially for manufactures (ETN 1+9 being machinery and consumer durables).

Clearly, the bulk of that trade is with the Soviet Union. Evaluated at the new exchange rates, the proportions are somewhat smaller but trade with the European CMEA nonetheless accounts for between 33 and 83 percent in 1988-1989.

As the two alternative series of table 1.1 suggest, there are several measurement problems associated with foreign trade statistics of the CPEs and MPEs. Especially important is that, because their exchange rates are rather meaningless and TRPs differ from east-west prices (EWPs), it is difficult to measure accurately relative trade dependence. Because the ruble - hence the TR - is generally overvalued in terms of convertible currencies, any realignment of exchange rates with underlying administrative costs tends to devalue the ruble as well as the TR, and hence lower the CMEA share in the country's trade. Nonetheless, the proportions given here are indicative of the substantial dependence of these countries on each other's trading capabilities.

The sheer trade magnitudes evoked suggest that it would be very difficult for these countries to disengage their economies quickly from the CMEA, even if they wanted to do so, perhaps for noneconomic reasons. Setting the latter aside, there have to be comparative advantages in the CMEA that should be exploited on economic grounds, provided the proper institutional, instrumental, and policy framework is put in place. This may, in Sachs's terminology, amount to "a poor man's club" (Sachs 1990, p. 24). But even effective commerce among the poor, under most common conditions, cannot but contribute to national wealth, provided it is not pursued at the deliberate denial of trade with other countries. The question of whether a high share of CMEA trade is self-destructive as it encourages technological obsolescence is one of these red herrings with which CMEA relations have been strewn for many years (see Chapter 9).

Apart from the sheer magnitudes involved, it is important to bear in mind what kind of commodities are being transacted primarily among the CMEA countries themselves. In that respect, CMEA links exhibit considerable asymmetries in the type of goods traded. Table 1.2 gives the broad commodity composition of trade of each of these countries with socialist partners, here taken as proxy for CMEA partners, and the rest of the world in 1987. The apparent asymmetry between their CMEA and other trade relations is more pronounced for the developed members than for others. On the whole, these countries (excepting Rumania) procure the bulk of their raw materials and fuels from within the CMEA in exchange for manufactures, basically machinery and consumer durables. In this connection it bears to stress that, excepting Rumania, all of Eastern Europe depends for the lion share of procurement of crude oil and natural gas on Soviet supplies. This applies to a considerable degree also to other critical raw materials. In trade with MEs, however, they on the whole export raw materials, fuels (often through reexports of goods procured in the USSR), and foodstuffs in exchange for a wide assortment of products. There is, of course, a substantial component of manufactures even in their export to MEs. The share attributable to finished machinery (say, group 7 of SITC) is, however, markedly smaller than what it is in trade relations with the CMEA.

For lack of data, this commodity composition cannot readily be shown for bilateral trade flows. However, both Hungarian and Polish trade statistics permit the computation of bilateral flows with various countries, albeit only in their own national trade nomenclatures, which are unfortunately not comparable to standard classifications. Nonetheless, whereas the structure of exports of these countries with socialist countries, CMEA, and the Soviet Union is rather similar, the commodity composition of imports differs considerably: In trade with the Soviet Union imports of fuels and raw materials dominate in contrast with imports from the rest of the CMEA where finished manufactures play a more important role. The magnitudes for Hungary and Poland are symptomatic of the asymmetries characterizing the other countries, perhaps more so for Czechoslovakia and the GDR than for Bulgaria and Rumania.

* * *

The paradox of the CMEA highlighted here by way of trade measures, although many other instances of regional dependence exist (see Chapter 9), illustrates one critical chasm between economic realities and political aspirations in the area. Not one European CMEA member presently appears keen on searching for a more effective regional or subregional integration framework. All find support for this attitude in the self-styled advice being ubiquitously proffered by some DMEs, IEOs, and western pundits. Yet, none of the CMEA countries can afford to disengage itself from the CMEA in a major way (say, by diverting half of its trade) in the short run even if potential partners in the west were prepared to absorb such a considerable incremental volume of trade on competitive conditions and the CMEA members were prepared to incur a substantial terms-of-trade loss for two-three years (say, of at least 10 percent per year). In fact, from an economic perspective it is doubtful that such a major trade diversion, as distinct from a thorough overhaul of the economics of foreign trade, should even be pursued with great determination. This is the message upon which I should like to expand through the rest of this volume.

2

Reforming CMEA integration

As intimated in Chapter 1, the CMEA has been the subject of numerous deliberations on how best it could be reformed and thus impart a new impetus to economic integration in Eastern Europe. The key forces leading up to this protracted examination, roughly since 1981, have been many, including: (1) the external imbalances, debt, and adjustment efforts of the early 1980s; (2) domestic economic disturbances; (3) inability to regain positive per capita growth on a sustainable basis; (4) lack of progress with SEI since the mid-1970s; (5) inconsistency between the trade and payments regimes of the CMEA and those required to support market-oriented reforms; (6) structural changes in CMEA relations (particularly the terms-of-trade fluctuations since 1975 and the restrictions on quantities of Soviet fuels and other raw materials that can be procured from within the TR regime); and (7) growing reluctance to honor the CMEA trade and payments regimes particulary to avoid arbitrage by private agents.

In the positioning about the CMEA's future it is often ignored that the debate on reforming the CMEA by no means dates from the new political reality in Eastern Europe, although this has unquestionably infused several new elements into the discourse. For all practical purposes, the CMEA as a regional organization has been in considerable disarray at least since the late 1970s. Hopes for its painful recovery have repeatedly been dashed under impulse of weak commitment to reforming the organization and profound doubts about the intrinsic potential of such an organization, even if reformed, to spur on factor productivity in key member countries.

Although hopes of introducing genuine reform for the region as a whole may by now have faded altogether, I see little reason to pronounce the CMEA dead without a careful analysis of the options available to the various actors. To clarify matters, the key difficulties that have stymied CMEA cooperation for so long are briefly restated in Section 1. Transitions in CMEA integration thinking over the decade prior to the two economic summits and since then are briefly recapitulated from the present vantage point in Section 2 and 3. The idea of creating a unified market at least for the European CMEA members is examined next. The chapter concludes with a measured assessment of the need for revamping the CMEA, a thesis argued in more detail in Chapter 9.

1. Core difficulties of CMEA cooperation

Although the CMEA trading pattern is not completely irrational, a substantial part of the asymmetry hinted at earlier stems from peculiarities of the core intragroup trade and payments regimes, as compared to conditions in world markets. Two are critical: (1) the CMEA members transact among themselves primarily on the basis of BTPAs and (2) these transactions are on the whole conducted at TRPs and formally cleared through the IBEC's facilities. These impart hindrances to intragroup trade, though there are many other obstacles that explain the CMEA's malaise.

Perhaps the most critical, certainly the one of longest standing, most obvious, and so far arguably the most intractable, obstacle has been on account of the TRP regime. Without going into great details (see Brabant 1987b), the TRP regime derives in good measure from the considerable degree of policy autonomy desired by CMEA members. To further this, these countries separate to a large extent domestic from trade transactions and do so chiefly through detailed BTPAs with predictable fixed trade prices. These can be negotiated more readily with countries that have a similarly felt need for *ex ante* arrangements than with MEs. The TRPs that prevail in these BTPAs, even in the best of cases, bear only a casual resemblance to WMPs. Perhaps the most important reason is that WMPs averaged over five years act as reference prices in CMEA negotiations. These can be obtained and enforced more readily for fuels, foodstuffs, and raw materials than for manufactures. Also, because TRPs are negotiated bilaterally, transaction prices are not uniform. Though the TR regime is in principle multilateral, it is on the whole a bilateral one, owing to the disarray in relative TRPs. Note that this does not invariably require that bilateral balance be set at zero. Comparatively small bilateral imbalances not due to *ex ante* loan arrangements are in fact accommodated through clearing credits available in successive BTPAs and *pro forma* through the IBEC's multilateral settlements scheme.

These bilateral arrangements with inflexible nonscarcity prices impose restrictions on the volume and commodity composition of trade, leading to the emergence of structural bilateralism. Here the constraints on the overall balance result only through fairly rigid limitations on acceptable commodity group imbalances. Perhaps the best known is the dichotomy between "soft" and "hard" goods. The latter are goods in short supply on CMEA markets. Most of these goods, but not all, can be diverted to world markets without significant price losses in the short run. Soft goods are those for which demand falls short and, as a rule, are difficult to sell in world markets without incurring substantial price losses in the short run. In this connection, it is good to bear in mind that goods specifically tailored to Eastern European markets may be in short supply, and hence "hard," even though it might be quite difficult to divert them in the short run because it is all but impossible to redesign them for world markets.

To maintain desirable trade flows in the face of such commodity group constraints, various deviations from the strict regime, including nonprice incentives, have emerged. The best known is trade conducted at WMPs and convertible currency. These are as a rule arranged in supplementary trade agreements, the TRP regime by convention applying only to "regular" trade agreements. Since the mid-1970s, this has accounted for a fluctuating share of CMEA trade of some countries (for example, 11.3 percent for exports and 3.1 percent for imports for Hungary and 3.8 and 2.1 percent, respectively, for Poland in 1988). For the CMEA as a whole, the share of convertible currency is probably around 3 to 5 percent. There are many other *iuntim* transactions conducted to circumvent inflexible TRPs, however.

For a long time now, some CMEA members have been agitating for reforming this archaic trade and payments system to promote genuine integration in support of contemplated domestic economic reforms, among other objectives. This move has gained considerable momentum since early 1990, following the seminal changes in the political, societal, and, in some CMEA countries, economic arrangements. In spite of the perceived need and the desire to move over to a different regime, so far no agreeable solution has been worked out. As noted, the latest CMEA Council Session (Sofia, 9-10 January 1990) failed to act decisively and deferred the matter once again to a high-level commission. Most likely, it will issue recommendations that will have their greatest repercussions by expediting the moving away from traditional bilateralism, artificial TRPs, and TR clearing, and it might perhaps obliterate the CMEA altogether.

Any such substantive transformation will have numerous repercussions on the level, commodity composition, and geographical direction of trade of these countries. It will also bring pressures to bear on industries unable to compete effectively on world markets without incurring substantial price cuts. Though the speed of austerity and the forceful restructuring resulting from such shifts compound those already being faced in the market-oriented economies, genuine CMEA reform and decisively moving forward with integration would all in all constitute a useful reinforcement of domestic economic reform. Its desirability would be considerably enhanced if the international community could support this process, if only to ease the most adverse short- to medium-term repercussions of the array of restructuring tasks to be undertaken.

Several CMEA countries have recently mooted the question of making their currency convertible. Particularly Poland has made serious strides with internal convertibility, thereby laying the foundations for current account convertibility in the near future. The GDR will soon be phased into the EC on the basis of its economic and monetary union with the FRG; with the disappearance of the *Mark der deutschen Notenbank* in July 1990, the issue of convertibility, as distinct from trade and payments controls, has fully vanished. Bulgaria and Czechoslovakia, and perhaps Rumania too, have committed themselves to establishing soon the foundations for moving toward convertibility. The Soviet Union has affirmed on several occasions its intentions to have a convertible ruble sometime by the late 1990s. But the prerequisites to support such a decisive step, especially price reform and the establishment of genuine wholesale trading among enterprises, are far from being in place at this juncture.

The obstacles to moving over to meaningful convertibility, in the sense of article VIII of the Fund's Articles of Agreement, are daunting as described in Chapter 4. Domestic prices have to be realigned with underlying scarcities, then linked to trade prices (with DMEs in the first instance), and subsequently to CMEA markets. There will certainly be large changes in exchange rates in terms of convertible currencies, but also with respect to CMEA currencies once they become flexible. In the process, the structure of these economies will have to be revamped. But before the foundations of convertibility can be laid, many of these countries need to work off the inherited disequilibrium (including the so-called monetary overhang) and to put in place the proper macroeconomic policies, institutions, and instruments to steer a decentralized, market-oriented economy without constantly running into domestic and external imbalances. Only then can they realistically hope to succeed with the transition toward genuine wholesale trading with flexible prices and enterprise independence on the basis of real economic accounting without unleashing powerful monopolistic and inflationary forces. Adjustments in the microeconomic sphere will be very considerable as managers will need to learn to react to market impulses rather than on the whole to administrative decisions.

In the end, these reforming economies hope to obtain a new impetus for domestic growth from greater participation in the international economy, utilizing competition at home and abroad as pivotal filters of economic decisions. Even if the political and economic will to move forward is present and a social compact making austerity acceptable to society can be worked out, these countries suffer from a totally inadequate infrastructure and comparative lack of experience with involvement in the international economy. In this respect, banking and marketing organizations seem to be most in need of rapid development. The international community could provide useful advice in these areas.

As argued in Chapter 1, one may well question whether the CMEA reform debates of the past decade or so, and their tentative solutions elaborated since 1987, are still relevant at this stage. There is no doubt that these options are no longer acceptable to the PETs. Yet, the debates and options examined until late 1989 are not altogether irrelevant. There are at least three reasons for this. Foremost is that the Soviet Union as the pivot of economic collaboration in the CMEA has not yet succeeded in enacting the key provisions of *perestroyka*. Even conceptually, the most coveted form of that policy as it stands today does not yet envision a genuine transformation of the economy anchored to market orientation. Various options along these lines have been vented in political circles in recent months. But action has so far been lacking. Second, some of the solutions looked at over the past several years, particularly those concerning the trade and payments regimes, may suggest improvements that the PETs in the end may feel impelled to acknowledge. Finally, although massive diversion of trade and payments away from the CMEA to the DMEs is being intimated as desirable, especially by the PETs, the prospects of accomplishing this in an orderly fashion are highly limited on the supply as well as on the demand side. By necessity, then, some *modus vivendi* will need to be formulated from within existing relations. Seen against this backdrop, as elaborated in detail in Chapter 9, it is instructive to bear in mind recent reform deliberations.

2. Gingerly acceptance of the need for renewal

In spite of efforts to bring about radical reform and completely new thinking in foreign policy matters, until late 1987, the Eastern European economic crises of the 1980s had strikingly evolved without exerting measurable repercussions on the CMEA organization, the collective development and integration policies enshrined in official documents, and the exceedingly passive policy instruments in place. This was especially surprising in view of the agitation for substantive changes launched in the early 1980s, which eventually led up to the June 1984 and November 1986 economic summits,[1] frequent meetings of the Central Committee Secretaries in charge of economic affairs (henceforth CCS for short),[2] and the convening of meaningful Council Sessions since mid-1984. Moreover, excepting the extraordinary case of Poland since 1981, even at the bilateral level, each CPE by and large has had to fend for itself since the late 1970s, including in the event of unanticipated CMEA supply constraints.

It is by now widely accepted that the policies, institutions, and instruments in place in the CMEA are not at all suited to buttress, let alone to enhance, the ongoing shifts in economic policies and mechanisms in some CPEs; they are even less able to assist MPEs. These shortcomings were undoubtedly felt widely in the process of warding off external pressures in the past decade. They were to have been tackled in the context of the arrangements enshrined in the document called: *Comprehensive program to promote the scientific and technological progress of the member countries of the Council for Mutual Economic Assistance up to the year 2000*, henceforth referred to as *Scientific-technological Progress*, which was endorsed in December 1985 (see CMEA 1986). As with previous integration programs, also this hastily drawn-up program came to naught almost as soon as it was endorsed and the CMEA found itself back to square one (Brabant 1989d, e). Yet until recently it proved too sensitive to conceptualize, let alone to promulgate, appropriate CMEA reforms. Certainly, the leaderships in place failed to come to grips head-on with the manifold institutional and policy-making aspects of the CMEA's immobilism, including in trade and payments.

At the latest since the preparations for the June 1984 CMEA summit (Brabant 1987d), which was the first since April 1969, there has been considerable agitation for enacting profound changes in the CMEA and SEI. Feasible alterations have been at the center of various investigations, including at the two recent CMEA summits (held in June 1984 and November 1986), most Council Sessions since 1983, and indeed the numerous meetings of the CCS. The range of issues for active deliberation can be grouped conveniently under three headings: (1) a broad-based debate about revamping the institutional and organizational setup of the CMEA with a view to rationalizing the bureaucracy, streamlining the mechanisms through which issues get tabled, and rendering the deliberative organs more effective; (2) the comprehensive reexamination of the ultimate purposes of SEI and means (institutions, instruments, policy coordination, and structural macroeconomic policies) to pursue; and (3) the institutional framework and the policy instruments available to enhance day-to-day SEI matters - in other words, the SEI mechanism in the strict sense - was to be

[1] This is known officially as the "Conference of First Secretaries of Communist and Workers' Parties and of the Heads of Government of the CMEA Member Countries." This gathering convenes intermittently on grave issues affecting fraternal relations among Communist Parties (see Brabant 1989a, pp. 132-4). When they do so mainly to deliberate about CMEA economic issues, I label the meeting "an economic summit" or simply "summit" if no confusion is possible.

[2] Incidentally, this emerged as a truly new, if unofficial, apex organ of the CMEA in late 1982 and early 1983 in connection with the tortuous preparations of the 1984 summit (see Brabant 1989a, pp. 134-5). Since then, it has played a critical role in propagating new thinking in the preparation of summits and Council Sessions.

the focus of probing inquiries, including in connection with then incipient reform initiatives in several member countries. A consensus on these three problem bundles was at best only slowly emerging between 1986 and 1989. Nonetheless, some important decisions were taken in 1987-1988 and implemented to a limited extent. There remained, however, an important layer of critical concerns that form part and parcel of the ongoing policy debate within the commanding political and technical policy-making organs of the CMEA edifice. The virtual collapse of democratic centralism throughout Eastern Europe has, of course, rendered this concept completely obsolete.

In spite of uncertainty as to what the CPEs were concretely aiming at, disclosures about intramural discussions have become noticeably more interesting roughly since mid-1987 and the important 43rd, so-called extraordinary Council Session, because of the admittedly extraordinary agenda and the critical, if still tentative, decisions reached there (see Brabant 1989a, pp. 140-2). This revealed *ex post* the seminal contribution of the November 1986 "CMEA working summit," which had earlier been written off as a failure, to polarizing the movement toward rationalizing the CMEA and enacting incisive SEI reform.

Without tracing this evolution in detail, before highlighting the decisions reached at the November 1986 summit and the CMEA Sessions of 1987-1988, a few words about the backdrop to the aforementioned 1985 program, its chief objectives, and the initial implementation attempts are warranted. At its roots were the disappointing economic performance of the early 1980s, continuing imbalances in many CPEs, growing problems in maintaining the traditional CMEA trade pattern, and lackluster progress with SEI since the abrogation of the debate on SEI around 1975 (Brabant 1987a, pp. 64-67). These constituted the bedrock of the 1984 CMEA economic summit, which, among other things, resolved that the CPEs work out a comprehensive technological cooperation program. The signatories had apparently agreed in December 1985 to progress quickly with its implementation.

Unfortunately, when it came to hammering out the all-important bilateral implementation agreements for these measures, obstacles arose almost at once. These manifested themselves especially in buttressing interfirm relations to foster the full cycle of technological progress and encouraging common capital formation in the CMEA. Certainly, some of the problems emanated from the fact that the program was endorsed after completion of the harmonization of the five-year plans and trade agreements for 1986-1990. The myriad of problems of how to reconcile with central planning the decentralized decision making in organizations involved in the realization of the program were thus compounded by already taut plans in place.

These inauspicious circumstances were behind the sudden convening of another economic summit slightly more than two years after the seminal one of June 1984 and just days after the long-delayed 1986 Council Session. Curiously, reports on the deliberations, were exceedingly brief and reticent; the communiqué (see *Izvestiya*, 13 November 1986, p. 1) of the two-day meeting, for example, comprised a mere 17 textlines other than the listing of participants! of which no fewer than six were devoted to endorsements of the then just concluded US-USSR summit in Reykjavik and the Soviet initiatives on disarmament. This cursory information was generally interpreted as a signal of another futile attempt to galvanize the obstacles to effective SEI. This impression was in fact reinforced by high-level assessments of the achievements of the Session and the summit of 1986. The lingering ambiguity was removed altogether when, after several postponements, the 43rd Council Session was finally convened in Moscow (13-14 October 1987). From both meetings it transpired that in the course of the year vigorous discussions on the reorganization of the CMEA and the prospective wholesale revamping of policies and instruments of SEI had been under way. Their importance can perhaps best be gauged by referring to the key achievements reported in connection with the recent Sessions.

3. The critical avenues slated in 1986-1987

In many ways the 43rd Council Session was a revelation as well as a disappointment. It was the latter because the meeting failed to resolve the central item of the SEI policy debate since 1980, namely how to transform the CMEA into an effective buttress for economic development. The Session was nonetheless quite informative. As noted, it confirmed that the November 1986 summit had been pivotal in charting prospective CMEA policies; it might even be elevated to the uniquely exalted place heretofore reserved for the April 1969 summit, where the very concept of SEI as the paramount objective of CMEA cooperation was finally adopted. Furthermore, the Session issued tentative recommendations, which were paramount in subsequent debates on SEI.

First, the Session agreed, apparently unanimously, to streamline the organizational structure of the CMEA by abolishing organs that had not performed well over the years, consolidating units that had in effect duplicated one another, retrenching the civil service, and generally gearing the tasks entrusted to the CMEA less to the day-to-day planning of resource allocation than to charting fully the medium- to long-term directions of structural change. Note that these objectives paralleled the intentions of Soviet *perestroyka* in 1986.

This first wholesale reorganization of the CMEA involved the abolition, amalgamation, or transformation of a large number of the formal CMEA organs (Ikonnikov 1988).[3] Although there is some confusion as to which organs were abolished,the ambiguities about the implemented transformations, save one,[4] can be removed. No fewer than 19 units were abolished or partly absorbed by existing institutions and six new ones were set up in early 1988. Three new Committees were created and one (on material-technical supply) was abolished, so that the number of committees subordinated to the Executive Committee rose to six. The number of Standing Commissions was very severely curtailed. Of the 23 extant at the end of 1987, only 12 were kept intact, two were merged, and two new Commissions were added. Finally, one of the Confer-

[3] The CMEA then consisted of 40 official organs (Session, Executive Committee and four Committees, 23 Standing Commissions, the Secretariat, seven Conferences, and three Institutes). By my reckoning as of the first half of 1988 there must have remained 28 organs.

[4] Ikonnikov (1988, p. 21) claims that also the Commission for cooperation with DEs was abolished, but I have never heard of such an organ.

ences was transformed into a Standing Commission (on legal affairs) and five others were abolished altogether, so that only the one on Water Administration and Shipping remained. The three Institutes were not affected.

Three features of these administrative changes should be retained: (1) the revamped or newly created organs were all headquartered in Moscow; (2) most sectoral organs were abolished, whereas all new and most reorganized ones were devoted to general purpose or macroeconomic problems; and (3) these organs were expected to tackle more and more structural, macroeconomic and longer-term development issues and facilitate indirect economic coordination.

Moreover, a sizable portion of the international civil service of the CMEA - 31.7 percent of the mandated contingent of late 1987 - was slated to be cut (*Hospodářské Noviny*, 1988:23, p. 11), primarily the Secretariat and Research Institute staff. Though staff cuts may have been enacted in early 1988, concrete evidence thereof is missing. Even after the originally envisaged reductions, there evidently remained considerable room for staff retrenchment and coaxing the CMEA civil service into greater efficiency (Shiryaev 1988a). These changes were apparently conceived as part and parcel of a much more sweeping reform of the CMEA, including the more informal affiliated CMEA organs.

Second, there was widespread agreement in Moscow, although the assent in some cases was rather reluctant, to rechart assistance policies to the non-European CMEA partners (Cuba, Mongolia, and Vietnam). Past economic and technical assistance efforts were deemed to have been less effective than they could or should have been. Disenchantment was evident for both recipient and donor. The donor countries committed themselves to elaborate a dovetailed multilateral approach to assisting these DEs with a view to measurably improving the medium- to long-term benefits accruing to recipients as well as donors. This effort was soon to be enhrined in a coordinated program that would become an integral component of a new integration strategy.

In a much similar vein, third, it was agreed to work out a new SEI strategy tentatively entitled *Collective concept of the international socialist division of labor for the years 1991-2005* (henceforth *Collective Concept*). This would advance SEI well beyond previous plans and programs on CMEA cooperation. In any case, the Session deemed it useful to take a fresh look at SEI objectives, policies, instruments, and basic institutional supports of regional cooperation. *Collective Concept* was to be in an advanced draft in time for the Prague CMEA Council Session in 1988. Its major objective was to lay the foundations for the "transition to a qualitatively new level of cooperation" that would eventually emanate in a "unified market." In addition to reiterating well-tested forms of CMEA relations and strengthening the role of central planning in charting guidelines for medium- to long-term structural development, the new program should foster economic efficiency and buttress the role of economics in all forms of cooperation with much wider use of commodity and financial relations and criteria of economic efficiency as solid anchors.

Fourth, directly related to the new SEI program were major decisions revolving around the precise mechanism of SEI to be elaborated in conjunction with, and perhaps in support of, ongoing economic reforms in key CPEs. Gaining concurrence on these matters has been much more convoluted than mustering support for any other item reportedly debated in Moscow. Although there was broad agreement on the need to revisit key elements of traditional CMEA planning and to overhaul monetary-financial cooperation in a significant way, members remained divided on critical economic issues. These included the introduction of a modified form of regional settlements; multilateralism in trade and payments; determination of unified exchange rates; revision of the TRP-formation mechanism; linking of domestic prices with TRPs and in turn closer with WMPs; and enhancing capital movements within the CMEA.

The Session also emphasized the need to reinvigorate the implementation of *Scientific-technological Progress* by measurably improving the economics of direct interfirm relations as well as the organizational prerequisites for such relations to enhance SEI. Within that context, firms needed to be invested with room to negotiate over prices and quantities within economic guidance rules and institutional instruments to facilitate microeconomic decision making. The measures envisaged include some highly limited form of intraregional convertibility. It was just that because, as a minimum, convertibility means that some class of transactions by some currency holders can be cleared anonymously and automatically with some provisions made for mobilizing imbalances by the surplus countries (Brabant 1989c, 1990e). The proposal launched by Ryzhkov to clear direct enterprise transactions automatically and ensure their convertibility over some transition period does not provide for final settlement, except via the TR accounts at the IBEC.

Although several agreements were signed in early 1988 to move forward with such direct enterprise relations, from the beginning, implementation was highly complicated, basically because of multiple technical problems associated with pricing, wholesale trading by firms, settlement of imbalances, and the selection of proper exchange rates.[5] Perhaps the greatest flaw of the "limited convertibility" proposal was the absence of a viable way of settling imbalances.

Finally, the Moscow Session paid lip service to the need to achieve better results with the habitual coordination of economic plans and indeed to provide support at the regional level through planning for direct enterprise relations. The GDR and Rumania voiced strong support for plan coordination in shrill contrast to the role accorded to these instruments by the other members.

4. Toward a unified CMEA market?

The above agenda makes it clear that expectations for the follow-up Session ran high. Not only were there to have been drafts of key new programs, including on attitudes toward the non-European members and the new SEI strategy. The CPEs had also committed themselves to elaborate details of the new SEI mechanism (including prices, direct wholesale trade, convertibility, exchange rates,

[5] Initially prices for such transactions were to be based on the TRP formula. Imbalances were to be settled via the regular TR accounting at the IBEC. Special exchange rates were set within the framework of the 1973, so-called Karl-Marx-Stadt agreement on joint investment coefficients (see Brabant 1987a, pp. 218-30; 1990b).

and regional settlements) and its institutions (including the two banks), and perhaps also the further streamlining of the CMEA organization.

The 44th Council Session was convened in Prague, 5-7 July 1988, after at least half a year of unsettling controversies about where to go from the recommendations issued by the 43rd Session. Needless to add that the meeting took place under some clouds and that the available reports, scanty as they are (see Kotouc 1988, Válek 1988), suggest that the real work would still be ahead.

Least open controversy existed over the stances *vis-à-vis* the three non-European members. Separate drafts of comprehensive cooperation with these three CPEs were presented in Prague. They were soon to be fused into a single coherent blueprint of the CMEA's stance on technical and economic assistance as part and parcel of *Collective Concept*. The basic objective was to further integrate these countries into the CMEA edifice[6] through concrete agreements about production cooperation and specialization, STC on more than a gratuitous basis, and generally further commercializing most but not all of their economic interactions with the European members. The programs reportedly also contained relatively extensive lists of specific development projects soon to be commissioned, but it was not clear whether all members concurred with these proposals. Either at the Prague Session or soon thereafter the European members offered to finance a CMEA-wide development fund in lieu of conventional assistance, but at least Cuba opposed any such move.[7]

The second bundle of problems examined in Prague concerned the further reorganization of the CMEA. But at least Rumania had second thoughts about some of these organizational changes (*Scînteia*, 8 July 1988, p. 5). Nonetheless, the Session welcomed the changes introduced in early 1988. It also called for continuing with vigorous restructuring. Further changes in the Standing Commissions and Committees subordinated to the Executive Committee were recommended. These were apparently part and parcel of a much more sweeping reform of the CMEA organization and personnel, including the specialized or affiliated CMEA organs, most of which were dismantled soon thereafter.

At this stage, the revamped institutional structure of the CMEA is much leaner than it ever was, excepting during the first decade of its existence, when the rump CMEA was essentially dormant. At least until mid-1990, the CMEA consisted of the Session, Executive Committee with seven subordinate Committees (on plan cooperation, engineering, STC, electronization, foreign economic relations, the agrocomplex, and fuels and raw materials), eleven Standing Commissions (electrical and nuclear energy, currency and finance, metallurgy, statistics, chemical industry, legal affairs, environment, light industry, transportation, standardization, and postal and telecommunications), the Secretariat, one Conference (on water administration), and two Institutes (on standardization and economic research), as detailed in Brabant 1989a, pp. 127-77; 1990c, g.

[6] Note that this is a significant shift of emphasis. As recently as early 1987, CMEA observers had identified these countries as not being quite ready for full cooperation in the context of the 1985 program (see Abolikhina, Bakovetskiy, and Medvedev 1987, pp. 139-40).

[7] Interview material. The size of the fund and other useful details were apparently never firmly set.

Third, as an integral link of the integration program discussed below, it was decided to specify soonest a new integration mechanism. The Prague Session emphasized the need to have in place economic instruments, institutions, and macroeconomic policies to foster substantially more intensive economic development through genuine regional integration. For that, the role of the economic tools of management, including the TR and TRPs, was to have been improved and the function of cooperation through the coordination of national economic plans modified. Firms as well as other lower-level planning tiers were henceforth to play a much more substantive role in the day-to-day pursuit of integration. Such elements of the refurbished SEI mechanism were to have been firmly in place in time for the inauguration of new five-year plans in 1991.

The Session also emphasized the need to reinvigorate the implementation of *Scientific-technological Progress* by measurably improving the organizational prerequisites and indeed the economic conditions for bolstering the ways in which firms from different CPEs can interact directly, including in the selection of prices and quantities. Investing interfirm relations with economic guidance rules and institutional supports was deemed critical to facilitate effective firm decision making based on real profitability calculations and financial self-management. In addition, it was envisaged to improve domestic and trade pricing, exchange rates, the credit mechanism of the IIB, trade and payments multilateralism through the IBEC, and other aspects pertinent to enhancing the indirect coordination of economic decisions.

Though all members but Rumania concurred on *Collective Concept* and anchoring SEI to the creation of a unified market, concrete measures regarding the TR and the TR regime, including reciprocal pricing, were left for future negotiations. The rather anemic response to the call for direct enterprise relations was probably responsible for this (*Pravda*, 24 April 1989, p. 2 noted that the volume of Soviet trade conducted through direct enterprise ties was less than 0.5 percent).

An unusual item on the agenda was the creation of socialist transnationals, which, as Oleg Bogomolov noted (*Komsomol'skaya pravda*, 23 July 1988, p. 3), would overcome "bureaucratic obstacles and the formalistic approach to tasks." The issue was thereafter discussed in the literature by a growing number of participants (Grinberg, Ligay, and Simanovskiy 1989; Shiryaev 1988b, 1989), but it was never clear what precisely was being envisaged. Whether this organizational form would differ intrinsically from the head or lead organizations that were to have spearheaded the implementation of *Scientific-technological Progress* remained fundamentally unclear.

As regards the SEI mechanism, the 44th Council Session paid lip service to the need to achieve better results with traditional forms of plan coordination and indeed to provide support at the regional level for interfirm relations. A critical role was slated to be played by production specialization, particularly in engineering, but not solely or even mainly through planning at the intergovernmental level. In addition to strategic planning coordinated at the regional level, sectoral cooperation, and, most importantly, interfirm transactions especially of parts and components were to have been measurably enhanced.

Fourth, a draft of *Collective Concept* was debated at the 44th Session. An integral part of this new SEI strategy, as noted, was the adoption of a new economic mechanism and the streamlining of economic policy in accordance with the new conditions for SEI. In this, a critical role was to have been allotted to effective production specialization, particularly in engineering. The draft debated in Prague was never published. The Secretary of the CMEA (*Rudé Právo*, 8 July 1988, p. 2) clarified that the document's focus was accelerating technological progress, intensifying production, broadening production specialization, and integrating more fully the non-European CMEA members; it also singled out the main branches, chiefly engineering and electronics, for accelerated integration and paid attention to the use of raw materials, social issues, and cooperation in environmental protection. More details were not disclosed, owing in part to *Collective Concept* having to be reanchored every five years together with medium-term growth strategies and corresponding plans.

The final issue on the agenda was the creation of a unified market in Eastern Europe - not altogether a novel idea. It certainly loomed large over the initial debates at the Council's inception and it was aimed at through various regional planning endeavors launched since the late 1950s. In 1987-1988, however, several differences were evident. One was the explicit endorsement of a common market for the first time in modern days by the Soviet Union at the 43rd Council Session; the creation of a region with free movement of goods, services, labor, and capital, was never aimed at, save perhaps by the most visionary of participants in the CMEA founding debates of 1949-1950 (see Brabant 1989a, pp. 12ff.). Also, the idea was placed at the heart of the elaboration of *Collective Concept*. Moreover, it was wholeheartedly endorsed at the 44th Session by all CMEA members, save Rumania. But it was by no means clear what a unified CMEA market might entail, even though some meeting of mind had occurred as to the establishment of the conditions for the free movement of goods, services, and other production factors within such a unified socialist market. Key elements of these preconditions were to be emplaced before late 1990, when the Executive Committee was expected to prepare recommendations for the further improvement of the mechanism of multilateral cooperation and SEI and ensuring their introduction as of 1991.

5. Toward radical changes?

As noted earlier, at the 45th Council Session in Sofia (9-10 January 1990), the CMEA members unceremoniously discarded the reform proposals worked out by the Bogomolov commission and decided to appoint another reform commission. It was also resolved to change relations within the CMEA in a number of respects. One was the trade and payments regime, moving TRPs much closer to current WMPs and replacing TR clearing with some form of convertible currency clearing or settlement. The other one was the complete revamping of the CMEA as a regional economic organization and the entire multilateral planning framework within which postwar economic collaboration in Eastern Europe had been forged.

The Bogomolov commission was installed in late 1987 or early 1988 to advise the CMEA's Executive Committee on how to shape substantive reforms of the purposes and means of SEI in the wake of the drift of the reform debate between the November 1986 "working summit" and the subsequent, 43rd Council Session in 1987. As a result of the understandings reached during the latter Session (see Section 3), the members of the commission elaborated a wide range of proposals. The first draft of some were first mooted during the 44th Council Session (Prague, 5-7 July 1988). These and their further refinement were to constitute the key inputs into the seminal discussions of the third economic summit of the 1980s. This had initially been slated for March 1989 in Prague (Brabant 1990c) with recommendations to be subsequently confirmed during the 45th Session, originally scheduled for June 1989 in Sofia. The first meeting never materialized and the second was postponed until January 1990, right after the extraordinary transitions in the sociopolitical landscape of Eastern Europe.

The new leaderships of Eastern Europe rejected the recommendations of the Bogomolov commission tabled at the 45th Council Session out of hand on the ground that they were far too timid, given the radical reform sentiment then sweeping the area. But they reneged on the promise made days before by the most ambitious of the Eastern European reformers temporarily drawn around Václav Klaus, Minister of Finance of Czechoslovakia. This contender for leadership in his country's reform debate and policies had earlier unceremoniously called for the abrogation of all treaties and indeed the *de facto* abolition of the CMEA, the multilateral features of collaboration that the organization allegedly represented for over forty years, and the complete revamping of the CMEA economies into MEs.

The Soviet Union at the Session proposed to move swiftly, beginning in 1991, with trading at current WMPs and at convertible currency or convertible currency clearing; but the proposal has, to my knowledge, not been spelled out in detail. Though there was some enthusiasm for such a shift on the part of Eastern Europe, there was also considerable apprehension about the clearing aspects and the fact that the Soviet Union, as other CMEA partners, would not have genuine firms to conduct negotiations for which they could assume full financial responsibility.

In the best CMEA tradition, the Session in the end resolved to appoint another CMEA reform commission (first under the chairmanship of Ernő Kemenes and now Béla Kádár), this time to formulate "radical" CMEA reform options. It is expected to focus its proposals in particular on what is required to revive CMEA trade and payments and perhaps provide an impetus to integration "from the bottom up," even if that means fragmenting the CMEA edifice into several tiers. This commission, which is independent of CMEA organs, is being assisted by a group of experts, who were to have prepared technical proposals by late April 1990. The commission was to consider them in May with a view to preparing its own recommendations to the "leading" CMEA organs sometime by mid-year. Soon thereafter, probably in September according to the original timetable, another full-scale economic summit or a substantive Council Session was expected to be called to order. By mid-1990, these various schedules appear to have seriously slipped.

The concrete proposals that may eventually be endorsed are not, of course, known at this stage. It would therefore be premature to state what the various positions on CMEA economic reform may eventually turn out to be. Yet, there is sufficient articulated evidence that the room for genuine economic reform in the CMEA as a whole is exceedingly narrow. The position of the PETs, especially Hungary and Poland, but also Czechoslovakia, is apparently twofold. On the one hand, these countries aim at downgrading the CMEA organization into something like the secretarial functions of the Organisation for Economic Co-operation and Development (OECD) at best, but more likely as an "open" regional secretariat. In other words, it would essentially become a facilitating organ entrusted with preparing briefs for consideration at the political level. It would not, however, possess any muscle in terms of enhancing regional economic integration. Furthermore, multilateral solutions are no longer seriously entertained at this stage. Instead, the Central European CMEA members as well as the Soviet Union appear to be promoting the idea of reinforcing bilateral relations through *ad hoc* solutions that fall short, at least for now, of placing the reciprocal exchanges on a convertible currency footing. Especially the reforming Central European economies covet conducting their trade on a full-fledged convertible currency basis. In relations with the Soviet Union, however, the drift of the discussions and recent events suggest that the TR regime will be replaced with convertible currency clearing of transactions evaluated at "imputed" WMPs, not necessarily prices that agents can support on the basis of their own profitability calculations.

Little thought appears to have been given to the possibility of introducing tiered integration within a CMEA enterprise endowed with a full-fledged constitutional framework, similar, for example, to the Rome Treaties that have been so important in fostering integration in the EC. By separating judicial, legislative, and executive aspects of CMEA integration through an overall constitutional framework, the boundaries within which individual members can advance their own cause would be clearly demarcated. A fairly flexible arrangement would then enable some countries ready and willing to move forward with integration more rapidly than others without harming the latter's fundamental interests (Brabant 1989f, 1990c). Especially the Central European countries, among themselves, would stand to gain measurably from actively pursuing regional integration, perhaps through a customs union. Finding the proper ways and means of exploiting their comparative advantages could, and perhaps should, constitute one key ambition of domestic reform.

* * *

Even if a swift decision with broad implications for integration in Eastern Europe were to be reached soon, one should harbor no illusion that the envisaged changes could be implemented quickly, even though virtually all CMEA countries are embarking on broad-based societal reform in a rather adverse environment, as examined in Chapter 9. Western assistance can only provide so much. What is really required is a broadly conceived structural adjustment effort for the region as a whole with the support of third countries. Whether this can be harnessed effectively, such as it was after World War II for Western Europe, remains to be seen.

3

The treadmill of reforms in Eastern Europe

Concepts about enacting economic reforms have been explored by the CPEs and MPEs for over thirty years. Indeed, modifications in the model and strategy of the orthodox CPE have been entertained roughly since the mid-1950s, after the first egregious bottlenecks with Stalinist-type, highly centralized economic administration had become glaringly evident. Since then, various substitute models have been formulated and many different types of MPEs have been tried. But none has even come close to what a PET at this particular stage is striving to become. It is instructive to obtain a firm grasp of the vastly different economic environment that the more ambitious of these countries are currently aiming at. Such an understanding is a prerequisite to discussing the transition from where these countries find themselves at present to the status they are coveting.

Section 1 briefly discusses why it is desirable to bear in mind the critical characteristics of CPEs and MPEs when discussing the transition phase of PETs. The chief features of the socialist development strategy are recapitulated next. Section 3 summarizes key features of the traditional CPE that have been mutated into the more streamlined variants of an MPE. The most important features of the latter that will need to be redesigned to carry out the program set by the PETs are set forth next. The chapter concludes with some indications on the starting conditions for market-oriented reforms, which themselves are detailed in the next chapter.

1. Relevance of the legacies of central planning

With the exception of Bulgaria, Czechoslovakia, and the Soviet Union, the CMEA countries under discussion here are all MPEs. Even the first three have had some experience with economic reform. This applies most notably to foreign trading activities in the cases of Bulgaria and Czechoslovakia. Certainly, the Soviet Union also explored reforms before the emergence of *perestroyka* since about 1986 (see Brabant 1990f). The first attempt was the regionalization scheme launched in 1957. Other reform variants were tried intermittently through the first mootings of *perestroyka* in 1985. Throughout all of these efforts, most conspicuous was that the foreign sectors of the Soviet economy were not at all affected by the various efforts to bring about managerial changes in the domestic economy. This changed abruptly with the sudden announcement in August 1986 that foreign trade reforms would be introduced as of 1987. This all too hastily conceived objective has thus far met with little success. As a result, the Soviet economy has remained essentially divorced from activities abroad through the classic instruments of the MFT. Few domestic economic agents have been exposed to reformed instruments in the foreign sector.

But Eastern Europe has had over two decades of involvement with reform, particularly in the foreign trade and payments sectors. In spite of this experience and the abandonment of the classical CPE model at a fairly early stage of postwar development, it is nonetheless useful to clarify briefly the traditional CPE model. There are several reasons that prompt me to do so. Perhaps the most important is that virtually all reform concepts acted upon over the past thirty years without exception have failed to address the core of economic decision making. Instead of pursuing the logic of economic decentralization, MPEs have invariably retained the heartland of central administration of the day-to-day affairs in macro- as well as microeconomic spheres. Genuine economic decentralization steered through dovetailed macroeconomic policies and their supporting instruments and institutions has never been targeted. This attitude may have crystallized because of apprehensions about the ability of market-oriented decision making to yield the desired output profile. It may also have underlined the pervasive lack of confidence on the part of the leadership in its own ability to guide spontaneous forces within a coherent macroeconomic control framework of its design and under its pervasive control. As a result, the PET at this juncture has to grapple with numerous legacies of the CPE model. These range from human psychology all the way through the nuts-and-bolts of ensuring macroeconomic coordination through other means than some variant of central planning.

There are many ways in which the traditional CPE can be stylized. I prefer to discuss these categories with reference to the more abstract, prototype CPE because it offers an opportunity for systematic analysis. Table 3.1 shows a systematic overview of the principal points that I should like to make here and in the next chapter.

2. The first strategy of socialist economic development

A growth strategy is a complex of measures to ensure that available resources are allocated with a view to attaining long-term development objectives. These as a rule cover a number of often conflicting goals of socioeconomic development, including the latter's speed, income distribution, and the earmarking of savings for the preferred capital-formation process.

Following the immediate postwar phase of economic reconstruction and consolidation of Communist Party rule, the quintessential socialist development strategy adopted by the Eastern European CPE was centered on industrialization in breadth of mostly backward, agrarian economies. This objective was slated to be implemented by manipulating key policy instruments, by transforming the economic institutions in place, and by prescribing some behavioral rules that together make up the model.

Socialist development processes anchored to the pursuit of forced industrialization in breadth played a crucial role during the first decades of the

Table 3.1. Key features of CPEs, MEPs, PETs, and RPEs

	CPEs	MPEs	PETs	RPEs
1. STRATEGY				
Industrialization				
- in breadth	strong	tempered	deemphasized	irrelevant
- income distribution	regulated	controlled	deregulated	fiscal controls
- investment	forced	regulated	deemphasized	market regulated
- accumulation	rising	tempered	eased	market regulated
- consumption	minimum assured	eased controls	assured	market regulated
2. MODEL				
- central planning	detailed physical	fewer details	strategic decisions	perhaps industrial policy
- nationalization of physical assets	all except land in some countries	all except land in some countries	property forms under review; start privatization	all property forms permitted; privatization
- collectivization of agriculture	fairly rigid, except Poland	peasant plots and markets encouraged	multiple organizational forms	chiefly private and cooperative
- labor regulation	strict wage fund and norms	wage fund controlled but norms fluid	controls under review	market set

- indirect instruments and institutions	poor	partly recognized	emerging	comprehensive
- micro	nonexisting	administrative regulation	relaxation	full
- macro	nominal	poorly developed monetary, banking, and fiscal systems	gradual build-up	full
- enterprise autonomy	poor	administratively regulated	emerging	full
- administrative coordination	overwhelming	strong, if weakened	vestiges left	not applicable
- informal personal initiative	important on margin but not encouraged	legal and illegal second economy	formalized	markets integrated
- market insulation	complete	weakening	weakening rapidly	no longer
- prices and exchange rates	fully delinked	detached	linked for some goods	fully market linked
- foreign trade organizations	full trade control	partly in control	gradually placed on market relations	market determined
- price equalization	all flows	loosened	marginally still	abolished

CPEs' evolution. This concern was so overwhelming that decision making about the overall allocation of resources was almost exclusively geared by the priority role of industry in the elaboration of a more or less autarkic economic complex. Autarky here is not synonymous with complete severance of all foreign contacts, however, although at one time a narrowly defined type of economic self-sufficiency was certainly immanent in the socialist concept of the best allocation of resources. The pivotal focus of economic policy is the creation of a diversified industrial economy that can function relatively independently of disturbances propagated from abroad.

Although there are many aspects of the economic model that ultimately derive from the metaeconomics of Marxist-Leninist precepts, this link is notably tight for the traditional development strategy pursued by a CPE. The core of the doctrine is the set of so-called "economic laws" of the historical path to socialist development (Brabant 1980, pp. 63-69). Using this body of ideological beliefs as inspiration or *ex post* rationalization of economic policy choices, the paramount strategic objective of the classical CPE is centrally steered balanced growth paced by extensive industrialization with the purpose of completing the material-technical foundations of socialist society as rapidly as feasible. That is to say, the CPE's initial development strategy aims, among other objectives, at full employment, rapid socioeconomic growth, extensive industrialization as the foundation for steady economic development, and a substantial degree of domestic policy autonomy. Regarding the latter feature, it is important to retain that policy makers in CPEs accord a pronounced priority role to selected industrial branches for which they mobilize material and human resources almost regardless of their true scarcity gauges. At least, most of the current "surplus value," that is the excess of normal revenues over fixed and variable labor costs, is appropriated not for present consumption but for the financing of the expansion of selected production sectors at the expense of agriculture and services in particular. As evinced during the early stages of industrialization, levels of living of the population could even decline for a few years, something that the planning authorities could enforce with impunity.

A growth strategy must be buttressed by an appropriate economic model or the combination of institutions, micro- and macroeconomic policies, behavioral rules, and policy instruments that help to implement the strategy. In the CPE, behavioral prescriptions are by definition normative, and sanctioned as such. Before entering a brief discussion of the key components of the traditional CPE model, it is useful to ponder the relationship between economic reform and the industrialization strategy typically embraced when the traditional CPE model was first installed.

As experience has demonstrated, forced industrialization through a highly centralized economic model was suitable for carrying out a consistent, rapid, and radical transformation of a relatively backward, predominantly agrarian economy, such as Russia's, into an industrial society by overcoming various chronic bottlenecks to steady growth. These included an unstable global economic environment, initially domestic strife over sociopolitical organization, inexperienced management, a labor force unaccustomed to the industrial production mode, a burdensome agrarian overpopulation, and others. But such an approach to socioeconomic development is less suited to ensure steady growth in a moderately to highly diversified industrial economy that can no longer extract the desired output increment chiefly from the addition of primary production factors to the production process. This sets the stage for exploring economic reform.

In its most general connotation, an economic reform has a component that seeks to reformulate the traditional socialist development strategy and another to implement the envisaged redirection of the development strategy. In the first instance, a reform is a process aimed at enhancing the way in which resources are allocated with the goal of satisfying present and future, private as well as social, needs better than before the reform. As such, its features may range from the philosophy of development policies to economic institutions and technical guidelines for economic behavior. These wide-ranging issues, touching upon social, political, humanitarian, economic, cultural, ideological, and other aspects of society, to a larger or smaller extent, are inextricably intermeshed with economic reforms. But they cannot possibly be discussed adequately here. Some of the more technical aspects of reform are detailed in Section 4.

The difficulty of rationalizing reforms stems from that fact that most often the immediate inducement to seeking such a change is flagging economic performance due to a slowdown in the pace of economic expansion, owing largely to sluggish factor productivity growth, or sociopolitical tensions resulting from persistent imbalances. The most direct objective is therefore finding ways and means of revitalizing the economy and generating economic growth primarily on the basis of factor productivity gains rather than through increments in physical factor supply, which is no longer feasible because of resource constraints. That is to say, the basic objective of the development strategy adopted when the CPE was first installed remains unchanged when policy makers first feel the need to seek reform. As indicated in Table 3.1, the leadership of an MPE is still hoping to generate rapid economic growth through industrialization, but this process is now to be anchored to factor productivity gains rather than the continuing injection of new factors of production or the reappropriation of existing factors. Neither of the latter options is feasible after a while or only to such a degree that the potential return is no longer worth the effort.

3. Salient features of the CPE model

A growth strategy must be buttressed by an appropriate economic model or the combination of institutions, micro- and macroeconomic policies, behavioral rules, and policy instruments that help to implement the strategy. In the CPE, behavioral prescriptions are by definition normative, and sanctioned as such. The CPE model is dominated by a hierarchical system of planning and management. Decision-making authority is vested at the center of national power to ensure a special kind of close interdependence between political and economic functions.

When first introduced, the economic model consisted of: (1) central planning in physical detail of nearly all economic decisions and restrictive regulation of the decision-making role of economic agents; (2) nearly exhaustive nationalization of capital, natural resources, and, in most cases, land; (3) collectivization of agriculture in combination with state agricultural enterprises; (4) strict regulation of labor allocation, though outright conscription remained the exception; (5) a pronounced disregard of indirect coordination instruments and associated policies and institutions for steering resource allocation; (6) managerial autonomy highly circumscribed by central planning and by the controls exerted by local Party and, in most countries, also trade union interest groups; (7) the channeling of most economic decisions through a complex administrative hierarchy, which tends to handle matters rather bureaucratically; (8) in spite of central regulation and administration, a minimum of personal initiative is condoned - in fact required - to implement plan instructions at all levels of production and consumption; and (9) rather rigid separation of the domestic economy from foreign economic influences. Some of these characteristics need to be clarified briefly.

1. Comprehensive central planning

As the core of the traditional model, planning means selecting development targets and allocating resources to fulfill those aims as well as possible. In the traditional CPE, the planning instruments and objectives are determined by a select circle of Party members, especially the Politburo, on behalf of the Communist Party as society's vanguard. Resources are essentially allocated by central fiat - not necessarily by one central administration. The plan endeavors to formulate instructions so that they leave no alternative to their execution. The objective is to ensure a close linkage between political and economic functions. For that reason, the plan assigns producers mandatory targets on inputs, outputs, pricing, wages, capital allocation, and other aspects of what would normally be within the compass of entrepreneurial behavior. In other words, questions concerning what is to be produced, how production is to be organized, what inputs are to be used, and so on are, in principle, settled by the norms specified in the plan, not by the foresight, risk taking, and creative ability of an entrepreneurial élite; the latter's initiative and leadership, if present, are not to impinge on the priority of fulfilling physical yardsticks.

Needless to say, the real world of production and consumption differs substantially from this paradigm. For one, conscious human activity cannot be reduced to the simple act of pulling a lever. Some scope for decision making needs to be reserved for agents because the planning center cannot possibly steer the economy in detail. Even if this omniscience is not already unrealistic at the outset of socialist planning, the appropriate functioning of an increasingly complex economy on the basis of coordinated directives and regulators demands that modifications be introduced. In fact, its compelling logic as a rule emerges very early on in the functioning of the traditional CPE, if only because the leadership quickly feels the compelling need to come to grips with various levels of uncertainty in economic decisions. This arises from the existing or rapidly growing complexity of steering an economy. It also emanates from planning being intrinsically a stochastic process if only because some sectors, including international trade and agriculture, depend on events that are largely beyond the scope of the information at the disposal of central planners and, moreover, beyond their control. Such uncertainty has to be mitigated either through more flexible planning or by *ad hoc* solutions formulated by microeconomic agents. Because the lower tiers of the planning hierarchy normally harbor preferences that differ from those of the central policy makers, their decisions coincide with the center's only by fluke. The plan must therefore eventually be supplemented with proper criteria for guiding the choices of economic agents.

2. Efficiency indicators and resource allocation

Technical rules on static economic efficiency are rather primitive and, moreover, passive. The theory of planning has generally crystallized around quantity calculations, as distinct from value planning. Ideological precepts and historical circumstances may have contributed to considering the dynamic results of economic expansion far more important than static efficiency. From the beginning of socialist economic organization, it has been accepted as axiomatic that socialism implies the effective control of the economy by society in pursuit of its objectives through appropriate policy instruments and associated institutions. The latter revolve around the planned steering of socioeconomic life by the state. Without this being necessarily well articulated, the accepted premise of central planning has been that tools of indirect regulation are not dependable; resource allocation must hence proceed largely through other, at times concealed, signals.

3. Indirect coordination instruments and institutions

Market-type instruments and institutions under central planning are rather primitive and passive. Socialist price policies provide a case in point of the subordination of value criteria to physical targets. Industrial wholesale prices are traditionally calculated by the center on the basis of average sectoral costs without making due allowance for capital, nonreproduceable natural resources, and land scarcities - hence the severe downward bias in prices with a high resource content (Petrakov 1986, 1987). Furthermore, the true cost of imports and real export opportunities are poorly reflected in administrative prices. Agricultural procurement prices are set differently depending upon the organization of agriculture, the specific goals the government intends to pursue with its agricultural procurement prices, and the planning center's influence over free peasant markets, which enjoy considerable freedom within self-policed rules on what is acceptable in the context of the CPE society. Consumer prices are, as a rule, divorced from wholesale prices by a complex network of subsidies and taxes that in part reflect government preferences. (There are, of course, other prices, such as for handicraft and free peasant markets as discussed in Brabant 1987a, pp. 129-63, but the three regimes outlined here will do.) In addition to these major dichotomies, prices are generally held unchanged for long periods of time for rather eclectic reasons (Brabant 1987b, pp. 34-62), but also to facilitate plan implementation and guide consumer behavior.

Note that each price regime is steered rather separately through particular institutional and policy choices. The disparity is maintained because the price regimes are modified according to criteria deemed suitable to reach social objectives or to enhance plan formulation, implementation, and control. Because prices are averaged over branchwide costs, there are always firms that incur losses and others that report a nominal profit. This calls for the continual redistribution of value added in each sector and also across sectors.

The deliberate choice to underplay value planning extended to nearly all familiar market-type instruments and institutions. In fact, the organization of the economy and macropolicy were simply to enhance the realization of priority goals expressed mostly in physical terms. Other instruments were not to interfere with the plan's execution, although they did to some extent. Thus, the CPE's fiscal policy is almost exclusively concerned with indirect taxation (that is, turnover taxes) to ensure some equilibrium between demand and supply of consumer goods. Incomes in sectors other than agriculture, services, and handicrafts are essentially limited to wages and bonuses, with little variation among workers or correlation with actual productivity levels. In cooperative agriculture, incomes depend on nominal profits derived from assigned output and sales at administratively set procurement prices. Additional revenues are obtained through sales on free peasant markets and the initially highly confined second economy. Both are regulated indirectly by the center, including through moral suasion and voluntary restraints on the part of agents. Because the center, in principle, controls wages and monetary transfers, which are the primary sources of disposable incomes in the CPE, it is a matter of indifference whether these incomes are regulated through direct income taxes or through the direct prescription of wage rates. In the orthodox CPE, essentially the latter method is embraced.

Based overwhelmingly on the real bills' doctrine, which posits that credits should be accorded only for real flows, in which sense credit becomes "productive" and hence conducive to monetary equilibrium, monetary policy has, at best, been passive. Accordingly, in most CPEs loans are extended for well-specified purposes, granted for fixed periods of time, secured by real assets, repayable, and centrally regulated or even administered on a planned basis. At the macroeconomic level, this model operates with a monobanking system. Money plays a passive role, particularly in the production sphere, where it simply facilitates the allocation of resources previously earmarked in physical terms in the plan. Financial assets for households are generally confined to cash, lottery tickets, savings deposits, and occasionally government or enterprise bonds; those of firms are as a rule limited to bank deposits. Fiscal policies are subordinated to the general aims of the plan and social precepts on income differentiation, profits, and price regulation. Most enterprise profits and losses are ventilated through the central budget. Managerial and worker incentives seek to overfulfill quantitative production targets, on which bonuses depend.

Credit policy is geared toward facilitating interfirm transactions. Capital investments, usually financed through the budget, which collects for this purpose virtually all enterprise profits, are undertaken with minimal regard for macroeconomic efficiency and scarcity levies are as a rule not applied. Credit institutions are expected simply to finance the investment targets chosen by the center, regardless of how these decisions are formulated. A more active monetary policy to equate consumer revenues plus net changes in private savings with the value of consumer goods earmarked for distribution during the plan period is sporadically instituted to counter dangerous open or repressed inflation, usually in the form of a monetary or currency reform.

4. Foreign trade and payments regime

The foreign trade and payments regime is passive in the selection and implementation of the development strategy. An integral element of the CPE model is the more or less complete disjunction of the domestic economy from external influences, especially in the microeconomic sphere, by means of special instruments and institutions. Interaction with other economies is compressed to the minimum still compatible with the overall development goals centered on rapid industrialization. For economies that cannot be autarkic because of size or resource endowment, severing domestic decision making from world market criteria has had several important drawbacks.

The institutions and mechanisms for conducting trade were selected as a direct consequence of the failure to adopt a comprehensive, internally consistent regional economic policy in the late 1940s (Brabant 1989a, pp. 25ff.) in the context of the CMEA. By compressing the interaction with other economies to the minimum still compatible with rapid industrialization, each CPE sought to isolate itself from the world economy, including other CPEs, in search of protection against foreign events. The MFT was expressly instituted to neutralize all influences from abroad, whether positive or disruptive, including with respect to other CPEs, and thus to further domestic policy autonomy.

External economic relations do not form a coherent component of the CPE. Organizationally, there is virtually complete disjunction of the domestic economy from activities abroad. This is accomplished by the nationalization of the foreign trade and exchange systems (Grote 1981, Konstantinov 1984). The former resorts under the Ministry of Foreign Trade, which is in principle in charge of the MFT, but usually delegates the authority to trade to a few FTOs organized by broad economic sectors, trade direction, and possibly currency of settlement. These organizations purchase domestic products for export and sell imports at domestically prevailing prices. Differences between fiat domestic and foreign prices expressed in domestic currency via the official or commercial exchange rate are offset through the so-called price-equalization account, which is a component of the central budget.

Trade decisions in the CPE usually result from a combination of economic and other factors. Trade serves chiefly as a means to fulfill the overall development goals. The planning of the level and composition of trade is intermeshed with the more general planning approach through material balances. Whether to import or to produce domestically is usually resolved by considering the domestic availability of inputs and the necessity to pay for imports. In any case, the central planner exhibits only marginal interest in reaping the benefits of export-led growth or in minimizing the real cost of the preferred import substitution. Planning of the geographical distribution of earmarked trade is largely a function of the home economy's need for noncompeting imports and their availability in alternative markets, export commitments, and consciously planned relative surpluses and shortages in the material balances to comply with commitments in BTPAs. Comparisons of prevailing prices as basic inputs into trade decision making are rarely undertaken as the price-equalization mechanism siphons off (covers) apparent trade profits (losses). Such differences are inconsequential for subsequent allocation policies. This near-irrelevance of prices applies, of course, also to the official or nominally commercial exchange rate.

Trade is by definition a sector that eludes the complete control of one planning center and that can hardly be managed in quantitative terms only. To gain greater stability in domestic economic activity, the CPEs aim also at forecasting trade flows as accurately as possible. But not all activities and fluctuations abroad are predictable. Born out of the postwar economic, political, and strategic constellation of forces, detailed *ex ante* BTPAs at relatively stable, if artificial, prices suited administrative planning. It also facilitated the implementation of the political aspirations of some CPEs whose realization would have been chancier in a multilateral environment.

The insulation of domestic processes from direct interaction with agents abroad in the real sphere is accomplished by letting FTOs separate home firms from foreign economic agents. Indirect influences are minimized as well. Actual trade events can impact on the domestic economy, but usually not through price pressures because domestic prices are set autonomously by administrative fiat; nominal gains and losses from trade are simply absorbed by fiscal means. But there are macroeconomic impacts. A disturbance from planned import cost and export return, if accommodated, affects the disposable budget, and ultimately consumer incomes, as well as the foreign exchange situation (see Brabant 1987a, pp. 110ff.; Lawson 1988; Wolf 1988). Planners attempt to neutralize the impact of this perturbation by sterilizing trade results that deviate from planned magnitudes. Alternatively, they offset trade gains or losses by varying other budgetary outlays or they postpone adjustment until a replenishment of foreign exchange reserves or servicing of foreign debt can be scheduled in the next plan. This potential indirect influence does not play an overriding role in decision making, however, because the bulk of trade is in any case regulated through comprehensive BTPAs with rather autonomous prices.

As a crucial implication of this trade model, macroeconomic decision makers are generally unaware of the real economic cost of their import-substitution policies. From the planner's point of view, this does not matter much so long as autarky reigns supreme. Although a state may successfully cripple the price mechanism on a national scale, if it allows external processes to actively supplement domestic availabilities, even if only for informational purposes, it is not quite clear how the inherently uncontrollable foreign opportunities can be dovetailed with the rigidly centralized internal economic relations.

There is, of course, a microeconomic equivalent to the lack of interest in trade results per se by central decision makers: Economic agents remain ignorant of the true scarcity cost of world market availabilities and requirements. This matter gains particular importance once the potential for extracting the surplus from the traditional sector nears exhaustion and policy options in the CPEs come to parallel those typical of MEs. In particular, the CPEs stand to benefit from improved allocatory efficiency and reduced imbalances.

4. Objectives of economic reforms in MPEs

As argued in Section 2, the centralized economic model was instrumental in fostering a consistent, rapid, and radical transformation of a relatively backward economy into an industrial society by helping to remedy various bottlenecks to steady growth. But such a centralized model cannot ensure steady growth in a fairly diversified industrial economy with limited reserves of production factors. In developed countries where this centralized planning model was tried, the outcome in terms of maintaining a significant pace of growth of per capita income levels was very disappointing. This set the stage for seeking economic reform. Although some changes in the development strategy away from rapid industrialization in heavy industry sectors are embraced in the process, the alpha and omega of the first reforms of CPEs have been piecemeal changes in the centralized economic model.

Not all aspects of the changes in economic model can be adequately discussed here, even when the purview is limited to the more technical tangents of economic reform. So many aspects of the economy and society have been affected in the process that it would not even be possible to list all of them in the space available. My aim is more modest: In addition to touching upon the core objectives of the reform, I describe briefly the most important aspects of reforms in enterprise behavior, wholesale trade, pricing, foreign trade, wage and related benefits, and the financial sector.

The MPE is primarily concerned about streamlining the economic model and ensuring that it capitalizes upon some of the sources of factor productivity growth that are difficult to exploit adequately under detailed central planning. Whereas the models embraced at the outset of the CPE exhibited considerable concordance and, in fact, a great deal of uniformity, the reforms sought prior to the inauguration of the current drift toward market orientation assumed various forms. These may be captured under two broad labels, namely the selectively decentralized and the modified recentralized economic models, whose key distinctive features are captured in Table 3.1. The latter were pursued from around the early 1970s until the current ferment, and in fact continue to predominate in several Eastern European countries, most notably the Soviet Union. The former constituted the backbone of the first wholesale wave of economic reforms undertaken in the 1960s, although some had important antecedents in experiments launched as early as the mid-1950s.

During the late 1950s and much of the 1960s, especially the European planned economies made generally nontrivial attempts to implant a selectively decentralized economic model with the intention of bolstering factor productivity growth. Although not quite uniform, the selectively decentralized models exhibited common transformations in policy instruments and some of the supporting institutions of the highly centralized economic model. But they kept intact the basic precepts that anchored the regulation of economic development in the centralized model. This applied especially to the broad goals of extensive economic growth. Such reforms therefore focused nearly exclusively on finding a more pragmatic division of administrative and economic duties between the center and local planning tiers. Changes were sought to activate an enterprise policy that could facilitate local decision making on the basis of cost-benefit analyses and in recognition of market preferences, especially with regard to external trade. But, as a rule, central planning and its administrative machinery were retained, with only some decision-making responsibilities delegated to lower-level organs. Firms could influence the formulation or implementation of the central plan. The number of directive plan indicators was significantly reduced. Gross output norms were replaced by other control levers such as sales, net output, profits, and net export revenues whose realized magnitudes corresponded to material incentives, usually tailored to the needs of individual firms. In this approach, only minimal reliance was placed on price indicators, as comprehensive price reform, to harmonize relative prices with underlying scarcities and put in place mechanisms for adjusting relative prices to shifts in demand and supply, continued to be eschewed.

Because central authorities no longer vied to determine enterprise policy unilaterally, as that assignment was partly entrusted to enterprise associations or lower-level planning organs, the task of overall planning became actually much more demanding. The most determined attempt to reach economic decentralization would logically have transformed central planning into macroeconomic policies to guide and control microeconomic units so as to ensure that the gap between the precepts underlying the central plan and the motivation of agents entrusted with day-to-day local planning and decision making would not become forbidding.

One of the key elements in promoting coordination between the center and local executors is the improvement of relative prices, as defined. Perhaps the most pivotal of the instruments to be enhanced when planners decide to devolve decision making to the lower planning tiers therefore is price reform, which has been envisaged since the mid-1960s. Establishing wholesale and retail prices indicative of relative scarcities prevailing in the economy, including foreign trade channels, may act as the fulcrum for reforming the entire economic mechanism, but few economies envisaged this transformation. As a result, one should consider separately the liberalization of the price regime, the information content of fiat prices, and the linkup between domestic and trade prices in evaluating the price reform component of an MPE. All planned economies sought to improve domestic prices at least on an intermittent basis by rescaling the principles of price computation, funneling real trade costs into domestic accounting, and letting enterprises to some extent react to changes in demand and supply via the price mechanism. But central control remained pervasive, and so confined flexibility in most countries to the periodic resetting of fiat prices.

Regardless of the chief aim of the price reform, actual calculations can be executed in many different ways. Even in the most conservative MPE the spirit of reform brought about the revision of administratively set prices on a periodic basis to take fluctuations in domestic as well as foreign demand and supply into account. Greater flexibility in administrative price formation was envisaged so that prices could continue to convey meaningful information to the plan executors. This assumed the form either of more frequent recalibrations of centrally set prices or the delegation of greater authority over price formation to the lower planning tiers, but with considerable ideological and political shackles.

A related issue is the degree to which revised or reformed prices can act as guidelines for the decision making of firms. In some cases, the latter had no direct control over price formation, although they were expected to react to the parameters issued by the pricing center. When they were introduced, these prices reflected somewhat better the true scarcities of capital, land, natural resources, and foreign currency. In a few MPEs, prices provided feedback on the state of product markets to central policy makers. In some, enterprises or their associations were allowed to revise prices from time to time in response to changes in costs. Firms were entitled to influence costs directly through a more careful selection of inputs and suppliers, by producing according to market demand, and, in some cases, by using their authority over price formation. Profits were to become more meaningful especially to determine premiums and social advantages to the workers, to provide for self-financing, and to guide entrepreneurial behavior more generally. But in all MPEs, including those in which price adjustments from then on became a quasi-continuous process rather than a once-and-for-all major undertaking, price movements were permitted only within pre-set narrow margins.

With respect to the information content of prices, all MPEs made room for a more active role of prices, even if set by central fiat, in regulating production and distribution processes. Although prices never fully reflected objective scarcities, they undoubtedly were moved closer to actual production costs. In some cases they even reacted to changes in supply and demand. Elsewhere, almost all prices continued primarily as parameters to transmit orders from the center to the lower planning tiers as well as units for accounting and control. An attempt was made by all MPEs to allot a more active role to prices and limited authority to set prices was granted to firms or their associations.

In some countries, fiat prices for some products were allowed to fluctuate depending on demand and supply, possibly within pre-set boundaries. Three generic price types came to the fore: administratively set prices as in the classical CPE, market-determined prices (although subject to informal controls), and prices that could move above a certain floor, below a certain ceiling, or between two extremes. Countries that allowed such partial flexibility committed themselves gradually to broaden the scope for periodic price adjustments by expanding the scope of the "from-to" group and, to a lesser extent, fully fluctuating price categories. But this planned evolution was adhered to only at the very beginning of the MPE environment for a number of reasons. Retail prices were also modified, but they have continued to be adjusted by the pricing authorities to ensure some semblance of balance in consumer markets and to hold inflationary pressures in check. These price-modifying processes have not entirely been devoid of administrative arbitrariness, however.

Though prices in most MPEs, therefore, continued to play much the same role as they did before, crucial for reaching proper decisions in trade-dependent economies was the linkup between domestic and trade prices. Most MPEs set pseudo exchange rates and gradually accorded a more important role to real foreign trade opportunities in the central recomputation of prices. Very few, however, have ever allowed trade results to influence domestic prices directly, even if economic agents obtained some pricing latitude.

A sharp distinction should be drawn between using trade results in domestic resource allocation and in profit calculations. The former type of streamlining was introduced in an attempt to motivate producers or traders to promote selected trade contracts. But firms were not necessarily entitled to pass on real costs. So their decisions on matters not covered by the plan were perforce reached on the basis of what appeared to be profitable from the microeconomic point of view. Although trade prices undeniably exerted a growing influence on domestic prices, the price system in most CPEs, on the whole, remained relatively inflexible, more so for consumer than for producer prices. For the former, various subsidies and taxes buffered the domestic price system against socially undesirable changes in the cost of living.

But a price overhaul was by no means the exclusive focus of the coordination instruments to be adjusted in replacing the CPE with an MPE environment. Extensive use of selective fiscal, credit, and income policies aimed at inducing firms and households to act in accordance with overall plan objectives was to be fostered too, although in these model variants authorities clung to direct control over a number of key economic processes. Most forms of nonprice resource allocation, some in concealed formats, might have been intended as transitory elements. But subsequent events and efforts launched to combat the perceived adverse consequences of reform, tended to inhibit their anticipated removal. Furthermore, even after the transition period, the preferences of the ruling political and administrative élites continued to enjoy a disproportionate weight. The link between imbalances and price movements in most of these reforming countries became somewhat more transparent, more so in the countries where prices could move within overall boundaries and least in countries that by and large continued to adhere to fiat pricing. External imbalances, as a rule, could not be transmitted to the domestic price mechanism because of the continuing focal role of the MFT and price equalization, albeit that the latter was now practiced with greater circumspection.

For example, credit and interest rate policies in the selectively decentralized model were intended to guide the allocation of capital funds. Instead of gratis budgetary appropriations, a greater role was reserved for banks, where firms could procure funds to finance improvements in production capacity and whence consumers could finance the purchase of durable goods. The interest rate policy associated with this devolution of financial policies was to foster greater rationality in the allocation of investment funds. Bank financing remained closely supervised by the central authorities, however. Moreover, key investment decisions, such as the establishment of new factories and their financing, were to remain the exclusive prerogative of the central authorities. None of the reforms envisioned the creation of autonomous financial markets in which local or foreign agents could mobilize voluntary savings.

Because of the concerns about increasing factor productivity, economic reform particularly in the smaller, trade-dependent economies sought to give high priority to trade expansion. Precisely because of their dependence on intragroup markets, a more trade-intensive growth strategy could mature only if CMEA partners were able to accommodate such shifts or if economic agents were entitled to explore outside channels much more intensively. Because the latter course was not considered advantageous, owing to the Cold War and Soviet predilections regarding regional cohesion, including within the framework of the CMEA, from the mid-1950s until the late 1980s a somewhat more positive attitude toward regional economic cooperation came to prevail, affecting both the strategy and the model of trade. But that stance on SEI has fluctuated a good deal over time and there have been substantive differences in the positions defended by the various members at any moment of time. Thus, in the partially decentralized framework, many enterprises retained the right to engage in trade directly, and the link between domestic and trade prices was not entirely severed. It was strengthened through the creation of surrogates for exchange rates that influenced at least the accounting of firms engaged in foreign transactions. At the policy level, this stance was affected by two important events. On the one hand, efforts to bolster SEI and regional interaction were explored with determination. Also an all-out drive was launched to upgrade production facilities by importing complete technologies especially from DMEs.

Foreign trade reforms as a rule affect four areas: (1) price formation, price levels, and relative prices, possibly including a more effective link between domestic and external markets through the intermediary of surrogate exchange rates; (2) the central regulation of trade largely on a macroeconomic basis; (3) the specific operation of the MFT, which finds itself being strengthened and weakened at the same time; and (4) the promulgation of links with foreign enterprises through some variant of industrial cooperation, including joint ventures. Although the various measures resorting under these four headings were loosely connected in partial reforms, innovations in the trade sector were intended to be harmonized with each other and with internal changes in the reforms that sought comprehensive administrative streamlining.

Virtually all variants of this selective decentralization came to an abrupt halt at the latest in the early 1970s. Hungary was in some respects the only major exception from this generalization. There are many reasons why the reforms were aborted. This policy stance jelled in part because the hoped-for stimulus to factor productivity growth did not materialize. To counter the perceived negative impact of reforms, on the whole, these countries sought to revert to the central allocation of resources, reduce the autonomy of enterprises, curb the flexibility of decision-making instruments, and sanction other retreats from partial reforms. The resultant modified recentralized models retained essential features of the MFT's transformation under selective decentralization of the preceding decade or so. In a number of respects, these efforts were actually strengthened, in marked contrast to the abrogation of reforms in the more domestically oriented segments of the economy. Although considerable recentralization occurred, there was no return to strict central planning because the original motives for seeking economic reforms did not, of course, evaporate with the abandonment, downsizing, or curbing of these movements. Particularly important in this regard was the continuing challenge of how to improve factor productivity, to provide sufficient resources for consumption, and to finance accumulation targeted specifically at stimulating factor productivity. For that reason, major and minor aspects of this modified recentralized model were revised rather frequently, chiefly to combat emerging imbalances. In searching for an appropriate positive adjustment strategy, especially payments problems with MEs played an instrumental role.

The modified centralized economy explores other means than indirect economic coordination to attain these goals. Two are important. First, many policy makers viewed political détente as a signal to import technology, if necessary through borrowing in DMEs. The second path taken by some MPEs harked back to the question of how to reconcile output maximization with certain rules and regulations on input minimization with a very incomplete coordination mechanism. This is the case in various experiments in virtually all countries that made intermediate economic units responsible for their own decisions.

In spite of the above modifications, the all-embracing control hierarchy of the centralized model, though reshaped, was essentially kept in place. The shift from sectoral planning to the creation of large units with economic accounting responsibilities in the 1960s and 1970s (in Czechoslovakia, the GDR, and Poland) or the fusion of economic agents engaged in related activities in the 1980s (as in Czechoslovakia and the GDR) did not affect the principle that all economic units must be administratively subordinated to the center as integral parts of one comprehensive hierarchy. The only exceptions occurred in Czechoslovakia in 1967-1968 and Hungary from 1968 on. Medium-level control agencies were either abolished or transformed into the central management of nationwide enterprises. The remaining firms were formally released from subordination to the state administration. Strict plan targets and physical norms were replaced by the general qualitative requirements to satisfy domestic demand, to meet obligations contracted abroad by the state or firms, and to achieve satisfactory export performance in MEs. Centralized resource allocation in many respects was to be complemented, but not generally replaced, by market-type transactions in the means of production. But the latter remained highly monopolized and strongly controlled by the state.

In some countries, this central control proceeded with changes in coordination mechanisms and institutions, including the administrative regulation of price changes. Though still under political control, frequent price revisions and changes in enterprise profit tax rates were to be enacted to reflect modifications in macroeconomic policy and the gradual moving closer toward genuine microeconomic decentralization. On the whole, the partially recentralized model was replete with hedges because no country passed the experimental stage or policy makers resumed the on-off partial reform cycle typical of the late 1950s.

It is important to stress that throughout the existence of the MPE models, the principal constraint on the output of firms was differential resource availability that could not be rebalanced through other means than the centrally imposed mechanisms. Moreover, whatever resources planners made available to economic agents could be modified somewhat through nonvalue indicators, such as informal negotiations about obtaining more inputs, a reduction in tax rates, easier access to bank credits, greater subsidies, and lower input or higher administered output prices. As a result, profitability was not a criterion in exit and entry of firms and hence did not really motivate enterprise managers.

Even though the reform formats embraced from around the mid-1950s until the mid-1980s as variants of the traditional CPE did not alter the basic precepts of central planning, they complicated the process of macroeconomic control in a number of respects. One potentially destabilizing factor was the decentralization of central planning authority in favor of regional or ministerial planning and budgetary centers. Such devolution was essentially sought to enhance decision making by central planning authorities, given that the ministerial, regional, and local agencies entrusted with wider responsibilities were presumably better informed about the real economic opportunities available to their subordinated economic units. At the same time, this called for another layer to coordinate decisions, ensuring that they were all reached with a view to enhancing the policy objectives of the country's leadership.

Perhaps graver problems of coordination were ushered into economic management with the devolution of enterprise decision making and the weakening of the strict administrative allocation of resources, be it by central, regional, local, or ministerial bureaucracies, in favor of horizontal relations among enterprises. Because the basic policy instruments of assigning comprehensive plan targets in some form remained intact, the economic rationale of such relations was rarely clear-cut. Oftentimes, firms had to procure inputs, including of labor, through other means than centrally prescribed norms. Lax credit control, monetary authorities simply continuing to finance enterprises in accordance with the central or regional plan regardless of economic justification, tended to exacerbate imbalances. In more than one respect, these resulted in stockpiling of unsaleable goods. Because central rewards for output fulfillment were more potent than those for attaining profit, however nominal, and there was pressure from workers to distribute retained earnings, enterprise management had also an incentive to circumvent wage scales or inflate bonuses.

In addition to complicating the process of ensuring domestic economic coordination, the largely administrative reforms also ushered greater complexity into the foreign trade sector. Although external imbalances could not influence domestic prices directly, they assumed such a scale that sizable macroeconomic repercussions ensued. Certainly, some of the causes for these external imbalances were rooted in mechanisms that remained largely beyond the control of central planners, in spite of the different rules prevailing in the CMEA context. Thus, an above-plan expansion in exports to contain external payments pressures tended to aggravate domestic consumer imbalances directly or indirectly. Similarly, shifting the composition of imports subject to volume constraints in favor of intermediate products strained consumer markets and exacerbated demand pressures.

In spite of these pressures building up, they could not automatically impact upon domestic price levels and relative prices. Central government control over domestic price policies under the reform variants introduced until recently continued to be either absolute or they took on a modified form. Absolute control prevailed in economies that adhered to orthodox price formation and stability, with perhaps the only change being the more frequent resetting of fiat prices. This worsened imbalances, however, as other-than-price mechanisms had to be found to close the gap. In the consumer sphere, this resulted in involuntary savings, resort to the second economy or transactions essentially outside central government control, rationing, queuing, product substitution, and other emanations of repressed inflation. In some cases, the second economy also interacted with the producer sectors, which yielded imbalances in interenterprise transactions and complicated macroeconomic control. The more central authorities accommodated these imbalances through the issuance of money without "commodity coverage," the greater the pressure.

* * *

This brief examination of the salient features of the CPEs and MPEs underlines that also these economies have been exposed to imbalances, whose magnitude in some cases has been very sizable. In spite of comprehensive policy control, these imbalances do not abruptly arise from nowhere. As in open MEs, sudden external shocks do, of course, also create disturbances that challenge policy makers in CPEs or MPEs into remedial adjustment. In most instances, however, rather than simply coming from the outside, the prevailing disequilibria are immanent in the inflexibilities of the planning systems in place. That is not to belittle the sizable external terms-of-trade and interest rate shocks that some of these countries have had to weather. But I attach more importance to domestic rigidities that are immanent in the system. These not only lead to disturbances, but also make it very difficult to respond quickly and properly to shocks from outside. Direct controls have certainly been more important than the indirect influence exerted by fiscal and monetary policy operating, for example, through the availability and cost of credit or inducements to save rather than to spend. The contribution of the banking system to containing imbalances has been minimal, owing largely to its passive dependence on prescriptions laid out in the central plan. The banking system's paramount task under the circumstances has been to control the monetary flows necessary to facilitate plan execution and thus keep them within planned boundaries. Open price inflation at times erupted in some markets as a result of the prevalence of differential price controls and the fact that the associated partial markets have remained unintegrated. It also took on various forms of repressed inflation.

4

On the economics of transition

Embarking on a market-oriented reform has, at least conceptually, two angles. One is the mutation process itself, during which the new environment crystallizes. This will usually require putting in place new policies, institutions, and policy instruments. An integral component thereof is the formulation of the transitional economic policy to ensure some measure of economic stability. How to avoid imbalances and the pressures they may bring to bear on prices and the incentive systems, or if they occur how best to come to grips with them, forms one important element of macroeconomic policy formulation and implementation. The other is how to operate optimally within the market-oriented economy once established. Here the scope of the discourse is no longer what can be accomplished in the form of transition policies. Rather, a new philosophy of macroeconomic policy and how to maintain steady economic growth at the desired rate primarily through fiscal and monetary management should form the core of what figures most prominently on the agenda of the PET's policy makers. The emergence of imbalances and how best to cope with them depend very much on what precisely market orientation aims to achieve.

This chapter is the logical sequel to the discussion of CPEs and MPEs. As such, it addresses the aforementioned two sets of questions. Section 1 briefly touches upon the main aims of obtaining an economy geared by market behavior. Next, I discuss the starting conditions for market-oriented reforms in PETs. The following section clarifies key policy concerns of the transition. The economics of transition, including its starting conditions and possible setbacks, forms the subject of Section 4. The final section examines the critical pivots of the market-oriented economy being targeted by the PETs, although this is discussed in detail in its own right in Chapter 8.

1. Key aspirations of market orientation

The pivotal aspiration of market-oriented reform, seen from within a technical discourse, is the acceleration of factor productivity growth and maintaining it at a comparatively high level through effective decentralization and macroeconomic policy coordination. All this is predicated on the sharp curbing of administrative guidance in the determination of output, resource allocation, and the distribution of incomes; eventually it should be abolished. Entrepreneurial activity is to be coordinated through market-type economic links rather than through vertical chains of administrative command. Supply and demand can influence more flexible domestic prices that are related to trade prices. They can thus help to guide decisions on inputs and outputs. Profit measures are now looked upon as appropriate indicators of a firm's contribution to the economy as a whole and the basis for rewarding personnel, provided adequate macroeconomic policies are put in place to reward "real" profits. Also, the supply rigidities so typical of the CPE or MPE will have to be worked off prior to relying chiefly on the operation of a full-fledged market mechanism.

Among the instruments of the decentralized economic mechanism, the following are the most critical. Rather than losing in importance, the role of planning for structural decisions on the basis of economic guidance criteria deserves to be reinforced. The transformation in planning necessitates downsizing the role of ministries and associations in the day-to-day affairs of the economic agents under their jurisdiction. This applies especially to the material-technical supply system, which is decentralized and transformed into genuine wholesale trading. As a result, economic agents obtain the responsibility to decide on the disposition of outputs and some inputs by themselves. Moreover, they are expected to react to changes in indirect economic parameters. These include prices, exchange and interest rates, and larger wage and income differentials. Furthermore, enterprise behavior is evaluated largely on the basis of net performance indicators with profits acting as the paramount criterion of success. Subsidies for wholesale and retail prices or for ailing enterprises are to be compressed and eventually abolished. Enterprises that cannot be turned around need to be discontinued, which requires a policy on bankruptcy. Finally, the decentralized economic mechanism necessitates changes in and additions to the traditional economic institutions of the CPE or MPE. Also, a credible monetary policy is predicated on the monobank becoming a bank of issue and lender of last resort effectively in charge of monetary policy. At the same time, commercial banking activities of the monobank are to be dismantled and replaced by a network of financial institutions that cater competitively to the financial requirements of economic agents.

In foreign trade, FTOs need to be transformed into effective self-accounting trading firms or their tasks assigned to producers, depending upon the best division of labor. The decentralized economic mechanism may change the character of cooperative organizations, including in agriculture. It invariably imparts an important role to small-scale private or cooperative enterprises, particularly in service sectors. Finally, the new economic mechanism seeks to promote new forms of ownership by encouraging small-scale private enterprises and also by attracting capital from abroad through joint ventures or special economic or trade zones. Needless to say, such a decentralized model ushers in many new policy concerns.

Perhaps the most outstanding commitment of PET policy makers is that they now rule out the earlier piecemeal approaches to reform. The present reform strategy reaches well beyond such traditional remedies as shifts in investment policies, partial streamlining of organizational links, and pressuring unprofitable firms into restructuring themselves by administrative means. It also aims at demarcating unambiguously the functions of Party organs, local government, and socioeconomic organizations in economic decision making. In the end success is predicated on fundamentally changing the working style of all sociopolitical and economic organs. As far as technical economics is concerned, the critical factors can be summed up into eight key items.

At the core of the reform provisions stands the creation of an economic environment conducive to enterprise self-financing and self-management. SOEs are expected to be fully responsible for their overall performance and how they discharge their obligations. Financing of enterprise investments from the central budget is to be restricted to selected projects only, mainly because bankruptcy and an effective capital market are still lacking. The success of this approach depends directly on access to inputs and capital goods, hence the importance of wholesale trade. Interfirm competition, domestically as well as through foreign trade, should be encouraged so as to cater to demand and ease the effects of the monopolistic position of producers in a sellers' market, including in the formation of prices.

Second, as a direct counterpart of the emphasis on enterprise autonomy, centralized macroeconomic control should motivate individual agents through appropriate economic levers to optimize the benefits to society as a whole. This will generally call for the radical downsizing of sectoral ministries, whose earlier tutelage role in the planning hierarchy and administration was paramount. Their vested interests are pervasive. Whittling this bureaucracy forms the topic of one of the struggles for power inevitably associated with the reform process. In addition to streamlining central planning for structural decisions, these levers include orthodox fiscal and monetary policies, in some cases augmented with price and income policies. Budgetary financing of investments is to be restricted to a narrow range of high-priority, goal-specific programs of national importance. Such flows are to be kept separate from loans issued by commercial banks or their equivalents on the basis of the economic viability of the projects for which the loan request is lodged. Money circulation and overall monetary policy are to be entrusted to the central bank. Commercial banking functions need to be increasingly discharged by specialized banks.

Third, the gradual substitution of genuine wholesale trade, including in the means of production, for major components of the present administrative distribution of resources is another salient feature of the reform. Only a comparatively small share of fuel and energy resources, raw materials, and perhaps some other scarce goods will continue to be centrally allocated. Public procurement should increasingly be carried out on a competitive basis through the wholesale trading network.

Fourth, directly related to the autonomy of firms and the sustainability of wholesale trade is the soundness of price signals. Because prevailing prices do not reflect scarcities and the mainstream views on price reform continue to stress only gradual adaptation of fiat or administrative prices to economic scarcities revealed through the operation of markets, the role of the price mechanism in the efficient allocation of resources will in effect remain subdued for some time. A major change can occur only if central policy makers decide to proceed with comprehensive price reform and to infuse greater flexibility into the price system. If the "big bang" approach is feasible, these two features will be merged for most, but not all, goods and services.

Fifth, the reorganization of banking institutions involves holding them fully financially accountable, creating for them adequate incentives to improve the return on loans, making the financial performance of firms a basic criterion for loan disbursements, and preventing in particular the intraministerial redistribution of circulating capital, depreciation funds, and profits among the firms they supervise until this vested interest of the bureaucracy can be sharply curtailed. Allowing firms to act upon their own profitability criterion, if that is what the reform aims at, is critical and should avoid a repetition of the redistribution of enterprise funds so pervasive in MPE reforms.

Sixth, provisions of the reforms call for strengthening the link between labor remuneration and productivity. This is to be fostered by gradually overhauling the traditional system of job guarantees and pre-set wage scales that are not widely differentiated and do not even approximately reflect actual labor effort. Firms should increasingly be able to set payment scales according to merit and productivity within the ambit of their own profitability and provisions on how to distribute profits, including through an adequate fiscal policy.

Instead of clinging to the *de facto* lifetime job guarantee so typical of the CPE and MPE, labor reform emphasizes the urgency of utilizing labor more effectively. This may require temporary layoffs, whose adverse implications need to be mitigated by providing, in effect, unemployment compensation; in some cases a full-scale social safety net may have to be erected. Labor mobility is to be encouraged to staff private and cooperative enterprises and indeed to foster entrepreneurship and initiative. At the same time, stimulating labor productivity through wage and related incentives places higher demands on the process of diversification of assets available to households and especially the supply of consumer goods with a high income elasticity. To meet these demands, the composition of output must be changed rapidly. An urgent task is to balance supply and demand in retail markets for which special incentives need to be created, including on the formation of private property.

Seventh, the philosophy of social ownership and how social property can be rationally allocated is being radically altered. Earlier views advocated that only the state could fully represent the preferences emanating from the social ownership of the means of production, including those appropriated in the microeconomic sphere. With reform, at first strong support emerges for the view that the firm as such represents the interests of public ownership. It is expected to utilize the means of production assigned to it for the benefit of society as a whole under the guidance of an appropriate economic mechanism. As an integral component of extricating the state from the direct exercise of ownership functions, control over the allocation of state-owned assets may be assigned to nonstate trustees; in some cases, such assets may be fully privatized through some sale mechanism, including auctions and, later on, stock-market operations (see Chapter 7). Furthermore, whereas previously the state arrogated to itself the right to be the sole owner of the means of production, firms can now be owned privately. Provided they are supported by appropriate and simultaneous adjustments in planning procedures and management practices, the practical ramifications of this doctrinal shift can be far-reaching.

Finally, a core focus of the PET reform is making more effective use of foreign economic relations. This takes the form of encouraging trade, joint ventures, FDI, movement towards currency convertibility, and others. Critical, as contrasted with the situation in most CPEs and even MPEs, is the decentralization of foreign economic decisions in favor of economic agents and changing the macroeconomic administration of foreign trade, including through a commercial policy and a more flexible foreign exchange policy.

Rather than separating domestic from foreign prices and allocating foreign exchange by central fiat, the foreign trade reform generally ushers in three important changes in the commercial regime. For one thing, firms are entitled to negotiate prices directly. Second, their profitability is codetermined by pseudo, and in some cases real, exchange rates. Finally, firms are being given wider access to foreign currency. These and other foreign trade reforms are bound in time to affect trade with all partners and the way in which these countries mutually cooperate, perhaps within a revamped CMEA framework.

2. The starting conditions for market-oriented reforms

Key is that broad-based market-oriented reform cannot be introduced within a vacuum. Instead, its take-off evolves necessarily in the presence of at least two legacies of the orthodox planning mechanisms. One is the coexistence of features of central planning with indirect coordination mechanisms, the latter in principle gaining ascendancy as quickly as circumstances permit. The other is the absence of firm macroeconomic policies, institutions, and policy instruments other than those of physical planning. Of particular importance are the tepid role of money, prices, wages, and other indirect coordination intruments in the inherited economic model, where their role is taken up by subsidies, payments in kind, material balancing, and other nonmarket instruments. Furthermore, as a consequence of the organizing role of the central budget in economic decisions, including in matters concerning foreign trade, there is little autonomy in consumption, saving, and investment behavior of individual economic agents. These factors are responsible for the absence or relative ineffectiveness of monetary and fiscal policies and their associated instruments and institutions. An important role in containing open inflationary pressures in these economies has been played through price dichotomies at home (industrial wholesale, agricultural procurement, and consumer prices) as well as in foreign trade matters (especially the TRP mechanism in CMEA trade in comparison with WMPs). As these buffers need to be gradually revamped, the question of how best to come to grips with the variety of phenomena known as hidden inflation becomes pregnant.

The demand and supply pressures that potentially disrupt market balances in the orthodox CPE or MPE are deeply embedded in the behavior of economic agents and cannot be rectified overnight. For one, the entrepreneurial élite was by and large appointed through administrative and political connections, rather than because the individuals in question demonstrated any particular managerial aptitude or promised soon to acquire the ability to manage economic units profitably. Moreover, the "animal spirits" of capitalist entrepreneurship are simply not present as the orthodox planning model fails to encourage the kind of decision making required in a market-oriented environment. Time is needed to inculcate the new spirit into existing and new managers and policy makers need to nurture along this transformation process too.

Similar constraints arise for households as providers of labor services and as consumers. Having been exposed for so many years to relatively low and stable prices for a wide range of basic goods and services, households tend to be reluctant to part with the implicit subsidies. This places formidable restrictions on the room for maneuver open to policy makers bent on revamping the role of the government budget. The principle of income differentiation, after it having been frowned upon for so long in response to an overly pronounced commitment to egalitarianism, is not likely to be tolerated quickly by the vast majority of the population. Finally, households may be reluctant to give up full employment and other social welfare and security guarantees.

Controlling income differentiation through fiscal means, rather than through strict wage and income norms set by administrative fiat, requires not only more sophisticated fiscal instruments, including value-added tax systems, a corporate profit tax, and progressive personal income taxation in lieu of turnover taxes; its success also critically depends on the acceptance of such new mechanisms by households. As regards labor and its remuneration, at the outset of the reform the emphasis necessarily has to be placed on restraint on labor remuneration, while at the same time lifting levels of average labor productivity and making room for instituting larger wage differentials to reflect corresponding variations in productivity levels. This *de facto* reduction, however temporary, in real wage and income levels will be accepted only if economic agents have confidence that short-term hardships will indeed soon give way to rewards according to effort. For that, the new policies must exhibit a substantial degree of credibility and consumer confidence may have to be gained through a new social compact.

Nearly all Eastern European countries currently seeking market-oriented reforms start from deep-rooted and sizable internal and external imbalances. Not only is the initial phase of the reform plagued by legacies of the central planning environment, it may also have to come to grips with the stock of excess demand in the form of repressed, and in some cases open, if perhaps muted, inflation that has been gathering momentum over the years. Unlike in the ME environment, disturbances such as those experienced in Eastern Europe could traditionally not be translated into upward price movements. In many cases, they did not even come about through the mechanisms that typically fuel inflation in MEs. Furthermore, the degree of success in containing these pressures and alleviating them over time has varied from country to country and from period to period. Oftentimes, the outcome has been determined overwhelmingly by the success of balancing the flow of purchasing power to households against the volume of consumer goods and services placed on markets through direct controls as well as Draconian credit ceilings for enterprises. The alternative policy measures available to come to grips with this overhang need to be evaluated with respect to their relative merit. They need to be implemented as quickly as circumstances permit during the early phases of the reform process so that the effort to bring about changes in economic structures and policies is not overburdened with the accumulated imbalances. This agenda is bound to entail more painful actions in countries whose previous attempts to reform primarily sought administrative decentralization.

But inflation is not the only potential concomitant of comprehensive economic reform that policy makers should be aware of. Such substantial societal changes have numerous implications, aside from exacerbating inflationary pressures, that may yield an entire range of macro- and microeconomic policy dilemmas to be tackled during the transition toward the coveted reformed state. The most important are: (1) the role of the government budget and fiscal policy, including of decentralized organs that have been granted greater fiscal and managerial autonomy; (2) the paramount function of monetary policy in maintaining stability and growth, and its autonomy when conflicts arise with other macroeconomic policies; (3) the central place and instrumental role of the banking sector in financing firms on a commercial basis and in mobilizing resources; (4) commercial decision making of economic agents throughout the economy and how to reconcile their interests with those held by central managers; (5) the crucial role of the MFT in setting commercial policies, opening up the economy to broad foreign competition, and bolstering overall trade; (6) the forms through which greater microeconomic efficiency is to be achieved and what this entails for the traditional tenets of socialized property; and (7) rationalizing prices to reflect more closely underlying economic scarcities.

Any transition toward market orientation begs the question as to what alternative to central planning as the core organizing principle of the economy should be embraced. Indeed, how best to coordinate decentralized economic decisions is arguably the central issue of moving over to operative markets without aggravating imbalances, and at the same time working off those inherited from past mistakes. This involves in the end the replacement of central planning, however applied in the CPE or MPE, as a coordinating mechanism by one that is congruent with the promotion of market-based decisions. Several variants of such a new coordination mechanism can be envisaged. There are even more ways in which it can be grafted upon the reforming economy, particularly in the presence of marked imbalances.

Whichever replacement coordination mechanism will in the end be preferred, it can be introduced only gradually but at different speeds. That is to say, changes in development strategy and, more important, in economic model can be introduced rapidly, as presently envisaged in Hungary and undertaken through the "big bang" in Poland since January 1990 and Vietnam since early 1989. They may also be sought more gradually, as appears to be the objective of the current reform ferment in Czechoslovakia. Finally, a third group of countries, among which China and the Soviet Union must be counted, have thus far been trying (as in China) or have been contemplating (as in the Soviet Union[1]) to phase in such a changeover during a protracted transition period, perhaps one or two decades. In contrast to the diversity in pace of reform envisaged, there is greater uniformity about the particular coordination mechanism to be designed.

With rare exceptions, one of the more striking features of the reform process in planned economies, beginning with the first feeble attempts to move away from orthodox planning (see Chapter 3), has been the rather casual way

[1] Rumors at the time of writing that the Soviet Union may resort to its own version of the big bang by late 1990, if substantiated, would, of course, relegate the above assessment to the dustbins of history.

in which the coordination problem has been dealt with (Brabant 1989b). How to ensure macroeconomic policy coordination during the fluid transition phase may call for different measures than those that form an intrinsic part of a coherent coordination mechanism for the reformed economy. Yet, ensuring that the decisions of sovereign economic agents do not run outrightly counter to what the macroeconomic policy maker is trying to accomplish during each phase of the transition is central in making steady progress with economic devolution in the expectation of thereby enhancing the efficiency of resource allocation and ensuring economic stability.

A key component of such a coherent coordination mechanism is how best to address the inflationary pressures that may be present when policy makers embark on the reform. Depending upon the nature of the pressures (such as those emanating from inherited imbalances, current macroeconomic policies that are not properly coordinated, or the price pressures arising from the desirable restructuring of relative prices), one element or another of the coordination mechanism will require greater emphasis.

The main propulsion of the inflation process stems from the incoherence or incompleteness of reforms, in part because they are being placed in an institutional environment that is not conducive to indirect economic coordination. Another important impulse stems from ongoing inflationary macroeconomic policies. There are, furthermore, country-specific circumstances that need to be carefully assessed. This is especially the case for inherited disequilibria or the stock of excess demand that may descend upon the rearranged market. In some cases, the devolution of decision making from the central government to provincial and local authorities, possibly also for foreign exchange allocation, has had important implications for macroeconomic policy control and the inflationary process, given the incomplete framework for ensuring rational decisions.

Yet, even the best laid-out reform program is likely soon to be in need of adaptation. The experience with modifying planned economies is unambiguous: Reforms are rarely viewed holistically, formulated into a clear blueprint, and then implemented by the political leadership according to a set schedule; they invariably face opposition and domestic as well as external obstacles that were not, or only incompletely, heeded at the time of the reform's gestation; and regardless of the ambitious nature of the reform, the results invariably fall short of the goals envisioned at its inception. A reform in essence involves a learning process. Hence the prevalence in all reforms of instability and sometimes outright vacillation in rules and regulations; disagreement or divergent views among reform managers on what is to be done and how changes should preferably be carried out; and willingness quickly to intervene through recentralization rather than tolerance for setbacks that are unavoidable in any societal transformation process, thus providing a learning process in its own right.

3. Key components of market orientation

In appraising the consistency and potential of moving meaningfully toward economic decentralization and evaluating the reform's performance, it is essential to gain a proper perspective on the evolution of how the tasks of coordination are being viewed by economic agents and the degree to which measures are taken to correct outcomes that do not correspond to the reform's intentions. This may require frequent fine-tuning of policies, institutions, and instruments in response to assessments of performance with a view to guiding the reform back on track. In the first instance, this clarification of the inevitable disruptions and adjustment costs implied in moving forward with reform, and what can, or should, be done about them, is a matter of technical economics. Whether these costs are acceptable and the remedial measures feasible are issues that derive importantly from sociopolitical precepts.

In this connection, the question arises of what statewide economic policy in a reformed economy should be all about. Clearly, differences between social and private preferences need to be bridged by guiding or intervening in purely privately motivated decisions; sociopolitical preferences need to be safeguarded centrally, though implemented according to new, possibly market-type, rules of the game; the nonmaterial sphere remains largely under central control; and infrastructural works, and perhaps other capital projects too, need to be initiated by the center, though by no means in an economic vacuum. There may be wide agreement about this division of priorities and responsibilities. But rarely are the implications of such a new constitutional arrangement, which moreover has to emerge from the economic model in place rather than in a vacuum, assessed fully.

Transforming these agreed-upon tasks into policies, institutions, and instruments that help to coordinate economic decisions through indirect means on the basis of what is in place is not at all easy. The many issues involved are not simply confined to the techniques of replacing one model with another. Market-oriented coordination can succeed only when economic agents have confidence in the framework within which they can pursue their own interest subject to a set framework managed by central policies. In particular, any suspicion that the current reform process may be retracted needs to be defused by reassurances and adherence to enunciated intentions. Strengthening confidence of the consumer in the Government's anti-inflation and stabilization policies, with a view to placing economic expansion within the context of genuine economic decentralization on a solid economic footing, could help to mobilize additional indigenous resources for development purposes. At the same time, the central authorities need to encourage the fast emergence of institutions and instruments to facilitate the smooth distribution of savings to projects that are economically viable.

In this respect, it is critical that those managing the transition toward a reformed setup institute comprehensive monetary and fiscal policies to steer the behavior of individual agents. Further, proper income and price policies are needed to enhance social priorities. In economies that wish to integrate themselves more completely into the global economy, these macroeconomic policies must also encompass measures and institutions in the commercial policy sphere. Instituting coherent macroeconomic policies in lieu of traditional central planning is an exceedingly complex assignment, if only because the traditional CPE, or MPE for that matter, has not been very much concerned about them, given the supreme role of central planning in economic affairs (see Chapter 3). Furthermore, the institutions and policy instruments in place at the outset of the economic reform are ill-suited to support market orientation. For example, once policy makers decide to commercialize economic relations, the institutional, financial, and legal infrastructure of the reform needs to be complemented by putting in place sufficient instruments to foster private initiative and to provide for the concomitant institutional supports. In contrast to stabilization, which calls for strong government policies, commercialization has subtler implications and thrives on minimal government interference. But there is a need to steer that activity through macroeconomic policies. For the planning mechanism to withdraw from resource allocation altogether with no clear-cut alternative in its place is a dangerous step.

The aim to harness the initiative and entrepreneurial spirit of the public so as to strengthen economic development forms the core of the more radical reforms currently being implemented. For allocation by a planning organization to be properly overtaken by allocation through markets, relative prices become key criteria of choice. The price mechanism can perform this function only if there is some reasonable degree of resource mobility and functioning markets, including foreign competition and labor mobility. The operating surplus of an enterprise indicates a productive use of resources only when the prices paid and received by firms represent the value of resources to their users and, perhaps through state policy or intervention, to society. For the price mechanism to function well, markets must be integrated and made up of a sufficient number of actors to ensure competition not only in domestic wholesale and retail trade, but also in foreign activities. This is not now the case in most countries under review. Ensuring the quick integration of the presently fragmented markets is an urgent policy priority. Efforts to decentralize decision making in several CPEs and MPEs, including most notably, but not only, the Soviet Union among the countries of direct concern here, have worsened market fragmentation.

The existing poor degree of market interlinkages has multiple origins, including the lingering divisions between rural and urban areas, between public and private enterprises, between central and local administrative organs, and the obstacles to putting in place an efficient transportation and communication infrastructure. It is to be expected that there will gradually emerge a full-fledged financial market to encourage savings and mobilize them for development. For that, it may be useful to design and regulate measures that enable households to accumulate and hold wealth in a diversity of financial assets.

The consolidation of fiscal revenue on the basis of minimizing distortions in microeconomic decisions, as through a progressive income-tax system, yet tax economic agents equitably and with a view to reflecting social priorities, is a question of some urgency. This is especially so because reforms are being sought by societies that place a strong value on limited income differentiation, nearly free education and health services, fostering the arts for the wider public, and other social services. That fairness may distort economic efficiency needs to be factored into the macroeconomic policy setting. To improve levels of living, it is necessary to use resources efficiently and for this purpose to reward persons unequally. To control income disparity, measures can be taken that minimize resource misallocation. The extent of income inequality and the means of keeping it within acceptable bounds are decisions that deserve priority attention to release creative ability, stimulate entrepreneurial spirit, and exploit prevailing and emerging opportunities with the goal of attaining a higher, yet sustainable, rate of growth.

But also fiscal revenues will need to be addressed. Up until now, the vast bulk of fiscal revenues has been generated through SOEs, indirect taxes, and below-market agricultural procurement prices. Once market orientation involves privatization of SOEs and the introduction of fewer distortions in indirect and direct taxation systems, there is a danger that the revenue side of the government budget will fall short of the level of expenditure that social consensus and parliamentary democracy validate. There is consequently some urgency in rethinking the entire fiscal structure of these countries with a view to maintaining adequate spending levels without introducing gross distortions in the economy or inequities in levying incidence.

In addition to domestic policies, the reforming countries also need to address their external sectors and hence commercial policy. This is important for a number of reasons, including the dependence of these countries on trade and hence the direct feed-through of external disturbances once the MFT is relaxed to permit direct trade relations, the hope of raising measurably their export potential on a competitive basis, the degree to which they are intermeshed in the CMEA context, and the external payments constraints for some of them. By themselves, these topics present an ambitious agenda for reformers. Excepting the CMEA conundrum,[2] the issues listed are to some degree under the control of policy makers from each country in isolation, although a resolution of the multiple tasks incumbent upon the most indebted planned economies is unthinkable without the cooperation of MEs.

To integrate themselves more closely into the global economy, these economies must come to grips with the dichotomy between CMEA and other markets, including the multiple policy issues associated with bilateralism, currency inconvertibility, price distortions, fixed trade quotas, and other obstacles to ensuring market operations in the CMEA. To pursue a more active foreign exchange policy, eliminate market dichotomies, and measurably raise trade levels, it is necessary to institute much more coherent trade and foreign exchange policies that differ by their nature from those pursued hitherto. Without strengthening the economics of intra-CMEA exchanges through efforts from within the group, the capacity of the members to gain a more competitive position in world markets is limited and its realization would imply an adjustment burden far in excess of what would have to be incurred through proper policy coordination. The latter is essential in orderly devolving decision making from the higher to the lower tiers of the economic hierarchy in the expectation of thereby enhancing the efficiency of resource allocation. Professional and technical appraisals of inevitable disruptions and adjustment costs cannot, of course, take ascendancy over the political process. But technically warranted advice phrased within the context of decentralized coordination should constitute one critical input into the decision making of the PET's political leadership.

[2] In principle, these countries could fully disengage themselves from the CMEA by diverting the bulk of their trade and payments to world markets. But this is not a very pragmatic solution, as examined in Chapter 9.

These and other policy concerns that arise in the course of the transition need to be streamlined into a coherent reform package and evaluated as to the best sequence in which the various measures envisaged should be introduced. This is not at all an easy matter. Suggestions are considered in Section 5, after briefly clarifying what the RPA should be all about, and in Chapters 7 and 8.

4. Key characteristics of the RPE

The RPE is essentially an economy anchored to fully functioning markets. In that respect, it is very much like an ordinary ME, as indicated in Table 3.1. Societal preferences in such an economy may be formed differently and vary sharply from those in traditional MEs. Macroeconomic policies must therefore be tailored in support of the realization of these specific societal preferences. To clarify the RPE, then, it is necessary to distinguish between policy objectives and how societal preferences are reflected in the application of the preferred economic mechanism.

For an RPE to allocate resources with a view to maximizing output as in an ME, it must have functioning markets. That requires not only markets for intermediate and final products, but also for primary inputs, including capital and labor, and their allocation over time. Furthermore, markets can only function more or less smoothly when there is an adequate institutional and legal framework for economic activity, ownership, enterprise formation, and other essential features of MEs. These rules and regulations, and their institutional infrastructure, need not be overly complex. Experience from MEs suggests that, to enhance the efficient allocation of resources, simplicity and clarity are beneficial features of the legal and institutional frameworks. Finally, activities of microeconomic agents need to be coordinated through macroeconomic policies that in part reflect the consensual preferences held by society's agents. This reflection should preferably be accommodated through a mechanism that enables agents to express their sociopolitical preferences, possibly through a parliamentary democracy or at least through representatives enjoying a substantial degree of confidence on the part of the majority of the people.

1. The microeconomic sphere

This consists essentially of labor markets, capital markets, price policies, enterprise behavior, and industrial organization.

a. Price policies. The alpha and omega of the ME revolves around the existence of flexible adjustments in prices or quantities, or both, as a result of the interaction of demand and supply in atomistic markets, including for capital assets. Prices provide a key signal for resource allocation and impose effective constraints on the behavior of economic agents in decentralized economic systems. Prices in this context refer to all resource and product prices, and thus include wage rates, interest rates, exchange rates, rents, and other scarcity indicators. Especially important is that RPEs must interact with other economies. This is not, of course, to deny the right to an own foreign exchange and trade policy in the RPE. On the contrary, such policies form an integral part of the macroeconomic framework chosen to reach societal objectives.

What needs to be emphasized here is that domestic prices in the RPE cannot function without some systematic built-in link with prices in trading markets. Such an unmediated synchronization of domestic and foreign prices is especially important for economies whose economic structure is unable to accommodate atomistic behavior in a wide range of domestic activities, even if the PET succeeds in moving rapidly with the breakup of state monopolies and large SOEs. To ensure proper response even in the latter sectors, foreign competition is essential. It should, therefore, be fostered with great determination by removing as many obstacles to effective market access as feasible without destabilizing markets. For this to work with maximal result, the interferences between domestic and foreign prices should be as simple as possible, given the macroeconomic framework set out below.

b. Enterprise behavior. As noted, atomistic behavior of producers and consumers is another key precept of the ME that the RPE needs to emulate. Under the planning models, consumers on the whole enjoyed a considerable degree of sovereignty. The weakest element of these markets has been the monopolistic behavior of producers because of centrally managed exit and entry procedures and also because SOEs have enjoyed the advantage of working for sellers' markets. The basic platform of detailed central planning subordinates enterprise management and finance to state decisions. Even in the MPE central authorities shied away from giving full autonomy to firms for political reasons and also because of inadequate appreciation for the technical aspects of economic policy, including the need to steer a firm course on entry and exit.

The most important goal in enterprise behavior, then, is to stimulate efficient productive behavior by granting nearly full autonomy to firms. This needs to be circumscribed through macroeconomic policies and institutions tailored to the goals society desires to pursue, including as specified in a comprehensive commercial code. The key feature here is genuine wholesale trade and liberal rules on exit and entry, including by foreign entities acting on their own account through FDI or in the framework of joint ventures. These activities are, of course, to be made subject to fiscal, accounting, and trading obligations laid out in the applicable laws.

The success of the competitive system not only depends on the autonomy of decentralized economic units acting in competition with each other, it also requires autonomy of management. This implies that the firm's leadership needs to be selected primarily on the basis of its managerial merits and held accountable for its performance by real owners of capital assets. Performance should be measured by the ability of management to increase the net worth of the firm while abiding by the rules of fair competition. For that to hold, managers need to be given strong incentives to administer firms efficiently. Likewise, owners of the firms through their supervisory or monitoring activities as part and parcel of their property rights need to be able to fire unsuccessful managers and to create the proper incentives to reward those who raise the firm's net worth for their creative merits (see Chapter 7).

c. Industrial organization. As noted, one of the hallmarks of economic organization in Eastern Europe has been state ownership of the means of production. There can be no well-functioning dynamic ME that explicitly excludes all forms of property other than, say, state ownership. On the other hand, it needs to be recognized that private ownership by itself does not always guarantee the most efficient use of resources. Furthermore, full privatization of state ownership is not really necessary to ensure more efficient use of society's capital resources. The purpose of privatization should in any case be twofold: a sharp improvement in the efficiency of the allocation of the services of the existing capital stock and providing for new capital accumulation in multiple ownership forms to maximize present and future levels of welfare in accordance with the social contract.

It may be helpful, at least for conceptual purposes, to accept two propositions for now; they are analyzed in much greater detail in Chapter 7. One is that it is useful to keep apart ownership of capital assets as such from the exercise of ownership rights other than alienation of the property; that is, the usufruct of capital resources in the narrow sense. The other focuses on the recognition of the principle that whatever ownership form is most conducive to improving the allocation of resources should be permitted within the overall macroeconomic framework, of course.

Full legalization of diverse forms of ownership and control is crucial for the effective functioning of economic agents through increased competition and hence for the full realization of the social benefits thereof. That includes the ability in principle of foreign firms, regardless of their origin, to enter the market with their own or borrowed capital and to establish their own firms or to form joint ventures within a well-defined and economically warranted legal framework.

d. The capital market. Efficient resource allocation can take place only when the trade-off between present and future consumption is properly accommodated through market relations. For that a flexible capital market, including for land and real estate, is indispensable. That requires a financial infrastructure, in the form of a competitive network of intermediating financial institutions of domestic and foreign origin, again placed in a well-defined and economically sensible legal framework. In the first instance, such financial infrastructure should consist of a competitive network of commercial, investment, and merchant banks (Brainard 1990). There should also be room for pension funds, including the management of state pension fund assets, and insurance companies providing all shades of risk coverage. It also requires a stock and bond market that enhances the intertemporal allocation of resources and regulates the acquisition and disposal of wealth in all its forms.

Two issues are of some importance here. One is that it would be foolhardy to expect a fully integrated financial infrastructure to be in place in a short period of time. In most PETs, in fact, one may well question whether policy makers should aim at a fully developed home capital market. There are some components that, for the purposes of resource allocation in PETs and RPEs are absolutely mandatory. This is certainly the case for a competitive network of banks and insurance companies of various degrees of specialization. Banks and investment houses may initially take care of issuing bonds and shares in companies without there being a fully operational stock market. The other topic revolves around what is required to ensure that such a market and its underlying financial infrastructure operate to the benefit of society. Capital transactions must be transparent. In other words, the capital market itself must reveal information to economic agents, partly in response to the latter's request. For that some regulatory powers have to be instituted. These may be similar to the supervisory activities to which private and public corporations in the DME are subjected.

e. Labor markets. As clarified in Chapter 3, labor markets in Eastern Europe have on the whole functioned with relatively mild interferences. That pertains in particular to the option of workers where to work during some periods of the evolution of the CPE or MPE. But it does not generally apply to the flexibility that ought to be available in negotiating labor contracts and accommodating in particular the trade-off between leisure and work. For that, it is necessary to restructure industrial relations through genuine trade unions that take to heart the economic interests of their members as well as of the country as a whole. But one should have no illusions that this can be set up quickly or smoothly. The experience of the trade union movement in some DMEs is not particularly encouraging in that respect. Some form of worker participation in firms through profit sharing or even employee share ownership plans (ESOPs) may be desirable. Whether this emerges depends very much on the place and role of trade unions and societal preferences for the kind of industrial organization that will be at the core of economic activities.

2. THE MACROECONOMIC SPHERE

This encompasses policies directed at ensuring that the interests of microeconomic agents are coordinated with a view to maximizing society's welfare through certain institutions and policy instruments. Society's preferences may be very complex, not necessarily a singular monotonic function of the availability of goods and services. There are, furthermore, competing claims on how individual preferences need to be reconciled at the aggregate level. To reflect these preferences for the country as a whole, a social compact is required to validate the macroeconomic mechanism, involving policies and their supporting institutions and instruments that seek to minimize the cost of implementing the social compact as rapidly and comprehensively as circumstances permit. The most important elements of the macroeconomic framework, as far as economics is concerned, are monetary and fiscal policies. Inasmuch as social preferences in the RPE are likely to differ from those characterizing the stylized ME, other components of the government's socioeconomic stance may have to be determined through price and income policies.

a. Monetary policy. Critical in operating a complex modern ME is a monetary policy that enhances resource allocation. Perhaps the core institution here is an autonomous central bank subject to societal oversight. The latter may be exercised directly through the parliamentary organs in place. Or supervisory authority may be lodged with agents acting on behalf of elected representatives of the people's will. Such a bank should be entrusted with regulating monetary intermediation with a view to ensuring steady economic growth and monetary stability. The bank also needs to see to it that macroeconomic policy stances do not entail fiscal imbalances or, when inevitable, that the latter minimize the crowding out of commercial demand for loans; under few circumstances (such as war or natural calamities) should a budgetary deficit be accommodated through the printing press. Actual financial intermediation between savers and investors can be discharged by a network of competing commercial, merchant, and investment banks. Also other financial institutions, such as insurance companies and pension funds, will play an important role in this process. In this connection, the foreign exchange regime needs to be firmly anchored. Whether the currency of the RPE should be fully convertible is a key item on the policy agenda of open economies aiming at integrating themselves into the global economy. These two issues can in principle be treated separately, although they are closely related.

The foreign exchange regime sets rules and regulations on the acquisition and disposition of foreign exchange. An RPE should at the very least allow for equal access of some class of agents (for example, domestic firms) to compete for scarce foreign exchange. This can be organized in various ways. One of the more efficient is through smoothly functioning auctions, unless the obstacles to auctions and a freer exchange regime have already been removed during the PET phase. Precisely because the behavior of agents competing for foreign exchange is initially unknown, it might be worthwhile to target the foreign exchange regime in such a way that the most outlying bids for foreign exchange are first accommodated through currency auctions; these should preferably be fully emplaced during the PET phase. Fairly soon, however, most foreign exchange transactions should be executed anonymously and automatically. The exchange regime should therefore be liberalized so as to enable all agents to compete equally for foreign currency. This should encompass in the first instance all transactions on current account. To improve the operations in capital markets, eventually also the restrictions on capital account transactions must be eased, if not liberalized altogether; initially, it might be wise to avoid the inflow of foreign capital exerting upward pressure on the exchange rate when in fact the already precarious competitive position of the country is being undermined. Both call for moving toward formal convertibility, in the first instance as defined by the Fund's article VIII.

b. Fiscal policy. The paramount task here is to create a system of revenue generation and outlays that allows the government to discharge its functions, as determined through the accepted political process, while maintaining macroeconomic balance, promoting economic efficiency, and ensuring an acceptable dispersion in incomes. These competing claims can be reconciled only through the minimization of distorting fiscal levies or subsidies.

A reasonable fiscal approach consistent with creating a market environment encompasses a combination of direct taxes on firms, natural resources, wealth, and personal incomes. Also indirect taxes will be required but preferably in the form of a value-added tax, supplemented in some cases with excise taxes on specific commodities, possibly a sales tax, and tariffs; whenever the cost incurred by government can be directly imputed to specific users or activities explicit user fees need to be set as equitably as circumstances allow.

c. *Price policy.* As already intimated, prices in an RPE should by and large be formed much like in MEs. That is to say, prices should in principle crystallize through the interaction of demand and supply in atomistic markets. Furthermore, domestic prices should be linked through an operative flexible exchange regime to trade prices, including in TR relations whenever trade there is *not* constrained through protocols negotiated at the governmental level. But there may be a need to go beyond the microeconomics of price policy. Even in the most liberal ME, prices are not always set freely in markets. That may be because of antitrust legislation, such as in the case of public utilities. It may also be needed to target specific societal preferences either through price subsidies or some social welfare scheme. In any case, just as in MEs, the government's pricing policy should aim at minimal distortions whenever possible to enforce its precepts through nonprice intervention; when price supports or levies cannot be handled otherwise, excise taxes and user fees should be set.

d. *Income policy.* Given the backdrop of the RPE and the egalitarian principles that those societies have traditionally embraced, it may be thought that an income policy should be seen separately from the government's fiscal needs. There may be some residual instances in which that will be so, just as in some MEs. But in general, government interference in the formation of gross incomes from labor as well as financial and other capital assets should be minimal. The chief aim should be to permit income formation according to the social compact and to realize preferences with respect to the desirable dispersion of incomes through fiscal and welfare policies.

e. *Commercial policy.* In considering the various reforms and the role of macroeconomic policy, it is frequently forgotten that the trade regime of the CPE and MPE has been critical in ensuring substantial domestic policy autonomy. It has also been an important obstacle to steady economic progress because it has inhibited effective competition from abroad and interaction among economic agents both of which are so necessary to channel effectively "information" in a decentralized environment.

As regards economic agents engaging in foreign economic activity, the logic of the RPE requires that any economic agent should in principle be allowed to compete anywhere within the rules and regulations in place. The latter are part and parcel of an orthodox commercial policy. From the point of view of enhancing competition and fostering export-led growth, commercial policy should be liberal and simple. It should be uniformly applicable to all, perhaps subject to certain explicit social preferences. Foreign competition should be looked upon as a major guarantor of market orientation. Putting in place high tariffs as a substitute for the forced separation of domestic and foreign economic agents in the past simply to protect uncompetitive domestic industries would be unwise. Once the transition in the PET has been bridged, the fears of foreign competition destabilizing the still fragile domestic ME should dissipate.

Protection has in the past also been maintained through the special trading and payments arrangements typical of the CMEA. Indeed, the very aims of SEI embodied forbidding protection of domestic activities. I see no need to do away with the CMEA in all of its possible cloaks. Especially the trading and payments regimes that it stands for need to be harnessed more effectively, perhaps within the context of a constitutional framework on tiered regional integration (see Chapter 9).

5. Legacies of central planning and the transition

A comparison between the features of the Eastern European economies set forth in Chapter 3 and the key characteristics of what most of these countries would like to accomplish as RPEs reveals a formidable chasm in policies, institutions, and policy instruments. Hence the need for designing an orderly transition from the economic structures in place to the desired RPE environment. This entails two broad sets of questions that must be resolved in designing the transition phase. One revolves around the objectives of economic policy, which is political economy in its true sense. The other is concerned with the technical aspects of getting the most out of limited resources, which is the subject proper of economics.

It is especially important to bear in mind certain features of the countries under consideration in designing this transition. The PETs are Central European countries, which for decades, including prior to the ascent of communist rule, tended to have a predisposition to egalitarianism and tolerated a considerable involvement of the state in economic life. That there is a trade-off between egalitarianism and economic efficiency should be made clear to all concerned. Where precisely this trade-off lies is a matter of societal consensus that may be building up at this juncture through the mechanism of parliamentary democracy.

Policies in the years ahead should be constructed around three major themes. One is economic stabilization. Gaining control over monetary and fiscal affairs in a decentralizing environment is an absolutely necessity. At the same time it requires that policy makers come to grips with the monetary overhang to ease legacies from the past that are choking ongoing flows. Second, the issues of reform and its transition phase *in se* need to be addressed, though they might usefully be linked to both stabilization and putting in place the groundwork for sustainable growth. Here price reform and genuine wholesale trade, as core components of enforcing greater autonomy upon firms, including SOEs, rank at the top of the policy agenda. Finally, formulating proper macroeconomic policies for an RPE continues to be a critical task. In this connection, questions arise as to the role of monetary and fiscal policies in a society that professes to be socialistic and the degree to which these policies need to be complemented with income and price policies to safeguard social priorities without exacerbating inflation.

One of the most banal platitudes of discourses on reform is that economists and others interested in reform know how an ME and a CPE work, and how the transition from an ME to a CPE was accomplished (Hewett 1989); but they know nothing, or next to nothing, about doing the reverse. It is, of course, true that there are no hard-and-fast rules about the transition, inasmuch as thus far no single CPE or MPE has succeeded in overcoming the multiple legacies of the planning environment. Admitting this is not quite the same as asserting complete ignorance of the transition.

Since World War II, several economies have made attempts to move over from a deeply engrained war-economy footing to a civilian, market-orientated mode of production with various degrees of success. Likewise, numerous MEs have made attempts to divest themselves of the most odious kinds of state intervention, including through privatization of state assets. Also a number of DEs characterized by weakly integrated markets and a limited resource base have gathered experience with transiting from variously regulated development and managerial models to one grafted onto major elements of an ME. Certainly, most of these changes were enacted in environments in which the basic market framework was still in place. Whether or not this makes a huge difference will need to be investigated.

The key components of an RPE are known. These assume that various actions are taken both in building institutions and in changing attitudes of all economic agents - management, workers, administrators, and households. Similarly, the ongoing policy agenda, as discussed in Section 4, is fairly clear. What is not so far known with any certainty is the best - optimal, if you wish - sequencing of the various elements of the transition, given the complexity of the prevailing macroeconomic policy agenda and its fragile sociopolitical setting.

I do not pretend to be in a position to offer a clear-cut solution. But it would seem logical to start with the very essence of what an ME is all about. The heart of it would seem to be prices that reflect relative scarcities and that respond to changes in demand and supply. These ought preferably to be set within a competitive environment, but that cannot always be secured for various institutional, legal, and economic reasons. Competition must therefore be accompanied by sensible regulation. Also critical is the enforcement of a "hard budget constraint," to use János Kornai's hackneyed phrase, particularly for SOEs and, with given fiscal constraints, for the state budget (Brabant 1990k). How to streamline these policy shifts, perhaps in the context of east-west economic assistance, will be spelled out in Chapter 8.

* * *

The preceding analyses have drawn a coarse picture of some of the daunting tasks faced by policy makers of PETs. Precisely because of the magnitude of the technical problems and the political interests of third countries in the democratization and marketization processes in Eastern Europe, various types of assistance are being made available to the PETs. Regardless of this unusual interest, the process of transforming Eastern Europe is bound to have two kinds of repercussions. One is the need and desire to divert part of CMEA trade. The other is how DEs will be affected by east-west assistance. Both sets of questions can best be addressed after looking at the kind of assistance that is being offered and what would be desirable, given the aims and circumstances of the PETs.

5

The political economy of east-west assistance

The astoundingly swift, mostly peaceful revolutions in Eastern Europe have been greeted with glee, approval, and understanding in many MEs. Especially Western Europe has been apprehensive about the shaky foundations upon which these anti-communist, rather than pro-democracy, sociopolitical mutations have been predicated. To buttress the budding democracies these countries have expressed considerable interest in providing various forms of assistance, ranging from purely cultural exchanges all the way to the nitty-gritty of international trade and finance. Because interdependencies in real life are rarely limited to two-way relations, one cannot adequately study relations between Eastern and Western Europe in a continental vacuum.

The forms of assistance earmarked for Eastern Europe and their ramifications broadly viewed form the subject of this chapter. Section 1 summarizes in a nutshell the core issues involved in this unprecented east-west exchange. Next I sketch the context within which one might usefully examine the western assistance efforts. In Section 3, I present an overview of the various kinds of assistance committed to date from within the western alliance. Whereas the brunt of the assistance effort has been conceived primarily within the context of cooperation between Eastern and Western Europe, it should not be forgotten that other countries have pledged help too. In particular, the initiative taken by the Group of Seven (Canada, France, FRG, Italy, Japan, United Kingdom, and the United States) at their Paris Summit in July 1989 and the subsequent steps set by the twenty-four full members of the OECD deserve to be highlighted. In some cases, these measures have been augmented by the interests shown on the part of other countries, including some DEs, which need to be touched upon here as well. Potential association of PETs with western integration schemes is one form of special assistance that may materialize as examined in Section 4. The ways in which western governments officially envisage to channel this assistance into Eastern Europe are summarized next. The chapter concludes with a brief invocation of the desirability of establishing a Marshall Plan for Eastern Europe, which forms the subject proper of the next chapter.

1. The core issues at stake

The avalanche of sociopolitical transitions in Eastern Europe since mid-1989 has elicited unprecedented interest on the part of the political leadership of many countries, particularly in Western Europe. This revolves around two buzzwords: democratization and marketization. Western leaders feel it appropriate to see to it that the processes of moving toward more democratic, pluralistic political decision making in PETs take firm root in the consciousness of the electorate of these countries. Related to this, but reaching far beyond the mechanisms and politics of democracy, is the attention given to the physical, legal, and commercial institutionalization of primarily market-oriented economies in Eastern Europe. Both features are as yet fragile and western assistance could be critical in ensuring that the ongoing changes do not get prematurely derailed. Other countries have on the whole been sympathetic to the transitions in Eastern Europe.

Although also most of the DEs have been on the whole supportive of the seminal changes taking place in Eastern Europe, they have recently aired a wide range of concerns and apprehensions. Their most serious preoccupations include the implications of the interest of DMEs in helping Eastern Europe in whatever way possible in three respects: access to western trading markets, the comparative attractiveness of private, commercial, and official foreign capital flows into Eastern Europe, and the possibility of diverting ODA in the process, at least in the short run. Short of obtaining assurances on these three acute concerns, DEs have expressed little satisfaction with the prospects of a single European market for trade and cooperation in the longer run (see Chapter 10).

In trying to ensure that the seminal changes in Eastern Europe do indeed contribute maximally to remaking Europe, a wide range of assistance efforts have thus far come to the fore. Some take the form of outright grants of financial assistance and emergency food and medical help chiefly committed by governments or intergovernmental organizations. Aside from these direct supports targeted at alleviating critical short-run problems arising from the abruptness of the political and social mobility in Eastern Europe, western governments have sought to provide also more indirect inducements. These include formal and other guarantees, as well as various supports, for private and official capital mobility toward the east, facilitating access to western markets for their exports, and even entertaining some form of association of the PETs with the emerging unified market in Europe, whether limited to the EC's Single Market or the "European economic space" provided by the Europe of the Eighteen.

2. The international context of assistance to PETs

Beginning with the unprecedented transition from a Communist-led Government to one formed by Solidarity in Poland in mid-1989, literally weeks after Solidarity had been allowed to emerge from the trenches into which the imposition of martial law in December 1981 had forced it, western governments have shown considerable interest in assisting a growing number of Eastern European countries, including recently Yugoslavia as well. With the decision of EC foreign ministers of 16 February 1990 to extend the program to the four other Eastern European countries as well as to Yugoslavia, the assistance package has now become regionwide. The so-called PHARE (*Pologne/Hongrie: assistance à la restructuration économique*) program has recently (June 1990) been formally extended to these other countries too.

Only Albania and the Soviet Union are still missing. If Albania were to enact some meaningful reform, it would undoubtedly be able to benefit from the same treatment as the rest of Eastern Europe. But at this stage, it is not at all clear whether such assistance would be granted to the Soviet Union; the recent row about furnishing financial and other aid to *perestroyka* is a vivid reminder of the lingering ambivalence on that score. The reasons behind this differentiation are many and complex. But the three most important ones are undoubtedly the sheer size of the Soviet Union, lingering suspicions of that vast country whose roots go far back in Russian history, and the fact that east-west détente has been chiefly the responsibility of the bilateral relationship between the Soviet Union and the United States.

Whether this *divide et impera* approach is wise depends to a large extent on the purposes of vast east-west economic, political, cultural, and humanitarian assistance. Thus far, the objectives are not very well defined. They are certainly not yet integrated with the aspirations of the PETs, the real needs to make the transition work at a tolerable cost, and the kind and volume of assistance that the west may eventually be willing to muster.

Nevertheless, the key issues at stake in the west revolve around a vast array of concerns that determine the engagement of the DMEs in favor of ambitious societal reform in Eastern Europe. These certainly include political, cultural, nationalistic, economic, historical, social, and demographic factors. Some may bring about palpable shocks on the European continent with wide-ranging social, political, economic, and security implications.

Among the politics of east-west assistance, ensuring that the democratic process in Eastern Europe proceeds with minimal setbacks has been one focal area of the multiple determinants of western support. Two stand out. Perhaps the most critical was further loosening the tarnished bond between these countries and the Soviet Union in all areas of interaction. Also, strengthening the forces that may soon lead most of these countries to assume the key features of PETs (including full-fledged market orientation, private property, and quick integration into world markets and the standard institutions there), as their leaderships are currently coveting, played an important role in the formulation of the western stance.

Perhaps the most sentimental assistance efforts have been mounted in the context of German unification. Of course, much more is at stake than simple empathy for a divided nation. German unification is a task of the highest political and sentimental order in the FRG; the GDR has simply resigned itself to being submerged into the FRG. The manysided GDR-FRG conundrum presents arguably the most challenging task of east-west cooperation as it is the logical endpoint of the outcome of World War II. The unexpected resolution of the German question is also a phenomenon that goes at the heart of postwar political, economic, security, and strategic arrangements in Western Europe and indeed the western world as a whole. Strategically and militarily, final unification can be achieved only with the withdrawal of Soviet troops from the GDR. It probably would still be too early to envisage Soviet troops on NATO soil prior to a full-scale military conflagration on the continent which, I for one firmly hope, has become a rather remote eventuality at this juncture! But beyond that narrow context, reunification has many far-reaching implications for western and eastern security arrangements. Indeed, the very *raison d'être* of the two military alliances in Europe and the particular configuration of postwar international economic security are being reconsidered. Some of these systemic repercussions are addressed in Chapter 10.

For nearly half a century, the idea of a (re)unified Germany remained a platitude toward which western leaders could commit themselves with ritual obeisance in the reasonable expectation that no deeds would be exacted. A reunified Germany now becoming a reality has led once again to uneasiness that finds its roots in historical anxieties. It has many implications for Western European integration - "1992" and beyond - as well. The topic is a special one. It does not touch upon relations between sovereign states with the purpose of one being in the position to influence the "environment" of the other.

Quite apart from the German issue, the stationing of troops in east and west has become a top priority on the negotiating agenda. The issues are clear: The Eastern European societies that have opted for market orientation and democracy deem it no longer necessary to condone a standing Soviet army on their territory. U.S. and Soviet leaders have negotiated a sharp reduction in their reciprocal troop strengths in Europe. Both powers are under some pressure to reduce military budgets and with the sharply curtailed military threat, the rationale of maintaining standing armies abroad quickly evaporates. On the other hand, the western democracies and some of the Eastern European countries fearful of a strengthening Germany have petitioned that foreign, chiefly U.S., troops be kept in Europe, albeit at reduced strength.

There is also a very serious demographic problem especially in the short run that deserves to be addressed with great immediacy, even though economic and monetary union was chosen as a key vehicle to stem the tide of migrants from the GDR moving into the FRG. But also people movements from other countries into Western Europe posed several problems (see Chapter 1). The hemorrhaging of the GDR's population as well as outflows from the Soviet Union continue at very high levels.

These cross-border demographic waves certainly pose serious problems, at least in the short run, for the countries of immigration. Repercussions are felt in job markets; strained housing, hospital, education, and related service facilities; and indeed in the entire gamut of problems that crop up when reestablishing cultural equilibrium in the host countries. Furthermore, it was mainly the able-bodied, younger, ambitious, and relatively skilled that have been moving westwards, particularly in the case of the GDR (about 64 percent of migrants in 1989) in part because of monetary incentives. These emigration waves as a result are having serious destabilizing implications for the countries of origin as well as the final destination. Finally, there is the threat that the new immigrants, because of privileges they can count on for historical or religious reasons, particularly in the case of the GDR-FRG population movements, will displace other migrants. These settlers chiefly from southern Europe and the DEs of North Africa and the Middle East will either have to move elsewhere in Western Europe or return to their home country. This would simply shift the burden of Eastern European emigration onto other countries, some of which are hardly in a position to come to grips with the reflux of people and the sharp reduction in worker remittances that would be entailed.

Of course, there are vast economic interests at stake as well. The presence of substantially underdeveloped markets of some size (about 288 million individuals in the Soviet Union and roughly 100 million in Eastern Europe, with Poland alone accounting for 38 million) holds the promise, at least in the medium to long run, of a marked expansion of effective European demand as well as supply, provided the eastern markets can be fully integrated and relative scarcities in the west can be replicated in the east. Eastern Europe offers a geographical area, where western countries in time hope to conquer sizable export markets and, through the intermediation of commercial and financial agents, especially the transnational corporations (TNCs), can expect to gain from a substantial presence. Inexpensive and relatively skilled labor in conjunction with capital, technology, managerial skills, and marketing acumen from DMEs may in time supply western markets with comparatively cheap goods, yield substantial profits especially to the TNCs with embodied comparative advantages, and enable these firms to "capture" eastern markets.

There are, of course, other reasons, most of which find their roots in historical relations or revendications. Three stand out. Perhaps foremost are concerns about recreating Europe which is frequently seen in the context of the post-Yalta interlude. Second, Western Europe has rapidly been gaining greater self-confidence in the international arena, particularly as exemplified by the behavior of the Commission of the EC. The latter has aspirations of big-power status at least in the all-European context, almost regardless of how "Europe" is defined. Finally, there is undoubtedly a genuine self-interest in Western Europe in regaining and sustaining greater stability in Eastern Europe than could reasonably be expected to prevail without active western support.

Eurocentrism among politicians and those who reflect upon international relations has a counterpart in the efforts of the catholic and protestant churches to reverse the godlessness that was assiduously fostered under Soviet-type communism. Also latent antagonisms within Christianity, particularly the catholic church as contrasted with the orthodox one, as in most of the Balkan countries, is playing a role. By providing material and other assistance, it is thought that the west can "recoup" Eastern Europe, as most of the Central European soul has historically been divided between catholicism and protestantism, particularly the Lutheran and Calvinist variants thereof.

Of course, these feelings are not only held by the donor countries. Also the recipient countries see in this western assistance a form of penance for the "wrongs" suffered by the east. Thus, as Prime Minister Tadeusz Mazowiecki recently put it in Brussels (*Neue Zürcher Zeitung*, 2 February 1990, p. 35) not without an astounding degree of naiveté, western assistance is a recognition of the magnitude of the political and economic changes in Poland and of the costs inflicted upon the country by all too rashly issued credits compounded with an interest problem of the western countries' making!...

3. Overview of western assistance to PETs

These factors and others not yet touched upon suggest that western "assistance" has by necessity taken on a wide variety of forms. Not all can be discussed here, if only because some forms are being provided informally, surreptitiously, or by discretionary means. Furthermore, there is almost always a gap between commitments and disbursements. But the precise picture of dollar and cents involved is much less important than obtaining a rough order of magnitude, a broad impression of what kinds of aid are being proffered, a perspective on who is proposing to do what, and some sense of how it all fits together, given the objective of the exercise, namely to support democratization and marketization of the PETs.

The most spectacular form of western assistance to the PETs is the multilateral assistance program put together by the Group of Twenty-Four. These countries have entrusted the coordination of their assistance and the concrete formulation of desirable aspects of the reform package to the Commission of the EC. Next in importance are the bilateral commitments by western governments, including Canada, France, the FRG, Italy, Japan, the United Kingdom, and the United States. Furthermore, there are efforts made by the multilateral financial institutions in Washington, notably the World Bank and its affiliates and the IMF, for those countries of Eastern Europe that are members or have recently petitioned for membership. Also the more secretarial international organizations, including OECD and some United Nations (U.N.) agencies, notably the United Nations Development Programme (UNDP), are helping, however limited their role must necessarily remain. Finally, a wide variety of support is being provided by private individuals and nongovernmental organizations. The latter complement the secretarial efforts just mentioned. The former in fact form an extension of the commercial and financial commitments of the various bilateral and multilateral donors cited above.

Seen against this backdrop, it may be useful to sketch the key pillars of the western assistance efforts and what would seem to be missing. The key elements of the Group of Twenty-four's assistance are six: (1) macroeconomic stabilization, (2) fresh funds in support of restructuring the balance of payments and the allocation of resources away from import substitution and domestic consumption to export sectors, (3) export facilitation, (4) technical assistance in part with financial support, (5) the promotion of foreign investments and joint ventures, and (6) debt relief.

The order in which I have listed the items reflects in part the priorities the west has accorded to various undertakings. Foremost therein would seem to be the adoption of macroeconomic stabilization to come to grips with the three kinds of imbalances discussed in Chapter 4, namely pent-up excess demand, current macroeconomic imbalances, and imbalances emerging in the process of restructuring relative prices. Such stabilization is to be undertaken by the country itself with the active support of macroeconomic programs negotiated with the IMF, and hence standby financial support. The aim is to reestablish viable domestic and external balances in part by significantly overhauling the budgetary and fiscal processes of these countries, to undertake the institutional changes required to enhance the functioning of markets, and otherwise to foster structural change in such a way that factor productivity becomes the key vehicle propelling economic growth without entailing major domestic and external imbalances. These efforts are being made with little regard to the critical role of the CMEA in maintaining economic performance and indeed in offering potentially lucrative trade opportunities. At best, countries are being urged to cut out export surpluses to the TR area, almost regardless of how this will be accomplished and its consequences for the well-being, or even the viability, of the domestic microeconomic structures (see Chapter 9). There would also appear to be too much emphasis on speed, comprehensiveness, and sequencing. Often it is not spelled out clearly that a comprehensive approach calls for sequencing, and thus for moderation in speed. Speedy reform can do without comprehensiveness and sequencing, but may lead to naught, and perhaps chaos. Sequencing without speed and comprehensiveness invites stalling the reform effort. I shall return to these issues in Chapter 8.

I decided to discuss first, and at greater length, the financial and commercial aspects of western assistance not because I deem these forms of cooperation by themselves far more important or intrinsically more attractive than the less tangible forms of technical or humanitarian assistance. Instead, there are two self-serving pragmatic rationales. One is that quantitative as well as qualitative information on financial relations, commercial policy, association with regional integration schemes, and industrial coordination is considerably more abundant and easier to place within an economic context than any of the other instances of assistance. Of course, because this is an economic treatise, the economic formats should in any case be accorded pride of place in this discourse.

1. Financial assistance

The macroeconomic stabilization efforts are being accompanied by new credits and grants in support of balance-of-payments adjustments and also to finance desirable shifts in economic structures, including to enhance environmental protection. Arriving at an accurate assessment of the financial assistance pledged, committed (for example, as approved through the regular legislative processes in the donor or creditor countries), and disbursed in some form is by no means an easy task. To the best of my knowledge, the available information is based on the culling of disparate news releases. Neither governments nor international organizations appear thus far to have gathered a complete picture, although efforts made in the context of the EC, the United Nations Economic Commission for Europe (UNECE), and OECD would seem to have yielded a fairly rounded picture (see UNECE 1990, pp. 212-23). The total estimated value of commitments by mid-1990 for 1990 and beyond amounts to some $16.8 billion for Hungary and Poland. How much will eventually be extended to the other countries is as yet uncertain as the PHARE program is officially being applied to them only beginning with late June 1990 and the other countries discussed here, except Rumania, do not yet have formal relations with the Washington financial institutions.

Structural shifts are being supported to make the PETs much more aware of foreign trade opportunities by favoring exports in the appropriation of resources. This is, of course, inextricably linked to the macroeconomic stabilization and positive restructuring efforts discussed earlier. Money is being committed through the international monetary institutions. The Fund is working out adjustment programs for which it is willing to provide standby support. Once this is in place, funds committed by other official financial institutions will begin to be disbursed. Loans are being committed too by international organizations and there various national financial commitments have been made to the PETs. Disbursements thereof too are predicated upon the PET reaching an adjustment agreement with the IMF. In other words, agreement with the Fund on basic features of the conduct of macroeconomic policy is the trigger that sets off a wide range of financial assistance efforts. The various financial measures can best be discussed under six headings.

a. Grants and loans by governments. Outright grants of currency have been of limited importance in the assistance effort. Several governments have extended official loans or have guaranteed commercial loans, however. I include here, which is particularly relevant for the GDR, the loans from Marshall aid counterpart funds available in the FRG.[1] In late 1989, the FRG agreed with the GDR to make available DM6 billion during 1990-1993 to foster private firms (*Dokumentation zur Aussenwirtschaft*, 7 March 1990, pp. 2-4). Without monetary union, the loans would have had to be repaid partly in local currency at a favorable exchange rate and carried an interest of 6.5 percent.

b. Loans from multilateral financial institutions. The World Bank, the International Finance Corporation (IFC), and the Fund are *the* key actors not only in funneling money into the PETs, but also in clearing the way for disbursement of other forms of aid, as noted. It bears to stress in this connection that only Hungary, Poland, and Rumania are members of the Washington institutions. The latter's seal of approval can therefore be extended only to these three CMEA countries (as well as Yugoslavia). However, both Bulgaria and Czechoslovakia have petitioned for accession. The GDR had been wanting to do likewise, but with monetary union Fund membership has become moot at best. Total commitments from the Fund to present members amounts to about $1 billion. That of the World Bank over the period 1990-1992, including what is likely to emerge for Bulgaria and Czechoslovakia once they join, is likely to exceed $5.5 billion, even if the newly founded European bank will come on stream quickly.

Two institutions of the EC have been granting loans. One is the effort of the European Community for Coal and Steel (ECCS) to support restructuring of these two interrelated sectors in the PETs too. This institution has been authorized to earmark up to ECU200 million for Hungary and Poland; but so far no amounts have been committed. But at least the facility is in place once the PETs decide to move ahead. The other is the European Investment Bank (EIB), whose mission is to finance mainly infrastructural projects in the bank's EC member countries or if otherwise instructed by those members. Because the EC has not yet in place an alternative channel for ascertaining through its

[1] The portion of U.S. assistance that Germany did not repay (some $2.2 billion) was kept in a special account (see Chapter 6) that eventually was entrusted to the FRG for issuing long-term loans most recently for small and medium-sized German firms, environmental protection, and the special promotion of Berlin. These loans still have to be repaid, so that the original fund would be kept intact (the total value at end of 1987 was DM16 billion). For a discussion of an equivalent fund in Austria, see Hoscher 1990, p. 36.

own means the creditworthiness of various proposals submitted by the PETs, the EIB has been instructed to start lending to Eastern Europe as well and was empowered in late 1989 to lend up to ECU1 billion to Hungary and Poland; this has recently been extended to the GDR as well. In all likelihood, however, the EIB's role in Eastern Europe will soon be replaced by a new financial institution.

Potentially the most innovative aspect of east-west assistance will soon emerge through the newly created European Bank for Reconstruction and Development (EBRD). This has been conceived as a regional development bank with the Asian Development Bank (ABD) probably offering the clearest precedent. Issuing from a proposal made by French president François Mitterand, the EBRD has been conceived as the key organization to guide the restructuring process in Eastern Europe. What the precise divisions between its tasks and those of the World Bank will be remains to be seen. Perhaps the two will succeed in synchronizing their efforts, with the EBRD focusing on project financing while the World Bank, in cooperation with the Fund, will zero in on structural adjustment lending and macroeconomic policy support.

There are 42 founding members of the EBRD,[2] which itself is capitalized at ECU10 billion (about $12.3 billion in mid-1990). Inasmuch as the EBRD's statutes were approved only in May 1990 and the bank will not start operations until April 1991, end March having been set as the deadline for ratification, it is difficult to assess in which directions the institution could be of greatest help to Eastern Europe. However, at least 60 percent of the bank's loans (up to its subscribed capital) will be earmarked to foster private enterprise, including SOEs slated for privatization. The USSR can draw upon the fund only up to its own paid-in share.

c. Commercial banking and related institutions. Individual commercial banks or related financial institutions sometimes in cooperation with their governments are setting up financial institutions to enhance east-west economic collaboration. There are two kinds. One is the creation of financial funds that will be managed professionally with a view to encouraging investments in selected PETs. Most such funds have thus far been conceived for Hungary by individuals of Hungarian origin with a track record in western financial matters.

Another form is the creation of investment or merchant banks or financing companies. An example of this form is Simest SpA, a merchant bank owned by the Italian Government for 51 percent, the remainder being distributed among various Italian credit institutions, business associations, and state companies. Its purpose is to take minority stakes in joint ventures and participate in other forms of industrial and commercial collaboration, mainly with small and medium-sized companies. This relative bias is built in simply because the large Italian firms have already amassed substantial experience and expertise in Eastern European markets through their own resources and well-developed

[2] All EC members, the EC itself, and the EIB; all European CMEA members; all EFTA members; Cyprus, Lichtenstein, Malta, and Turkey in Western Europe; Yugoslavia; Australia, Canada, Israel, Japan, New Zealand, and the United States as the remaining DMEs; and Egypt, Mexico, Morocco, and the Republic of Korea as DEs.

contacts with financial intermediaries. Simest will also provide services to small and medium-sized companies in Italy intending to invest in Eastern Europe.

d. The convertible currency debt. For some countries in Eastern Europe, most notably Hungary and Poland, but the problems of Bulgaria and the GDR should not be underestimated, the convertible currency debt is a Damocles sword hanging over any kind of open market-oriented economic reform. This is particularly so if the reform is to prove its mettle fairly quickly in terms of yielding visible benefits to the population at large. It would probably be hopeless to provide assistance to the fledging market orientation of PETs without doing something about that debt. Various measures are being taken to seek debt relief for the PETs, which not coincidentally happen to be the most chronically indebted Eastern European countries. These efforts are being undertaken in the context of the Paris Club as far as official debt is concerned and under the umbrella of the London Club in the case of the commercial debt. Applying the Brady plan to the PETs is being considered within the context of the London Club's activities.

Poland, for example, has asked its 17 creditor governments that it be allowed to suspend debt-service payments of principal and interest (the latter recently amounting to roughly \$1.5 billion or 17 per cent of convertible currency earnings in 1989) immediately, freeze its foreign debt at present levels, and seek a long-term solution that would go in the direction of outright debt reduction (*International Herald Tribune*, 10-11 February 1990, p. 9). In the first instance, this petition is directed at the Paris Club negotiators, who are responsible for rescheduling the government-held debt. By now, this accounts for the bulk - about three fourths - of the Polish convertible currency obligations, simply because the government-guaranteed commercial debt contracted in the 1970s has had to be covered by the guarantor.

On 16 February 1990, the 17 official creditors that form the Paris Club agreed to reschedule a record \$9.4 billion of debt payments for 14 years (*Neue Zürcher Zeitung*, 17-18 February 1990, p. 35). This total includes \$3.4 billion in late payments outstanding at the end of 1989, as well as all the interest and debt repayments due until the end of March 1991. At the time, Poland's official debt amounted to some \$27 billion (as opposed to a total of \$40 billion).

It is hoped that this favorable reaction on the part of Governments will provide the necessary impetus to leniency on the part of the London Club negotiators of the commercially held convertible currency debt. After the protracted negotiations of the past decade, some modified Brady-type debt-reduction program may be envisioned in this regard. This has not so far occurred. The Vienna negotiations in the context of the London Club, which are ongoing at the time of writing (July 1990), has thus far only come up with a proposal that Poland service its commercial debt for 15 percent of the interest due in 1989-1990, the rest being capitalized. Poland has tabled a counterproposal to enable it to repurchase its debt at market value (between 14 and 17 percent of nominal value) or to obtain a sizable reduction in interest rates. Commercial banks do not seem eager to opt for either proposal.

e. Transfers in the German monetary union. Transfers from the FRG into the GDR are undoubtedly the largest of all the kinds of assistance that can reasonably be anticipated. For the period 1990-1994, the FRG is counting official transfers, mainly for the support of budget deficits and welfare payments, of about DM115 billion, of which at least DM24.75 billion will be disbursed in 1990 and DM38 billion in 1991. Should the economic fortunes of the eastern part of the union remain well behind expectations, that volume of assistance will in all likelihood increase substantially.

f. FDI and portfolio investments. Again, the GDR is likely to be the most substantial beneficiary of commercial capital flows from the FRG. Also the other PETs are hoping to attract especially FDI through wholly-owned or joint ventures. The initial response of TNCs to the sociopolitical changes in the PETs has been muted at best. But once basic stability, including on the political front, in the PETs will be regained, more than a trivial opportunity for FDI is likely to emerge through two channels. One will be the privatization in the context of the creation of basic vestiges of a stock market. The other will be in making the PETs an attractive location for FDI and portfolio investments in comparison with alternative outlets for foreign capital.

2. Commercial policy facilitation

Western assistance efforts are also being underpinned with various concessions made to improve the access of PETs to western markets. These take the form of tariff cuts, usually by removing hidden and other restrictions on most-favored nation (MFN) treatment or simply the granting of such a status for the first time or revoking earlier interferences with the MFN status; obtaining preferential access to EC markets under the provisions of the General System of Preferences (GSP); abolition or the easing of quantitative restrictions; narrowing the restrictions imposed under the aegis of the Coordinating Committee for Multilateral Export Controls (CoCom); and assistance with marketing and other aspects of reaching a firmer foothold in MEs. Not all forms can be discussed at length here because the measures are rather qualitative and their impact can only be assessed in the far-off future.

a. Roll-back of discriminatory tariffs and other restrictions. In the context of trade and cooperation agreements negotiated between the EC and Hungary and Poland, arrangements were made finally to abide more closely by the prescriptions of article XIII of the GATT, to which the three parties, of course, have belonged for a long time (Brabant 1990a, pp. 190-3), and nontariff barriers. The parties had agreed to a timetable (end 1994 in the case of Poland and end 1995 for Hungary) for eliminating the discriminatory quantitative restrictions maintained by the EC. It was decided fairly quickly to move that deadline forward, and in early 1990 most of these restrictions were lifted by the EC.

Of course, there are also a host of nondiscriminatory quantitative restrictions and sectoral market controls that have been under consideration. However, progress with respect to Eastern Europe on discriminatory restrictions would in principle be tantamount to extending such preferences to all GATT partners, because of the MFN clause. But some restrictions on passenger cars, footwear, and toys have nonetheless been relaxed, probably in the GSP context. Regarding sectoral market controls, in some instances, particularly the EC is entertaining preferential allocations in quota determination. This has already resulted, for example, in the PETs obtaining a larger steel quota of 15 percent (the United States has increased Hungary's quota by 30 percent) and increments in quotas for textile and clothing outside the provisons of the Multi-fibre Arrangement (MFA). Furthermore, the EC has relaxed its import restrictions for agricultural products.

b. MFN treatment and GATT status. Most Eastern European countries enjoy MFN treatment with most MEs. The only major exception is the United States, which for various reasons (see Brabant 1990a, pp. 182-3) has traditionally regulated its relations with planned economies outside the GATT framework, even for those countries that have acceded to the General Agreement. It has already granted MFN to Czechoslovakia and has reconsidered its on-off MFN stance for Hungary and Poland, and may eventually regularize these relations within the GATT framework.

Only the GDR and the Soviet Union remain outside GATT. Bulgaria has been an observer since 1967 and petitioned in 1986 for full accession. This process was stalled, largely owing to the fact that Bulgaria was not really making progress toward marketization until recent measures and the Chinese request for reaccession has been causing many difficulties (Brabant 1990a, pp. 188-90). Both the GDR and the Soviet Union have petitioned for observership in the GATT. The latter obtained this status in May 1990. The GDR's status in GATT will probably be full accession as a result of German economic union.

c. Association with EC and EFTA. Facilities have been discussed to bring the Eastern European countries under some kind of Western European integration umbrella (Kostrzewa and Schmieding 1990, Krenzler 1990). Initially, a special status for Hungary and Poland was being mooted, although these countries were really hoping to obtain the green light for eventual full membership (Adamiec 1989, Giscard d'Estaing 1989). Because of the wave of changes in and the number of PETs, the Commission of the EC has now been empowered to negotiate a formal association status, which I shall discuss in detail in Section 4 below. Whether in the end something similar can be worked out with the EFTA countries remains to be seen.

d. Facilitation of marketing. This is essentially an area of technical assistance, the focus being on what it takes to broach markets and tailor domestic products, or items previously designed overwhelmingly for the Soviet market, to tastes and habits in "new," much more sophisticated markets. Traditionally, the CPEs and MPEs have shown a poor understanding for "investment in marketing," the entire gamut of material (such as distribution points, maintenance centers, and outlets for spare parts and sales) and other (such as advertisement and gaining goodwill) infrastructure to underpin a successful penetration of a market.

e. CoCom arrangements. Exports of sophisticated manufactures from most DMEs have been under various kinds of CoCom controls since the late 1940s. Although these lists have been under review on many occasions in the past, there is presently a move under way to substantially curtail the restrictions on exports to the PETs. How much will be liberalized and what its impacts will be are matters of definition and conjecture, respectively. Of the roughly 120 product categories under controls, at least 30 are being removed and for another 20 restrictions will be sharply relaxed. Furthermore, the PETs have also obtained assurances that the issuing of licenses for listed goods will be speeded up. This change in attitude toward strategic controls stems not only from the fact that DEs have made inroads into such markets in Eastern Europe. Also, the very structural modernization that is being advocated by DMEs can be introduced quickly only through the importation of equipment, most of which has been on CoCom restrictive lists. A typical example is modern telecommunications without which it is not possible to create a modern ME and to attract sizable FDI.

3. Industrial cooperation

Enveloping various efforts to promote technical assistance, this has thus far revolved largely around managerial and financial infrastructure and the training required for that purpose. Measures have been discussed to lend various kinds of private, corporate, and institutional assistance to individual sectors. They are too numerous and disparate to be detailed here. Once joint ventures and FDI will start flowing into the PETs, presumably this aspect of east-west assistance will be increasingly managed through regular channels of technology transfer in its widest sense.

Governments of MEs can in principle do very little to enhance the flow of FDI, including in the form of joint ventures, into the PETs. But they can set important markers that may indirectly foster such capital flows. Thus investment protection agreements and the PET joining pertinent multilateral programs, such as the Multilateral Investment Guarantee Agency (MIGA) under the World Bank's auspices, can strengthen the climate for the foreign investor. Also, various government investment guarantee schemes extended to the PETs may be important in swaying FDI flowing into, say, the PET rather than elsewhere. Similarly, export credit guarantees for goods destined for joint ventures may be a highly important ingredient in steering FDI flows. There are also special funds to assist small business undertakings by and for the PETs.

One important component of industrial cooperation in the broad sense is environmental protection. Eastern Europe has been heavily polluted as a result of the burnt-earth type of industrialization pursued under central planning. Coming to grips with the multiple problems at stake with western assistance is not only in the interest of the PETs but also Western Europe's.

4. Emergency assistance

Especially in the cases of Poland as the most indebted economy and Rumania as the sole country where blood had to be shed in late 1989, the west has assisted with emergency aid. In the case of Poland, this has taken overwhelmingly the form of foodstuffs from surplus stocks in the EC and the United States. Given the bloody nature of the Rumanian revolution, however, assistance has been more varied and initially focused on medicine and related emergency healthcare items, in addition to foodstuffs. Whereas emergency aid can still be provided, it will essentially play a marginal role in the overall effort in the next few years.

5. OTHER TYPES OF ASSISTANCE

One of the commodities in shortest supply in the PETs is expertise in the nuts and bolts of an ME. By that I mean essentially the financial, institutional, and legal infrastructure, in its widest meaning, upon which an orderly coordination of microeconomic decisions motivated by private market considerations is predicated. Some aspects of this technical assistance have been addressed by the Group of Twenty-Four undertaking, but more could be done as regards the "institution building" that is so necessary for the smooth functioning of markets. One can think here of the problems of regulation, the need for an organic evolution in the financial infrastructure, the role of pension funds and insurance companies in buttressing market behavior, the legal framework that guarantees property and ensure a stable framework within which commercial undertakings can be built up, the complexity of fiscal structures and the desirable combination of direct and indirect tax structures and how they can best be enforced, and many other aspects of what appears to be required to function properly in a market environment. These elements are examined in detail in the next three chapters.

a. Management and financial training. The EC has set up a special training center for young professionals from PETs. Recognizing the importance of having a financial infrastructure for the smooth operation of market relations, such assistance is being given especially by France. But other are also involved in advising on operations of commercial, merchant, investment, and central banks; insurance companies and pension funds; and bond and stock markets.

b. Other forms of technical training. These include assistance with converting CMEA norms to western standards, bringing statistical practices in conformity with international conventions and usances, combating pollution, rectifying potential hazards in nuclear reactors, and coming to grips with many other inconveniences of modern life. There is also a considerable component of straightforward education and research that is currently being implemented.

4. On associating PETs with integration schemes

The decision of 1985 finally to move resolutely toward the creation of the Single Market in the EC, largely for its own prestige and competitive reasons (Pinder 1989), in itself elicited great interest on the part of CMEA countries well before the recent political events there. The economic incentives of seeking association are enormous in view of EC's size, level of economic development and wealth, economies of scale, the proliferation of regional preference schemes, and perhaps confidence that regional transfers would in the end work in favor of Eastern Europe. The prospect of the creation of a unified "European economic space," namely the more complete fusion of the EFTA and EC members, has only further heightened the attraction of being part of it all. Of course, the association with EC or EFTA, or both, should be seen together with the current assistance efforts of the Group of Twenty-Four. But it also raises issues that transcend these efforts, inasmuch as the very character of regional integration schemes in Europe is concerned.

For all practical purposes, interest in seeking some relationship with EFTA did not really crystallize until the first eastern feelers toward a special EC status were extended in earnest, and quickly rejected by key EC members, and indeed the Commission for reasons to be clarified below. Such accommodation was then explored as perhaps the vestibule of eventually finding a proper place into the EC's palace. However, any type of association of the PETs with the EFTA has been rejected by the latter, at least for now, owing to the fact that the CMEA countries are not really MEs and will not soon be able to gain that status; they are therefore not in any position to grant operative tariff preferences, which form the backbone of EFTA's activities and *raison d'être*. But in July 1990, agreement was reached between Czechoslovakia, Hungary, and Poland on the one hand and the EFTA on the other to start negotiating free trade agreements. This and more formal arrangements may come about once the EC and EFTA reach their own accommodation for the European economic space.

As far as the EC is concerned, there have been several overtures whose outcome is only now materializing. A special case is being made for the GDR, which in any case has been the unofficial (n+1)th, if incomplete, member of the EC. German economic and monetary unity will mean full participation in the EC. This entitles the former GDR to obtain access to various regional funds, including the social fund, the EIB, the regional development fund, the structural fund, and perhaps something akin to the integrated mediterranean programs designed specifically for Eastern Europe (Pinder 1989, pp. 318-9). For the other CMEA members, however, they can at best hope to force through their core interests in the context of the special association status, presently being offered to the five Eastern European countries, in the first place the "suitable" PETs, of course, and also Yugoslavia, though the latter's problems fall outside the compass of this study; the offer to Rumania is presently in limbo on account of the convoluted politics of the post-Ceauşescu regime.

In the session of the Foreign Ministers in Brussels of 5 February 1990, the proposal of the Commission of the EC to formulate fairly far-reaching association agreements with selected CMEA members was endorsed; reservations were then still made for the GDR. Also the case of the Soviet Union is being dealt with separately, owing to the size and political significance of that country. Such agreements would be formulated under the legal provisions of article 238 of the Rome Treaty (*Neue Zürcher Zeitung*, 5 February 1990, p. 35). Interestingly enough, however, it has been made crystal clear that such an association agreement cannot be taken to mean that these countries will have a "higher" claim on future membership (Ehlermann 1989, Giscard d'Etaing 1989, Krenzler 1990).

Such an association agreement would encompass a number of provisions regarding the degree of economic interdependence in the east-west context that can realistically be envisioned. However, these possible benefits of gaining association status will accrue only if several prior conditions are met. These will reportedly include respect for the rule of civil, commercial, criminal, and constitutional laws; commitment to upholding basic human rights; the creation of a multiparty political system and the holding of democratic elections at the earliest possible moment; and decisive progress with market-orientation in macroeconomic policy, economic institutions, and policy instruments.

The features of the association agreements are many. They can usefully be discussed under the heading of the six core items of trade, economic cooperation, technical and financial assistance, common projects, political dialogue, and cultural collaboration. The basic provision aims at the gradual introduction of a free trade agreement, much similar to the EC's agreement in place with EFTA. That one, at least for the time being, concerns only trade in manufactured goods but notably not agriculture and fishery (although individual EFTA members, such as Iceland, have in addition concluded their own free trade agreement, including on major fishery aspects); and it does not deal with the other three freedoms on labor mobility, capital mobility, and services. The discussions around the Europe of the Eighteen envisage, however, the widening of the association agreements in many respects, short of cutting into the many complicated issues of fiscal, monetary, and political sovereignty. The association between the EC and EFTA may in due course extend fully to the core of the four freedoms within the context of the European economic space. Presumably, these items too would be considered in the promised association agreements for the PETs. The institutionalization of free trade over time would necessarily call for the abolition of the MFT in the PETs, at least in the sense of separating domestic from foreign economic activities through centralized institutions and administrative procedures as examined in Chapter 3, and otherwise the very far-reaching liberalization of their successor trade regimes. Note that it would be difficult to envisage a very liberal association regime for labor mobility as that could exacerbate the kind of problem that German economic and monetary union was originally designed to rectify.

Second, in the area of more general cooperation the association agreements would comprise what is already in place in the bilateral trade and cooperation agreements and scaling up the "lower" agreements with Czechoslovakia, Hungary, Poland, and the Soviet Union to those negotiated more recently (including Bulgaria, the GDR, and Rumania). They would, however, expand thereupon in light of the agreements in place for other areas, notably EFTA, Turkey, and Yugoslavia. In addition, the association agreements would seek to create new instruments for steadily enhancing these forms of interregional cooperation.

Third, a new element is financial cooperation tailored to economic realities, especially the absorptive capacity of each country. This will take several forms, including infrastructural loans but also transfers from the EC budget perhaps in support of export credit and investment promotion. There are naturally budgetary implications of such an association agreement. The Commission of the EC has therefore been soliciting greater flexibility in its own budget by persuading EC members to contribute generously toward the multi-year financial support of the PETs. The association agreement would also facilitate loans from the EIB and the ECCS. Not yet mentioned in the suggested draft terms of reference, but something that cannot possibly be overlooked, is the promotion of loans from the newly founded EBRD.

Fourth, a considerable variety of technical assistance programs ranging from simple statistics to all forms of training should be included in the project. Many of the items listed in Section 3 under "other types of assistance" could presumably be included here and more concretely spelled out.

Fifth, an unspecified political dialogue (perhaps in the context of the Council of Europe and later possibly the European Parliament) is held out as a feature of the association agreement. This would presumably ensure that Eastern Europe will eventually fall into the mainstream of political organization and behavior in Western Europe and in some cases even join. This holds especially for the Central European countries.

Finally, the association agreement would endeavor to facilitate the "Europeanization" of the PETs. A good dose of (western) Eurocentrism would certainly be foiled upon recipient countries.

Together these core items of the association agreements could have considerable ramifications for the political stability in PETs as well as luring foreign investors and traders into these countries. The association agreements are, however, to be negotiated with each country separately, which should embody sufficient flexibility to enable the negotiators to fine tune the agreement according to the needs and potentials of each country.

5. On providing foreign assistance to PETs

It is true that there are few guidelines available that together add up to a custom-made model of how to transform planned economies into PETs and subsequently into RPEs. Nonetheless, there should be little doubt about what precisely it is that, from a purely technical point of view, needs to be done once a consensus exists on what it is that the reforming economy hopes to accomplish. There may be disagreement about the precise sequencing and the speed at which changes are introduced. But certainly a desirable sequencing and pace of introduction can be arrived at, and modified if need be, through some societal consensus. Alternative options with their possible consequences should be submitted to the political leaderships, which must subsequently accommodate their choice with specific popular or social mandates as to what is tolerable and feasible.

The first consideration in mooting the subject is to ascertain what precisely it is that the country purportedly in need of assistance is hoping to accomplish singly and perhaps in its regional context. If by consensus the country does not wish to evolve into a full-fledged ME, it would be foolhardy to make assistance contingent on recipients reaching a status it does not even covet. Once the objectives are ascertained, potential donors should decide for themselves whether or not it is in their political, ideological, humanitarian, or ideological interest to support that effort. Of course, potential donors may wish to influence the decision-making process and indeed the reform intentions of recipients. Assistance may be made conditional on these ideological or other foreign policy precepts. But that is a subject for foreign policy rather than technical economics. This is not to endorse the case for providing unconditional assistance. On the contrary: Donor countries should aim, at least in part, at strengthening the process of reform as formulated through a consensus-building process that they can support after it has been made clear what the purpose of the assistance should be.

The second phase revolves around technical advice. Under no circumstance can foreign assistance be considered a substitute for sound macroeconomic management through appropriate institutions and policy instruments, given the set of policy objectives embraced. One can see this when placed in the threefold interrelated structures of an economy popularized by Robert W. Campbell (1966). Aside from production possibilities and the normative elements embedded in the objective function of the economy as a whole, there are administrative structures. These can be either hierarchical, as in the CPE or MPE, or organized largely through markets and the price system. The essence is that some administrative structures are required to ensure that economic agents act in harmony with society's objective function, however derived.

The third phase of an assistance program, in my view, involves determination of the amount of the assistance donor countries are willing to muster for the PETs and in which forms they are disposed to transfer it. A substantial amount of the assistance currently envisaged is not unconditional. The reasoning is that in such a way donors can target the groups most in need of help. Also, this procedure allows donors to transfer surplus goods (such as foodstuff stocks held through massive state subsidies) at a relatively small incremental cost. However useful such targeting may be, both to reach the envisaged recipient quickly and to make the commitment politically, fiscally, and psychologically acceptable at home, this mode should primarily be limited to emergencies for which customary economic accounting and efficiency criteria do not apply.

Finally, there is the problem of how best to arrange for the efficient transfer of resources and to ensure that the recipient utilizes the transferred assistance with maximum result. For that, a coherent approach to delivery of assistance under at least some coordinating and supervisory agency would seem useful.

Inasmuch as most forms of assistance are "targeted" rather than transferred in lump sum, inevitable distortions in pricing mechanisms and incentives are introduced, perhaps unwittingly. For example, food aid given free of charge will discourage domestic producers and may encourage shifts in consumption and work patterns that, from a longer-term view, may be quite dysfunctional. All efforts should be made to improve domestic resource mobilization and, thus, to conceive of foreign assistance as offering planks directly in support of local efforts rather than substituting for them.

Even when a foreign assistance package is conceived in this manner, domestic administrative structures and institutions in place in the recipient country may be highly deficient and thus inhibit the envisaged reform course. Likewise, it may take some time before the benefits of the adopted reform course can be reaped. Without stabilization, the reforming country may find itself in chaos, which itself destroys the reform efforts. It is in these two areas that foreign assistance can provide a catalytic role in fostering the reform process by supporting the stabilization of fragile institutions, human resource development, and the implementation and sustainability of policy reforms. First and foremost in coming up with such a technical proposal is, of course, the requisite knowledge of the recipient countries as well as a broad understanding of the problems of transition. The CPEs or MPEs are not the only economies that have introduced major changes in recent years. True enough, many of the unprecedented changes in economic systems and policies sought over the past two decades or so in MEs have been qualitative rather than quantitative. In some DEs, however, institutional and policy changes have been very substantial, in some cases even quite dramatic. Likewise, the aftermath of World War II made room for a wide range of experiences with how to switch from a war to a civilian economy. I suggest that these experiences, while all perhaps *sui generis* in their final application and outcome, can nonetheless help to bridge the gaps in knowledge that should currently be critically felt by those interested in lending unprejudiced assistance to the PETs.

* * *

Over the past two years or so, many commentators from east and west alike have argued for the re-creation of the Marshall Plan, this time for Eastern Europe, as the organizing forum for placing western assistance within a coherent framework. The Marshall Plan threatens to become a hackneyed code, a euphemism for appropriating large sums of money for large economic, social, and political problems, however well-intended they may be (Cerami 1989). In that sense, it loses much of its original connotation and hence historical reference. But it bears to underline too that not everyone has been in favor of dispensing massive foreign aid to Eastern Europe. The pro-assistance advocates have been countered by both those who criticize development assistance as well as revisionist readers of the Marshall Plan. In my view, the advocates as well as the detractors of the proposition are tackling the wrong issue.

The core task of whether or not to grant assistance - and if so, how much, in what forms, and how quickly - is not the emulation of the Marshall Plan for Eastern Europe, perhaps on the dubious grounds that the ERP was successful and that Stalin forcibly denied Eastern Europe the benefits of that effort. Rather, the core question should be whether the Marshall Plan launched in 1947 addressed issues that are relevant to the situation of Eastern Europe today and whether it discharged the assigned tasks expeditiously and effectively. On both counts, I believe there are major differences between the Marshall Plan in 1947 for Western Europe and what is required at this stage of Eastern Europe to be taken into account, as examined in Chapter 6.

6

The Marshall Plan and Eastern Europe

The Marshall Plan occupies a singularly exalted position in postwar international relations (Wood 1986). Traditionally, the program has been hailed as an imaginative act of far-sighted statesmanship. Its contribution to European economic recovery and its internal consistency to tackle the problems initially assigned to it have recently been questioned in a politically more dispassionate, if not always diplomatic, frame of reference than what was typical during the immediate postwar decades. These analyses have been arguing for more realistic appraisals of the achievements of the Marshall Plan and the multiple, often conflicting, diplomatic, economic, humanitarian, political, and strategic motivations that may have been prevalent at the program's inception. Whether the Marshall Plan was instrumental in bringing about the Western European economic recovery that lasted into the 1970s is a matter for the economic historian. Whatever the nature of the chafing at the unique mythology of the Marshall Plan, virtually all observers agree that the assistance program launched by the United States in the aftermath of World War II was well-intended and directed at rectifying the perceived economic stagnation or slow pace of postwar recovery, among a host of mostly foreign policy and security considerations.

The point here is that Marshall Plan assistance has recently been invoked as an example of how the west's response to the needs of Eastern Europe (for example, Roth 1989, Winiecki 1989, Würzen 1989) at this juncture could usefully be organized. I disagree with this proposition. To illustrate the reasons why I feel the Marshall Plan is not a very good example for Eastern Europe, I examine in Section 1 the circumstances under which it was formulated and its principal effects. The next section summarizes the basic facts about this ambitious assistance effort. The critical components of the ERP are recounted in Section 3. Next, I inquire into the achievements of the Marshall Plan. The chapter concludes with an evaluation of whether the experience of Western Europe could be indicative of what a Marshall Plan could do for Eastern Europe. Inasmuch as my answer is rather negative, I examine in Section 6 the basic differences between Eastern Europe now and Western Europe then.

1. The overall environment of the Marshall Plan

Most of Europe in the second half of the 1940s featured a highly unbalanced supply of primary production factors. The prewar capital stock had been severely eroded because of war destruction. Although also the labor force had suffered from the protracted military conflict, by and large the levels of skilled and unskilled labor at war's end in most countries were disproportional to the productive capital stock. This should have made private fixed capital investment highly profitable. Inasmuch as capital was more abundant in third countries, primarily the United States, Western Europe should have become a magnet in the international capital market. The promise of a solid profit margin should also have encouraged private savings in Europe itself.

Yet, private capital formation did not grow as rapidly as anticipated in part because of domestic economic policies in Western Europe. These rested on four pillars. The first envisaged only a very gradual loosening of wartime controls, some of which had already been imposed in the 1930s as a consequence of the beggar-thy-neighbor policies pursued in an effort to counter the worst impacts of the Great Depression. As a result, these controls over wide segments of production and prices of major goods were continued in many countries; major exceptions were Belgium and Italy. Second, many of the Western European countries had suffered heavy human and capital damage during the war. To counter this, policy makers accorded paramount importance to investment in support of reconstruction and redistributive policies. This in itself became a motivation for the continuation - in fact, the sharp expansion - of the role of government in economic policy. That was then understood to comprise far more than simply setting up the macroeconomic framework and tinkering with its policies and institutions as warranted by circumstances. Third, in efforts to bolster demand and avoid the negative effects on employment of changing economic structures swiftly to a civilian environment, many countries pursued a relatively easy monetary policies, and thus resorted to money creation. This built-in inflationary bias was not very conducive to saving and encouraging investment. Finally, most countries sought to maintain a fixed exchange rate regime. This entailed exchange rate targeting, usually at an overvalued level *vis-à-vis* the U.S. dollar. This bias was compounded by these countries having embraced a foreign exchange management regime that forced them to maintain currency inconvertibility and foreign exchange controls through export licensing for much longer than required (Kostrzewa, Nunnenkamp, and Schmieding 1990).

The consequences of such a policy mix were a very inefficient allocation of resources within the countries, an inherent bias against reshaping the division of labor amongst them, and failure to attract private resources for reconstruction and growth from outside. Not only that, because of currency overvaluation there was an inherent bias in demand in favor of importing "essential" capital goods and foodstuffs, whose domestic prices were held artificially low.

Because of the policy commitment to adhere to fixed parities, which was reinforced through the Bretton Woods agreements, and ill-advised precepts to return to prewar parities, the inevitable differential inflation in the postwar period made for eventual inconsistency in fixed exchange rates. This led to an artificial "dollar shortage." It also made traders prefer exporting only for dollars, and hence the perceived need to embrace barter arrangements with other countries to permit trade at all. All this and other ill-advised policy measures culminated in 1947 in a severe current account crunch.

The ostensible purpose of Secretary of State George C. Marshall's proposal of ample American assistance to Europe was to break the vicious circle wherein vital long-run structural adjustments were being frustrated by intractable short-run problems. Marshall emphasized that U.S. assistance was meant to provide a cure, not a palliative for this built-in dilemma. At a broader level, the Marshall Plan was a belated recognition that policy makers had been far too optimistic about the time required for the world trade and payments system to return to "normality," however this was to be understood in the constellation of forces at the time. At the very least, countries were expected to return quickly to a system of multilateral settlement and free trade, as incorporated in the postwar IEOs. The initial postwar optimism to the effect that this new structure could be rapidly put into place evaporated as a result of a series of dollar crises in Europe and by the premature, abortive adoption of sterling convertibility in 1947.[1]

The Marshall Plan recast the postwar adjustment process into a more realistic timeframe: It set 1952, some six years after the end of the World War II, as the date by which internal and external balances would be reestablished. Aid recipients were expected to take special measures to boost their reciprocal trade as a step toward restoring a "working" world economy based on multilateralism and a liberal international trading system. During the transition period the United States effectively allowed the Western European countries to discriminate against U.S. imports to conserve their dollar balances. The program also emphasized the need to boost output and productivity growth, and to develop economic cooperation and integration within Western Europe.

Most of these features of Western Europe in the second half of the 1940s look very much like those that the Eastern European economies have been suffering from in recent years; the problems stem also from the foreign exchange regime and the substantial disjunction between domestic producers and trading markets typical of CPEs and MPEs. Just like most of Western Europe after World II, Eastern Europe finds itself in a double bind. One is chronic structural imbalances. These can be corrected only through fundamental changes in the makeup of these economies and in the behavioral characteristics of their economic agents (households, firms, as well as various levels of government). This usually requires a protracted period of positive structural adjustment policies, some of which can be introduced only in conjunction with important changes in the political landscape to make the painful process socially acceptable and to distribute its burden equitably. Earlier efforts to come to grips with these issues failed essentially because of the inability of the planning process to react effectively and in a timely fashion to important changes in the economy, including modifications in the primary input supply, shifts in terms of trade and in foreign trade opportunities, and the almost complete lack of success with SEI. The other set of issues can be summarized under the label of

[1] A condition of the 1945 loan from the United States to Britain was that the latter would, immediately and unilaterally, implement the various clauses of the proposed IMF. Implementation was, in fact delayed for one year, following Congressional ratification of the IMF legislation in June 1946. Under U.S. pressure, currency convertibility at an overvalued exchange rate was promulgated. In 35 days (from 15 July until 20 August 1947, when sterling convertibility was once again suspended) the U.K. treasury lost half of its foreign exchange reserves in a vain effort to prop up sterling.

short-run stabilization problems. This involves essentially efforts to bring domestic absorption in line with resource availability, that is equating *ex ante* aggregate demand with aggregate supply. These measures can be enacted without them being tied in with the conscious process of structural change and supply-side reforms.

The distinction, at least conceptually, between short-term stabilization and long-term structural adjustment problems is important in devising the kinds of assistance that the international community may wish to render to the PETs. The purpose would be to support the unprecedented sociopolitical changes in these countries and to help in determining how quickly and at what socioeconomic costs these reforms should be implemented. I mention the need for conceptual clarity. This is not to deny that failure to deal with short-run imbalances promptly and effectively is apt to exacerbate structural problems.

It would be desirable to avoid inflation, economic stagnation, and a progressive decline in levels of economic development. Precisely because a growing number of commentators, statesmen, and IEOs in east and west alike have been publicly airing their concerns about these topics, there might be some room for creating a Marshall Plan for Eastern Europe. This terminology is, unfortunately, used loosely all too often. In view of the considerable similarity between the current economic environment of Eastern Europe and the experiences of Western Europe in the 1940s, a repetition of the Marshall Plan, this time organized mainly by Western Europe for Eastern Europe, has been proposed. To evaluate its underlying merits, it is of more than passing interest to reevaluate what was done in Western Europe in terms of the objectives set and to assess how relevant this experience might be to assisting PETs. Such an inquiry would appear warranted also because there is a substantial difference between easing constraints on a growing and dynamic economy and restoring a broken-down and nonfunctioning system to working order.

There were basically three kinds of economic problems in Western Europe after World War II: conversion, changing supply, and avoiding inflation. First and foremost was the question of conversion, that is, of reprofiling the production structure so that it could increasingly meet civilian demand at a time of rapidly receding military needs. Although the physical destruction of plant and equipment had been much less than originally feared, productive infrastructure was in poor shape. This was not only because maintenance and repair during the war years had been neglected. Also, the capital stock was run down, old, and ill-adapted to the newly emerging structures of domestic and foreign demand. Furthermore, transportation and communication infrastructures were either destroyed or in poor shape for want of investment and inadequate repair and maintenance. Similarly for the housing stock, a large portion of which had been destroyed during the war and its aftermath. Finally, supplies of foodstuffs, energy, and manufactured consumer goods had been sharply curtailed in favor of catering to military needs during the war. Although a return to heeding civilian supply was programmed, it took several years of physical controls before the market could take care of its own required adjustments.

Second, in addition to these supply-side problems, the western countries had to come to grips with other constraints on the long-term adjustment process, including the dollar shortage on account of a chronic and large structural deficit in their current accounts. Also, the external debt contracted during the war to finance needed imports weighed upon postwar economic policies. Because of constraints on their trade, stemming from trade controls and inconvertible currencies faced abroad, these countries sought to maintain their own trade controls and in fact felt a need to reinforce bilateral balancing.

Third, during the war money had been put in circulation for which there was an insufficient counterpart in goods and services, hence excess savings. This monetary overhang, upon war's end, threatened to fuel demand well beyond levels that supply adjustments could support for some time to come. There was therefore a threat of serious inflation spilling over into social unrest and political instability as controls were removed. The solution adopted in several countries was to continue the system of direct physical controls through rationing whose extent was to be relaxed only gradually.

2. Basic facts about the Marshall Plan

Given the state of the Western economies in the second half of the 1940s, the much slower economic recovery than had been anticipated, and the perceived threat of economic instability making communism attractive to Western Europe, France and Italy in the first instance, U.S. policy makers felt it desirable to funnel substantial foreign aid into Western Europe. This U.S. commitment to vigorous promotion of regional political and economic cooperation within Western Europe was made clear by then Secretary of State George C. Marshall on 5 June 1947 in his famous Harvard University speech. It was soon thereafter translated into the ERP to be supervised by the Organisation for European Economic Co-operation (OEEC) set up in April 1948 in Paris (Gordon 1988) and a number of counterpart national institutions in the United States and Western Europe.

The Marshall Plan officially ran for just under four years, from April 1948 until the end of 1951, after which the program merged into the defense-related assistance provided under the Mutual Security Act (MSA). This scheme had been formally established on 30 December 1951, in the wake of the complications caused by the Korean War and the escalation of the Cold War, although actual assistance flows under this program commenced only in mid-1952. It was around that time that final disbursements under the Marshall Plan commitments were running out for most participants. Marshall Plan financial transfers, which started in April 1948 reached a peak in the second half of 1948 and the first half of 1949.

Marshall Plan allotted aid of $12.4 billion (current values) over that four-year period (Wexler 1983, p. 249) to the sixteen Western European member countries of OEEC. Most of it, about ninety percent, was in the form of grants. There was also a large grant-element in the loans, which were usually for 35 years at 2.5 per cent interest with repayments starting in 1952. Marshall Aid was also used to finance the two intra-European Payments Agreements of 1948-1949 and 1949-1950, and the European Payments Union (EPU) which ran from late-1950 to the end of 1959.

These magnitudes should be kept in their proper perspective, both when evaluating the original Marshall Plan and what would be involved in emulating this assistance to the benefit of Eastern Europe. As a proportion of the aggregate output of the United States, Marshall Aid averaged just over 1 percent of GNP for the four-year period, although it was as high as 2.4 percent in 1949. For the recipient countries, ERP aid averaged just over 2 percent of GNP, but with considerable variation among countries and from year to year. In the first year of the program, this aid was an important addition to national resources in all the recipient countries, except Belgium and Sweden. As a proportion of national income, the assistance ranged from 2.4 percent in the United Kingdom to 14 percent in Austria (Milward 1987, p. 96). The largest shares of total aid were received by Britain and France (23 and 21 percent, respectively), a reflection of the fact that the principal criterion for distribution was the size of the recipient's dollar deficit: The larger the deficit, the larger the country's share of total aid. The FRG's share of Marshall Aid was relatively small (about 10 percent), but it received considerable sums under a special aid-in-occupation program. This was the so-called GARIOA, or "Government Aid and Relief in Occupied Areas," program. Between July 1946 and March 1950 the value of goods financed under this program was $1.62 billion, slightly more than the $1.6 billion that the FRG received in Marshall assistance (*Dokumentation zur Aussenwirtschaft*, 7 March 1990, pp. 2-4).

Estimates can be prepared of the amount of aid that would be required at this stage to equal the total commitments disbursed by the United States in 1948-1952. Taking the change in the U.S. GNP deflator between 1948-1951 and 1989, the total aid of $12.4 billion would be equivalent to $65.4 billion or $16.4 billion a year expressed in 1989 prices (UNECE 1990, p. 13). In terms of aid per head of the recipient population, the 1989 equivalent of what was originally transferred to Western Europe would be about $57 a head giving a total of some $22.25 billion a year at the present population. If the present western aid program for Eastern Europe were based on this figure of $57 per head, total aid would be around $6.5 billion a year; inclusive of the Soviet Union, the total would rise to nearly $23 billion a year. This figure, based on the transfers under the original Marshall Plan but adjusted for price and population changes, provides one hypothetical magnitude for which precedents could be invoked.

Recently the President of the Commission of the EC provided some idea of the scale of aid that the EC might provide to Eastern Europe.[2] He suggested that if Eastern Europe were given the same support as provided by the EC to its own depressed regions, the EC's budget would require an additional ECU 14 billion a year for the next 5 to 10 years, depending on the pace of transformation in the eastern countries. In addition, a further ECU 5 billion a year in resources would be required for the EIB. Such a level of assistance would amount to roughly $23 billion a year, which is 3.5 times larger than the Marshall Plan equivalent for the six countries quoted above. In fact, the data being mooted in this EC proposal are more or less the same as the Marshall Plan

[2] Press release of the address by Mr. Jacques Delors to the European Parliament, presenting the Commission's Program for 1990, Strasbourg, 17 January 1990.

equivalent for the group inclusive of the Soviet Union. Since the program suggested by the EC President could run for 5 to 10 years, his proposal, still for Eastern Europe itself, would require financing on a scale some 4.5 to nearly 9 times that of the Marshall Plan adjusted for price and population differences.

In terms of western GDP/GNP these are not very large numbers: The value of the Marshall Plan at U.S. prices and recipient population of 1989 ($22.3 billion) is a little more than 0.4 percent of the GNP of both the United States and the EC; if Japan is added to the potential donors, the magnitude would be less than 0.2 percent of GDP. Mr. Jacques Delors's proposal of $22.8 billion is very similar, at 0.45 percent of the Community's GDP in 1989. These numbers suggest that, with some good will, there is not much of an obstacle in financing such a large-scale program. Whether the PETs will be able to absorb such a volume of resources in the short run is a different matter, however (see Section 5). This hypothetical amount can usefully be contrasted with the requirements for external financing and the absorptive ability of the PETs.

3. Critical components of the program

The ERP's key feature was that each recipient had to draw up a four-year plan for economic recovery. Each plan had to include estimates of output, import requirements, and anticipated exports, and it had to demonstrate how the recipient country expected to achieve adjustment and economic balance by the end of the four-year period. To coordinate these plans and the allocation of aid, the aid recipient countries established a Committee for European Economic Co-operation (CEEC), which was quickly converted into the more permanent OEEC in April 1948. This framework reflected Marshall's insistence that the European countries themselves should assess their requirements for aid and take the initiative in making action-oriented proposals, and that there should be a degree of united and cooperative effort among the Western Europeans themselves.[3]

As part of its objective to raise output and productivity levels in Europe, the ERP included a technical assistance program whose purpose was to demonstrate to Europeans various aspects of the U.S. production structures that could be emulated with a view to raising productivity levels in Europe (Hogan 1987, pp. 19ff.). These included production techniques and management-labor relations. Efforts were also made to persuade participating countries to set up national units to foster factor productivity - the so-called productivity centers (Diebold 1988). The most prominent element of this program was the sending of teams of personnel from European industry to visit their counterparts in the United States, the idea being that direct experience was an effective way of gaining

[3] In the United States, the ERP was established by the Economic Cooperation Act of 1948, which entered into force on 3 April 1948, and was administered by the Economic Cooperation Administration (ECA). In October 1951 the ECA Act was superseded by the MSA and the ECA was replaced by the Mutual Security Agency. In practice officials of the ECA played an influential role in the preparation of the European proposals and in advising on what would be acceptable to the U.S. Administration and the Congress.

insight into the methods that afforded the United States higher levels of productivity. European managers and technical personnel were also sent to the United States for special training and U.S. experts were posted to Europe. However, the technical assistance element of the Marshall Plan actually remained quite small and was little more than a "fairly modest informational program" (Wexler 1983, pp. 92-93). Nevertheless, this part of the ERP in particular is the one that should not be ignored when the Marshall Plan's relevance to current problems of Eastern Europe is being assessed.

Another feature of the ERP worth noting is the use of counterpart funds. The mechanism embraced was that the domestic currency value of imports financed through Marshall Plan dollars was deposited in special accounts placed at the disposal of national governments who, with U.S. "assistance," could utilize them to bankroll specific investment projects on concessional terms. Marshall Plan aid, thus, in principle had a dual character. It provided additional capital investments. It also made it easier for the Governments in most recipient countries to direct resources into desired sectors and projects, which helped to strengthen state control over economic affairs.

Utilization of these national currency equivalents of Marshall Plan grants was subject to approval by the ECA. The ECA tried to use them to influence the composition of fixed investments, but its success appears to have been limited. For one thing, not all European Governments used the fund for fixed investment (Norway and the United Kingdom used them entirely for debt retirement), and in those that did they played "a useful but by no means indispensable role" (Milward 1987, p. 111). The use of counterpart funds tends to be a two-edged sword from the point of view of recipients: On certain occasions they can strengthen the government's hand in overcoming domestic opposition to certain projects considered worthwhile or essential; but in others the authorities may be weakened by the charge of permitting too much external interference in domestic affairs. There is also the risk that counterpart funds may distort indicators of relative scarcities.

It is important to stress that the basis for the allocation of Marshall Plan funds was essentially a country's balance of payments situation with respect to the dollar area, not an evaluation of the overall investment requirements or the desirable allocation of resources. As a result, the bulk of the assistance went to the two countries - France and the United Kingdom (Gordon 1988) - that encountered recurrent external payments crises in the early 1950s, almost regardless of whether these deficits were incurred largely on account of capital goods' imports. The effectiveness, then, of the Marshall Plan depended to a considerable extent on the determinants of the current account deficits.

4. Paramount achievements of ERP

In trying to assess the relevance of the Marshall Plan experience to current problems, it is useful to have some idea of what it achieved, especially relative to its objectives. But this is easier said than done as the whole question is now a matter of considerable controversy among economic and diplomatic historians. For many years the standard account was that Marshall aid succeeded in lifting Europe out of its postwar morass, as intended, or at least that by 1952 it had created the conditions for sustained growth in Europe by recreating viable markets and stable democratic institutions. The extent to which this interpretation should be revised is the subject of the controversy mentioned earlier. One view is that, while accepting that the Marshall Plan cannot be given all the credit for the postwar recovery and reconstruction of Europe, it provided "the 'crucial margin' that made European self-help possible. It facilitated essential imports, eased production bottlenecks, encouraged higher rates of capital formation, and helped to suppress inflation all of which led to gains in productivity, to improvements in trade, and to an era of social peace and prosperity" (Hogan 1987, p. 432).

Whether the Marshall Plan contributed critically to economic recovery and the rapid rebuilding of Europe's economic strength and political stability - constants of the postwar Atlantic credo - has recently been contested. Revisionist historians argue that Europe was already well onto the path of economic recovery before the infusion of Marshall Plan aid. The pace of growth had gained strength in 1946-1947, partly under impetus of domestic private investment, although the foreign trade regime and the overvalued exchange rates inhibited even stronger growth. Even so, these observers contend that the impetus to sustained growth in the early 1950s came essentially from the all-around devaluations, in terms of the U.S. dollar, of most European currencies in 1949 in conjunction with the reemergence of the later FRG as the major European trading partner. Both bolstered the arena for intra-European trade and thus reduced the need for U.S. imports.

One major piece of evidence in this contention has been that the FRG, which obtained relatively little Marshall Plan assistance, resumed rapid domestic and trade growth after the monetary reform of June 1948. By contrast, the two countries that obtained most Marshall Plan aid - France and the United Kingdom - struggled continuously with external payments constraints and their growth remained rather sluggish. The explanation has been that by allowing recipients to run imbalanced policies, the Marshall Plan in fact encouraged the continuation of domestic policies of state regulation, demand expansion, income redistribution unrelated to performance, and the maintenance of currency inconvertibility and bilateralism for far longer than would otherwise have been enforced upon them. In the short run, however, domestic absorption exceeded domestic output capacity, but this may in the medium run have had deleterious effects on efficiency because of the structural aberrations tolerated in the process.

A different interpretation accepts that Marshall Plan assistance enabled Western Europe simply to finance its dollar deficit, but argues that the deficit was due to the strength of the recovery in European output and that the boom would have continued even if U.S. aid had not been forthcoming (Milward 1987, pp. 465ff.). Without going into the details of this argument, whether or not a strong recovery was already under way in Western Europe in 1947-1948 impinges upon the decision of what might be expected from similar large-scale programs of aid to the PETs. This derives importantly from the big difference between easing constraints on a growing and dynamic economy and restoring a broken down and nonfunctioning system to working order. The evidence

(UNECE 1990, p. 12) suggests that postwar Western Europe fell into the first category rather than the second and that fairly rapid progress was made as a result of domestic initiatives in solving many of the problems described earlier.

The setbacks of early 1947 proved to be temporary. By the time Marshall delivered his speech at Harvard, rapid recovery in Europe was being resumed in part because the damage to industrial assets sustained during the war was much less than thought at the end of hostilities. In fact, Europe's industrial capacity in 1945 was greater than before the war. Especially the increased size of its engineering industries was well placed to meet postwar needs. In addition, the need for replacement investment and the profitable opportunities presented by postwar shortages led to a rapid recovery of fixed investment to prewar levels and as a share of aggregate output, excepting the United Kingdom (UNECE 1953, chapter 5). This rapid recovery and strength of capital formation underlines that business expectations quickly improved (Milward 1988, p. 240), in part on the grounds that the ME structures were still essentially intact despite their suspension or dilution during the war years.

On the other hand, this recovery and growth led to external deficits, chiefly with the dollar area. This was a global, structural problem that could not be solved quickly. By enabling Western Europe to maintain high rates of growth of output and capital formation without having to resort to consumption austerity, the Marshall Plan played an important role. This may well have helped to reinforce political stability in postwar Europe, although this statement can hardly be tested with any confidence.

Some (as Mee 1984, Milward 1987) argue that the chief motivation for ERP was the solidification of the U.S. political and economic presence in Europe, in other words one component of the *pax americana*. Whatever the motivation behind the Marshall Plan may have been, there is little doubt, even in the mind of revisionist historians, that U.S. aid promoted political stability in Europe, made the reintegration of the FRG acceptable to the victorious powers, and provided a nonnegligible buttress to policy experimentation. Thus, the monetary reform in the FRG in June 1948 led to a turbulent adjustment period, during which the velocity of money rose much faster than anticipated and would, without an infusion from abroad, have produced sharply larger price pressures than were in fact experienced at the time.

5. A Marshall Plan for Eastern Europe?

PETs are willing to pursue greater market orientation, including by integrating themselves much more deeply into the international division of labor. Perhaps the most critical element of reform is the need of these countries to rid themselves of interventionist, paternalistic policies set centrally on questionable economic grounds. Efforts should be made to eliminate gradually the pervasive distortions of relative prices and incentive systems that do not reflect the best technical way of catering to social preferences. Furthermore, an outward-oriented economic system, regardless of the degree of commitment to marketization, requires appropriate economic, legal, and political institutions. As argued in Chapter 4, the institutions and policy framework in place in CPEs or

MPEs leave much to be desired when contrasted with what is required to support indirect economic coordination.

The case for viewing with some confidence the future of the PETs that have embraced radical reform can be made on three grounds. First and foremost, the political leadership of the PETs, with the support of the population at large, appears to be willing - and indeed determined - to pursue far-reaching economic and political changes. There is overwhelming support for shouldering the adjustment burden in the short to medium run provided there is some hope that the future may bring positive growth. The weakening of the entrenched power structure, particularly the pressure exercised by the pernicious *nomenklatura* and Party apparatus, as in M. Olson's (1982) paradigm of the decline and rise of nations, would seem to favor drastic change, although it may have to be spread out over time. Furthermore, Eastern Europe has a very skewed factor endowment relative to its potential participation in the world economy. The capital in place is relatively obsolete, not very well maintained, and in any case not well suited to produce quality products for global markets. On the other hand, labor tends to be relatively abundant, fairly well disciplined (with some exceptions of militant pockets that have given rise to some social conflicts in recent years), and very well educated for the level of development of these countries. This relative factor endowment is comparable to Western Europe's after World War II.

As described in Chapter 4, the core of the economic reform efforts of PETs consists of a dovetailed package of actions in internal and external sectors. The domestic parts of the reform hinge on the introduction and maintenance of scarcity-related prices, the creation of genuine wholesale and retail markets, the recognition of property rights and hence the revival of the private sector which may or may not be accompanied by full-scale privatization (see Chapter 7), the creation of an effective monetary policy and its associated infrastructure, the revision of fiscal policies so as to minimize interference with price and incentive systems, and the creation of capital markets (see Chapter 8).

On the external side, reforms aim at trade liberalization, the linking of domestic with foreign prices, the establishment of a unified effective exchange rate that is flexible, the gradual abolition of trade controls by liberalizing the trade regime and reconceiving it within the market context (which requires effective customs duties), and currency convertibility by drastically revamping the orthodox foreign exchange regime. One of the more contentious issues of the reform debate has been whether such a package ought to be introduced all at once - the approach being essentially the so-called "big bang" - or whether there is a way in which genuine economic reform can be phased in over time, perhaps two to three years. The experience with reforms in Eastern Europe when the MPEs emerged has been rather discouraging in that respect: Any gradualism in reform blueprints has provided an invitation to the ruling leadership of Government, Party, and the bureaucracy to introduce fairly quickly revisions in the intended reform course at the first sign of adverse consequences.

It is probably true that the most effective way of destroying the influence of the leftover political, economic, and managerial leadership or pressure groups is through the big-bang strategy. That would disable them from seeking to reorganize themselves and provide resistance at the first sign of adversity during any stepwise reform. But this widely held position can neither be corroborated nor disproved on the strength of past experience. The reform ambitions of the PETs are held by radically renewed political structures that have to come to grips by and large with the old-style economic, managerial, and bureaucratic cadres still in place. What can be done about this?

The dilemma is clear: Dismissing everyone all at once and thus reconstituting society from the bottom up is simply impossible. Yet organizing the big bang in a situation where the economic, managerial, and bureaucratic élites remain in place offers its own dangers. By leaving it ostensibly up to the "market" to settle old scores is a display of gross naiveté in the powers of the market. Particularly in the CPE's or MPE's environment, such a big bang may lead to all kinds of nonmarket events that are as undesirable from the point of view of the orderly allocation of resources as the administrative interferences in people's lives in the *ancien régimes*.

There is simply no costless way of suppressing old structures, particularly when they are so deeply entrenched in the psyche of economic agents who are now expected to operate according to completely different rules of the game. It is precisely at this juncture that strong central leadership is required to ensure that the legacies of the old environment do not altogether derail the reform movement. This requires political renewal, perhaps in the form that has been coming to the fore since late 1989. It also requires strong action to "reform" the bureaucracy, macroeconomic leadership, and managerial decision making. It is naive to believe that rapid privatization in and of itself will elicit the changes in mentality that ensure stability in a market environment.

It would be critical to link foreign assistance directly to the core elements of the reforms as perceived by the reformers themselves. Western assistance could take on various forms. One would be to clarify for the reformers that the desired economic regime may imply distortions. Thus, the trade-off between efficiency and equity for countries that continue to place considerable ideological emphasis on egalitarianism needs to be made crystal clear.

But a more congenial attitude toward east-west assistance has to be a two-way street. Much of western advice currently being proffered to Eastern Europe is simply "a mix of irrelevance and magic," as *The Economist* (20 January 1990, p. 30) recently put it. Even the west does not have a secret formula that simply needs to be acquired and adapted. On the other hand, there is inevitably an element of mutual deafness in dialogues between seasoned western politicians or managers and Eastern European dissidents just out of jail or up from underground.

Inasmuch as the perceptions of PETs in the west may be seriously distorted, the process of reequilibrating relative factor supply through inflows of FDI or portfolio capital may be unduly delayed. Ensuring that the environment for such transfers is as competitive and market-oriented as possible constitutes an important arena for western assistance. Initially it may be preferable to emphasize somewhat more the former, if only because recent experience with unconditional bank loans, especially when promoted through government assistance, has been none too encouraging.

As noted, whatever the eventual format of the reform program, some agents will be offered opportunities and make a gain in the bargain, while others will be disadvantaged or simply not seize the opportunity. A bout of stagflation is almost certain to result unless very strong macroeconomic policies are followed. The unemployed may have to be retrained and relocated. Some will simply not be up to such changes any more, perhaps because of age or fundamental psychological inability to accept incisive changes for themselves. It is very important to have in place a system of social safeguards during the early phase of the transition. Apart from humanitarian reasons and society's obligation to mitigate adversity by common means, there are at least two unique features of the PETs that thereby need to be heeded. One is that the circumstances ahead have been unknown for over forty years. Also, for decades the leaderships of these countries inculcated in the population the belief that such types of social adversity would never again have to be imposed upon society at large. Providing a social safety net would not only avoid needless suffering on the part of vast layers of society, it would also ensure that social tensions can be held in check, thereby gaining the all-important stability during a breathing space upon which the reform program is in part conditioned. It would also provide an important psychological fillip to the population at large, hence belief in the credibility of the reform program.

Should a Marshall Plan for Eastern Europe be formulated? If for some reason it is thought to be opportune at this stage to invoke the historical association with the experiences under the Marshall Plan, so let it be called a Marshall Plan for Eastern Europe! Far more important is the latter's substance and this differs in many ways from the postwar experiences: The need to support short-term emergency measures, to aid with the retraining or schooling of bureaucratic, managerial, and economic cadres that would otherwise take too much time in the PET environment, and the emergence of the institutional framework necessary to encourage market-oriented decision making. But the accent should clearly be on the overriding *purpose* of the assistance measures: Ensuring that the reform package holds socially, politically, and economically at the smallest cost that socioeconomic techniques know how to design. If in addition donor countries wish to transmit their own values to the PETs, that is a matter of their foreign policy choice on whose intrinsic merits technical economics has little to offer by way of advice. Personally, I would like to see a platform that is as free of ideology as circumstances permit and politicians can afford. But that may be hoping for too much rational decision making invoked by an armchair economist, critical observer, and opinionated commentator, who may unwittingly posit "that politicians should behave like rational people for a change" (Hanson 1988, p. 75). This is a rather unrealistic hope. But in the case of assisting the PETs, the widely diverging philosophical methods and motivations of western actors have infused so much muddle in the debate and so little evidence of careful thought that even a realist might hope for some improvement.

6. Key problems of an Eastern European Marshall Plan

It is worth remembering that the international economy is now, after the lethargy experienced during much of the 1970s and early 1980s, far stronger than when the ERP was introduced; one of the objectives of the Marshall Plan was precisely to strengthen the working of the global economy. These trends are expected to continue in Western Europe, supported by expectations about the benefits of the Single Market by the end of 1992. If these expectations will be realized, not only should the burden of assistance programs be relatively light, but so should the dismantling of protectionist barriers against imports from PETs. At the same time a buoyant world economy provides the PETs with the opportunity to strengthen export-oriented policies and thereby underpin the marketization process.

Rather than inquire into whether DMEs can afford financial assistance, the paramount concern should be whether Eastern Europe can absorb a massive inflow of financial resources. Throughout the 1970s, most of these countries borrowed heavily from the west, gross debt rising by some $62 billion in Eastern Europe between 1970 and 1981 and in the Soviet Union by nearly $28 billion. This considerable inflow of resources had little impact on the productive efficiency of these economies. On the other hand, this external burden has considerably exacerbated macroeconomic management.

The pivotal technical objective of the radical changes now under way in the political and economic systems of Eastern Europe is, of course, to obtain a marked improvement in economic performance. This will require, *inter alia*, a greatly increased capacity to adopt new technologies in a broad range of economic activities. This depends in part on the availability of the resources necessary to acquire such technologies; capital inflows from the west may hence be very salutary. But improving the capacity to absorb the new technologies is contingent on fundamental changes in economic structures and behavior that can be introduced only over a protracted period of time. Furthermore, there is no reason to presume that the capacity of the PETs to assimilate western resources on the scale described earlier has radically changed from what it was a year ago or so.

A basic and critical difference between the reconversion tasks faced by Western Europe in 1945 and the transformation problems of the PETs today is that the former did not have to reconstruct markets from first principles. Whereas war-related controls had suspended or even interfered with the free workings of the market mechanism in many countries, unlike the ideology of central planning in Eastern Europe, there was never any serious doubt that this was a temporary solution inspired by pragmatic considerations about how best to mobilize resources to achieve a limited number of well-defined objectives. Moreover, at no point was there ambiguity about property rights and enterprises never lost touch with foreign markets. Furthermore, the basic incentive structure of the ME, though constrained, was not eliminated by wartime planning: Entrepreneurs still sought to improve efficiency. In fact, labor scarcity, the difficulties in accessing foreign markets, and the ability to display ingenuity under wartime adversity contributed to better management and rising factor productivity (Worswick and Ady 1952, pp. 7-8). These developments also help to account for the rapid response of domestic investment to the bottlenecks and other shortages of the immediate postwar years.

The basic economic organization of a CPE and MPE is very different from that of an ME. Their incentive structure is deficient, leading to endemic microeconomic inefficiencies and pervasive shortages, at times even at the macroeconomic level (Brabant 1990k). More fundamentally, firms have no strong incentive to adopt new technologies and raise allocative and productive efficiency. New firms cannot be set up in response to profitable opportunities and the failures of established concerns as entry and exit remain under the central control of planners and industrial ministries, whose SOEs tend to be large, inefficient, and inflexible. These features on the whole remained intact throughout the MPE reforms, as detailed in Chapter 3. This is one of the reasons why the events of 1989 represent such a radical break with the past.

The transformation of a CPE or MPE into an ME is clear as regards the direction to be pursued, but it is exceedingly vague as to the precise destination. It is often overlooked that the actual functioning of markets depends on a detailed infrastructure of property rights; corporate and other law; an extensive array of specialized financial institutions with proper supervision; regulations and regulatory bodies also in nonfinancial areas; labor laws and procedures for settling disputes, including the role of new trade unions; and other components of the "infrastructure" of an ME. Much of this is, of course, embodied in institutions. But important elements emanate from cultural and social traditions and are embedded in business conventions that vary from country to country. Moreover, most MEs have demonstrated considerable capacity to adapt their institutions and behavioral conventions to changing circumstances. In other words, beyond a number of core elements there is no single, homogeneous model of an ME for the PET to emulate. The transformation of the PET into a full-fledged ME, then, requires a detailed specification of how institutions should be changed or constructed and how the behavior of all economic agents should be adapted.

Following the above logic, rather than recommend a repetition of the Marshall Plan with substantial financial flows, the appropriate thing to do is to focus western assistance on the inadequate or absent structure of institutions and economic incentives that are so vital to make the market environment succeed in the PETs. There are, in fact, several gaps that must be bridged soonest in the interest of the very forces that one is trying to nurse along. Four such areas can be distinguished. Perhaps foremost are informational insufficiencies. Since the onset of *perestroyka* in the Soviet Union and especially the revolutions in Eastern Europe, the data base upon which the old-style leadership placed its decisions has been revealed to leave much to be desired. Not only that, in some cases the data were deliberately falsified to mislead the population and opposition groups. There is simply no way in which a modern economy under reconstruction can be run effectively without having available decent quantitative and qualitative information. Second, there are considerable professional lacunae. An ME stands or falls with the presence of a number of features of markets that exhibit a minimal degree of integration. These are not just product markets, such as in wholesale and retail trade; markets must extend to labor and capital and indeed to the entire gamut of services. Third, there are organizational requirements of operating markets. Perhaps foremost is the entire gamut of the nuts and bolts of coordinating activities of individual agents within a well-defined arena for seeking private profit in whatever form legally authorized. Finally, there would seem to be ample scope for cooperation in education and research, if only to catch up with the long divorce between the west and especially the PETs that have basically a western historical orientation. A carefully chosen number of scholarships for promising graduate students to obtain training primarily in Western Europe would not be very costly. Such a scheme would provide a targeted group of young professionals the opportunity to attend university or business school. It should also include time to travel and to work in the commercial or professional atmosphere of a western company or institution.

The details of a program of technical assistance is something to be drawn up by the PETs themselves according to the particular arrangements that they consider most suitable to their own preferences and traditions. Such a program could also indicate needs for financial assistance, but it would be necessary to show that it could be effectually absorbed.

What types of technical assistance could best be provided to the PETs? Many suggestions were already embedded in the earlier discussion. Certainly, management training and expertise in specific technologies are required. Perhaps most urgent, however, is assistance with establishing the infrastructure of market behavior. The transformation of a PET into an RPE requires a major change in the rules according to which a society conducts its economic activity. It needs expertise on legal, economic, financial, and many other aspects of how markets operate. Especially experience with privatization, regulation, market failure and how governments can intervene, the financial wherewithal of functioning markets, and the like is required to avoid having the PETs traverse the nearly 200 years' experience with markets and their setbacks all over again.

Such behavioral advisory service could be obtained, not really from businessmen or engineers, but economists, politologists, and antitrust lawyers. These specialists are readily available in western official (national and international) and academic institutions of higher learning. Furthermore, western specialists on Eastern Europe could make an especially valuable contribution. In spite of their often being of a disputatious temperament, the advice and assistance that these specialists may bring to bear on the early stages of transformation could be invaluable. Coopting such a range of experiences into a technically sound assistance program could provide invaluable information to the PETs. It certainly would not be expensive and the long-run returns could be very substantial indeed, if only because of the starting conditions of the transformation process: Markets are segmented and inefficient; market structures tend to be monopolistic or, at best, oligopolistic; there are pervasive imbalances in these economies; the sentiment for privatizing state assets is profound, yet the framework for the orderly and equitable transfer thereof is simply not in place; economic information in the broad sense is sparse and/or inaccurate and there may not be sufficient familiarity with the kind of information, quantitative and otherwise, that is required to monitor progress with the reform and indeed to foster the marketization process; experience with marketing abroad by firms is limited; and many other features that provide the ground for domestic and foreign firms to make above-normal profits. Although such may be unavoidable in the short run while a competitive market framework is being constructed, care should be taken that this "profiteering" does not lead to strong social reactions, which could harm the reform process.

The foreign trade aspects of the radical reforms under way in the PETs are obviously critical not only to restore balance in these economies but also to ensure that steady progress can be made with productivity growth. However, marketing, the collection and use of market intelligence, and the whole range of skills required to compete effectively in world markets are areas that have been neglected for many years. But they are crucial for improving export performance. They provide obvious areas for technical assistance, especially given the desire of donor countries to see to it that the PETs become much more intricately interlinked within the global economy; the obvious need to dismantle major components of the MFT in the PETs; and the commitment of notably the EC to make removal of its quantitative restrictions on imports subject to continued progress in economic and political reform. Since the immediate supply responses in the PETs may not be very rapid, a gradualist approach on the western side may be implemented quite easily and could ease the adjustment burden of having the PETs shift a substantial part of their trade to MEs.

* * *

Throughout this chapter, I have emphasized that the transformation of PETs into RPEs is a much more difficult task than the reconversion of Western Europe from wartime controls, basically because the root structures of the ME have to be largely (re-)created in the PETs. Even so, postwar adjustment in Western Europe was for the most part ushered in gradually in an effort to avoid producing inflationary shocks. The transition phase for the PETs is bound to be even more protracted as efficient markets do not simply spring to life on the retreat of central planners and bureaucratic controls. Markets can function properly only if there exists a complex infrastructure of laws, financial systems, as well as certain habits of economic behavior that materialize only slowly under impulse of competition, risk taking, financial probity, and other features of regulating markets, some of which can be taken for granted in MEs. Markets also require a certain size distribution of firms, a degree of openness to the world economy, and a measure of supervisory regulation if they are to be competitive and to encourage innovation and economic adaptability.

These and other considerations led me to suggest that the PETs might benefit most from a broad program of technical assistance from MEs formulated in support of each PET's path toward radical reform and what is required to carry it out. Once the PETs are clear on what it is they want to achieve and the obstacles ahead, and MEs see such a programs as being viable and supportable, western assistance should be provided not the way the Marshall Plan was carried out, but by aiming at the maximum of coherent technical assistance that can be reconciled with the aims of the reforms and the capacity of reformers to assimilate such new knowledge. In other words, much depends on what the PET is and wants to undertake by way of transforming itself into an RPE. That is the topic of the next two chapters.

7

Property rights and privatization

One of the pillars of the current sentiment for comprehensive economic and other reforms in Eastern Europe is privatization. This is usually lumped together with property rights reform, although the two may be quite distinct. With some vengeance, not coincidentally, of course, this debate has taken on the obverse character of the role played by nationalization and the formation of state property at the beginning of the socialization process. The protracted discussions about ownership in PETs indicate that the multiple, at times intractable, issues involved are currently seen as an inalienable component of property rights' reform, which has several dimensions. It is an unalienable component of what policies in PETs are all about (see Chapter 8).

Property rights' reform is an integral component of moving rapidly with orienting economic relations in the PETs fundamentally on the basis of market indicators. This has many tangents (Brabant 1990h, i), but here I focus on its economic aspects. For that reason, it is useful to recall what markets are all about (see Chapter 4). Section 1 clarifies the relationship between ownership and property rights, and why property rights' reform is a necessary, if insufficient, condition for succesfull market orientation. The same is done with respect to privatization in Section 4. But first I clarify what precisely this term should connote and how I address the issue, given that there is at best only a very weak positive theory of privatization (Murphy 1989, p. 67), and in Section 3 I clarify some methodological issues about privatization and property rights. Section 5 examines alternative ownership forms that are available and their various implications. Next I discuss problems inherent in privatizing state assets in Eastern Europe. Section 7 ponders alternative forms of privatization from three angles: competition, fairness, and speed. Conclusions regarding the desirability of privatization in Eastern Europe follow.

1. On privatization and property rights

The original *raison d'être* of socialism was to overcome exploitation of labor by owners of the means of production without overly encroaching upon efficiency. After World War II Eastern Europe solved this dilemma peremptorily by fully socializing property, which should have permitted rapid development, eliminated alienation, and facilitated a just income distribution (Tardos 1989a).

But far more than socialization is at stake. The broader debate about privatization of SOEs has inevitably been influenced more by political philosophy and expediency than by the niceties of economic analysis (Vickers and Yarrow 1988, p. 2). Yet, it would be instructive to separate economic rationality from the more emotional, political, and ideological *obiter dicta* so pervasive in the reform literature than by economic rationality. As far as economic management is concerned, a host of questions revolve in particular around the overwhelming influence of the erstwhile political monopoly of the Communist Party, the enormous power of the government bureaucracy over macro- and microeconomic affairs, and the highly monopolized economic structures in place.

Property is concerned with assets in one form or another. These may be tangible, such as machinery, or intangible, such as the right of access to airwaves. In that sense, property can be looked at from three different angles. First, there is a question of how best to allocate the existing assets with a view to maximizing some returns. Especially here it is useful to distinguish between ownership per se and the usufruct component of property rights. For all practical purposes, virtually the entire capital stock in place in PETs at the inception of market-oriented reform belongs to the state or society as a whole. Although this established clear property rights, the preponderance of the state's monopoly on property was confounded by state power, much like in feudal times (Kanel 1974, pp. 828-9). Converting them into secure property rights protected by orderly judicial and legislative procedures limits arbitrary decisions by the powerful. In some cases, however, efforts to improve economic performance through administrative devolution introduced in the mid-1980s resulted in ill-defined property rights: Enterprises dispose of the capital stock but it is not at all clear whether they are, or should be, the owners with all consequences for the alienation of such property. Second, whatever rights are assigned and however they can be separated, mechanisms must be put in place to ensure that the value of capital assets is not eroded at the expense of the ultimate owner. As noted, this may necessitate the creation of insurance schemes in addition to legal redress. Finally, there are questions concerning the formation of new capital from amortization funds as well as new public and private savings and how best to ensure that these funds are appropriated so as to yield maximum economic benefit. In postwar Eastern Europe, private saving for capital-formation purposes was not actively promoted as the bulk of capital assets was withheld from individual households. Similarly in the case of enterprises: They were not encouraged to raise their net asset value as central planners financed investment from the budget or through "soft" bank loans according to their own criteria.

Technically, socialization is neither necessary nor sufficient for proper resource allocation. But neither is there a sound technical argument that justifies privatization as invariably offering a superior alternative to social ownership. Certainly, state ownership has a poor record in encouraging technological innovation and adequate maintenance of most assets, and it inhibits venture capitalism. For that there must be the possibility for individuals in principle to found their own firm and, hence, to assume the full risk of succeeding or failing with their own or borrowed capital.

There are unquestionably instances in which it would be advisable to encourage private ownership, if only because of the horrendous cost of ensuring proper allocation of user rights to state assets. An example would be private housing, small retail outlets, or service enterprises. On the other hand, precepts on income and wealth distribution and access to a certain social dividend, as the "scientific socialists" referred to it, may well counsel for rather than against maintaining state property of basic sectors of economic activity. The same prevails in the case of market failure, notably natural monopoly and externality (Thompson 1988, pp. 41-42). But that does not necessarily mean that it would be justified to have the state exert its property rights directly through central planning. The core question would be how to ensure that the service flow from such assets gets maximized as measured by some objective function.

2. Alternative ownership forms and their implications

Social interactions among individuals, corporations, and government agencies are conditioned by two broad sets of constraints (Grosfeld 1990, Ickes 1990, Kanel 1974, Moser 1989). One is a physical one, arising from the limit on resources. Behavior in society is also influenced by rules or institutional arrangements that govern the choices of individual actors. Rules essentially define the framework within which these ordinary choices are made. Because they shape the structure of incentives, they have an important bearing on outcomes. The postulates of constitutional economics imply that if the limits to individual behavior are well defined and the rights are recognized and accepted, social interaction proceeds orderly. That is to say, an order will emerge within which the interdependent behavior of individually motivated agents is reconciled with the gradual pattern of tolerable outcomes (Kanel 1974).

It may be intuitive how property rights impact on economic decision making (Alchian 1987, Demsetz 1967, Furubotn and Pejovich 1972, Pejovich 1983, Ryan 1987). But there are major differences in the literature. Without a doubt, alternative property rights exert different effects on the allocation of resources. That the owner of property rights should be entitled to the residual benefit thereof is also clear. But what does ownership mean and what residual benefits are targeted? In what follows, I consider a property right to be a socially enforced right to select uses of scarce goods. Any mutually agreed contractual terms are permissible, though not all are necessarily supported by governmental enforcement. That is to say, ownership cannot be satisfactorily defined unless the right of property is the right of dealing with things in the most absolute fashion the law allows (Ryan 1987, p. 1029). The crucial element, in Roman law, is the *ius utendi et abutendi*, that is, the right of use and disposal of the object of ownership. The latter is very important both as an integral component of property rights and one that can be separated from user rights as such.

An efficient property rights' system can be established only by fulfilling at least three conditions (Comisso 1989, pp. 214-15). First, property rights must be lodged in the hands of actors with purely economic responsibilities. In a market context, such rights would of necessity be attributes of the behavior of private individuals. Although some will also emerge in PETs, a good part of the public capital stock for years to come will be used by SOEs and their "shareholders," such as Tardos's foundations (1989a). Second, property rights must be enforced by a neutral party based on an effective judicial system and modern civil and commercial codes. This should aim not only at issuing a guarantee that the state has no intention to nationalize property, except perhaps under extremely adverse circumstances. It should also provide a guarantee about the framework in which property owners can increase their property. This includes the fiscal regime on the distribution and accumulation of income and wealth. Above all, administrative institutions and Party organizations must renounce their powers of direct supervision and restrictive regulation. These are considered basic ingredients of the institutional infrastructure for creating and maintaining an ME. They are especially so in the context of the PETs, where "The most powerful upper limit on accumulation is uncertainty and the fear of future nationalisation and confiscation" (Kornai 1990b, p. 11), as occurred in the past with memories of such repression remaining very much alive. Finally, policy-making authority, including the ability to prescribe what kinds of activities the bearer of property rights can engage in, must be entrusted to institutions that themselves neither exercise property rights nor enforce them. This is normally the role of the legislative branch of government.

There are two key features of property rights' reform. One may be obvious to most observers. But in the context of what is currently happening in Eastern Europe it is useful to underline that property rights have to be clearly demarcated. This necessitates that the limits to individual, corporate, or collective behavior have to be well defined and mutually recognized, possibly through a social consensus on the trade-offs between private gain and social welfare. When ownership of property is clearly defined and resides with specific economic agents, the latter benefit from using that property in the most productive manner or personally bear the cost in the form of reduced returns (Walters 1987, p. 36). At the same time, property rights should not be subject to unpredictable changes resulting from government intervention, confiscation, or nationalization (Goldberg 1974). The probability of any of the latter eventualities emerging must be limited to extreme circumstances that are constitutionally and legally enshrined as clearly as possible. After all, the western legal doctrine on property rights emerged precisely as a counterweight to the capriciousness of royal favors under feudalism (Kanel 1974).

Property rights are important in explaining the direction and coordination of uses of economic resources in a private property system. Ownership affects allocative efficiency in the market place and has repercussions on the internal efficiency of firms (Vickers and Yarrow 1988, p. 3). The assignment of property rights determines the objectives of the owners of the firm, whether private or public, and the systems of monitoring management. Public and private ownership differ in both respects. Changes in property rights, as a result, materially affect the incentive structures, hence the behavior, of management.

The transfer of ownership, here understood as entitlement to the residual profit from operating an enterprise, from public to private sectors necessarily engineers a change in the relationship between those responsible for the firm's decisions and the beneficiaries of its profits. In general, changing the allocation of property rights entails a different structure of incentives for management and hence modifications in both managerial behavior and company performance. The allocative efficiency implications of property assignments depend very much upon the competitive and regulatory environment in which a given firm operates, with the latter two typically having substantially larger effects on performance than ownership per se. It bears to stress, though, that ownership, competition (hence the monitoring system), and regulation are intertwined influences. The efficiency implications of any change in one set will, as a rule, be contingent upon the other two. Hence, effects of privatization cannot properly be assessed in isolation from these other determinants of incentives.

For the decentralized coordination of economic decisions about production and distribution to work well, that is, along established principles of comparative advantage, in a society with diffused knowledge, economic agents must have secure, alienable property rights in productive resources and products. These should be tradeable at mutually agreed prices in reliable contractual transactions that can be negotiated at a fairly low cost. Each type of contract implies different costs of supervision, measurement, and negotiation. Also, the form of economic organization, along with the function of the visible hand, changes with each different contractual arrangement (Cheung 1987, p. 56). The partitionability, separability, and alienability of private property rights (Alchian 1987, p. 1031) enable the organization of cooperative joint productive activity in specialized economic units, such as the complex corporation.

3. On privatization in Eastern Europe

Various options for property rights' reform in Eastern Europe have been entertained. Many observers take this by definition to mean divesting state assets, involving the transfer of *all* angles of property rights, including the alienation of assets (sale, destruction, inheritance, leasing, give-away, and others). This is misleading for two reasons. Sale need not at all be involved as in the cases of intangible assets such as the awarding of franchises for the running of public facilities (for example, naval dockyards) or publicly maintained legal monopolies (for example, broadcasting rights). The same can apply to tangible assets when ownership per se is divorced from exercising most ownership rights (Kent 1987b, p. 13; Swann 1988, pp. 3ff.) or when SOEs are enjoined to maximize profits, to provide goods and services only if the price covers the cost involved, and to adopt cost-minimizing procedures in employment and procurement. Note that, though ownership may not change, privatization alters the balance of power between government as owner and private agents as executors to the latter's favor. Even where asset sales occur, much of the impact of policy may arise from decisions taken about regulation rather than the mere transfer of ownership. The immediate effect of privatization is to substitute shareholder for governmental monitoring and control of the SOE's management. The impact of that shift in the monitoring function, therefore, depends very much on the degree to which the new shareholders can motivate management to become more responsive to maximizing net asset values. It is not necessarily the case that a simple change in title produces this kind of responsive chord.

Privatization can as a result be described as an umbrella term for a variety of different policies that are loosely linked by the way in which they are taken to mean the strengthening of the market at the expense of the state (Vickers and Wright 1988, p. 1). More specifically, in what follows I take privatization to mean the transfer from the public to the private sector of entitlements to residual profits from operating an enterprise, because that seems to be the mainstream preoccupation of the ongoing reform debate in Eastern Europe. This step is usually accompanied by changes in regulatory policy affecting, among others, controls on entry, exit, prices, outputs, services supplied, markets served, consolidations, and profitability in particular industries.

4. The desirability of privatization

The issues raised by privatization need to be examined from various angles to arrive at a balanced assessment of its pros and cons. There are many arguments in favor of privatizing state assets especially in the PETs that strive to establish functioning markets as quickly as possible. Some are based on unimpeachable economic considerations. Others derive essentially from a range of metaeconomic assessments. There are furthermore questions regarding whether privatization refers to the stock of state assets or new capital formation, and what could be done to ensure that the value of state assets is maintained rather than appropriated for private purposes. There is certainly no unanimity of views on these issues.

The most cogent arguments for rapid and comprehensive privatization in PETs derive from failures of past reforms and two anomalies of socialism. Foremost in favoring substantial and rapid privatization are noneconomic considerations, although they undoubtedly exert repercussions on economic affairs too. There are two critical ones: the overpowering influence of Party politics over economic affairs and the hold of government bureaucracy over a highly monopolized enterprise sphere. The *nomenklatura* management may have earned its spurs in Party or bureaucratic politics, but rarely has it managed state assets to maximize their net worth. Small wonder, then, that the focus of privatization has been to dissociate political and bureaucratic powers from far-reaching controls over resource allocation (Winiecki 1990, p. 65). This presents a powerful argument for privatization as an integral component of a broader-based reform movement, even in circumstances where "market failures" exist, and pure theory might suggest more nuanced approaches (Lipton and Sachs 1990). Oftentimes, however, this apodictic statement hides rather than clarifies the political background.

Breaking the back of Party and ministerial control over the enterprise sphere is the single most important argument in favor of privatizing capital formation, maintenance, and allocation when the erosion of the grips of the Communist Party over society gets under way. Once that is accomplished, as would now seem to be the case in the PETs, it is essentially up to the new government and its parliamentary and legislative bases to ensure that economic arguments now receive a fairer, more technical reading. State-owned assets represent in essence societal savings enforced through socialist precepts, as seen through the eyes of the ruling élites of the erstwhile planned economy. Although political precepts of PETs change, prevailing state assets form part of society's wealth. The custodians of society must therefore ensure that these resources are utilized as efficiently as possible. This raises two broad areas of inquiry. One deals with the allocation process. The other one revolves around earmarking a proper value for those assets if they are to be privatized almost regardless of the allocative implications of such a highly politically charged decision.

Second, the turn taken by reform socialism, entrusting assets essentially to the enterprise collective in some variant of worker self-management, has been a great disappointment. The highly monopolized structure of production in these economies led to economic rents that the SOEs themselves rather than the state captured. It also encouraged raising wages to ensure loyalty to management, which would not, of course, put at risk its own assets or entrenched position. Markets cannot function well without competition, including for the utilization of assets, and thus require some measure of exit and entry motivated by economic incentives. Furthermore, this decentralization of ownership has left the legal basis of property rights ill-defined. Markets can function well only if rents accrue to those having property rights - not necessarily the ultimate owners who may content themselves with a fixed rate of return or other measure of their opportunity cost.

Finally, to ensure some equilibrium between social equity and economic efficiency, it is not necessary to restrict property rights invariably to state ownership. In fact, as argued, the entire gamut of ownership forms should be fully recognized.

Governments interested in divesting themselves of direct involvement in SOEs, yet bent on retaining ownership, can explore at least two alternative organizational forms without disturbing ownership structures. One is arranging leases of SOE assets to the highest bidder or to a party determined as the most appropriate in given circumstances; another option is the recognition of management contracts. The advantage is that the benefits of ownership are retained in the public sector, but the operations are, in effect, privatized (Ramanadham 1988b, p. 9). It allows the government time to decide on denationalization which helps to establish the comparative advantage that the SOE has in the public or private sector. Alternatively, the government could make a genuine declaration to the effect that, irrespective of its ownership, it undertakes not to interfere in the commercial decisions of the SOEs so identified.

These alternatives presuppose that it is possible to devise criteria of managerial behavior as surrogates of markets that force an SOE to operate as if it were a private firm, that is, bound by market discipline in investment, cost minimization, pricing, and production function. Such criteria would include, for example, a specification of a minimum required rate of return on capital, targets of overall and perhaps of disaggregated net returns, unit costs and productivity, and the obligation to resort to commercial markets for funds. This leads to a paradox (Zeckhauser and Horn 1989, pp. 55-56): Although privatization may seem most appropriate for SOEs operating in competitive markets, these are precisely the firms whose internal efficiency performance can be most readily improved by reforms in their public monitoring systems.

5. Advantages and drawbacks of privatization

Since the early 1980s, there has been a wholesale wave of privatization attempts in MEs, including most notably France (Bauer 1988), Italy (Bianchi, Cassese, and Sala 1988), the United Kingdom (Ashdown 1989, Buckland 1987, Heald 1988, Kay and Vickers 1988, Ramanadham 1988a, Vickers and Yarrow, 1988, Yarrow, 1986), the United States (Kent 1987a; MacAvoy, Stanbury, Yarrow, and Zeckhauser 1989; Swann, 1988), and a host of other countries (Drumaux 1988, Nankani 1990, Pera 1989, Vickers and Wright 1988). Two questions can usefully be asked in this connection. What were the motivations of these privatizations and could they could be applied to the PETs too? How successful have these privatizations been and to what extent could lessons be derived for Eastern Europe?

Various motives have argued the case for privatization in MEs, although they have not always been publicly aired. Basically four can be distinguished (Heald 1988). One is improving the use of scarce resources. Another is to plug budget deficits and seek budgetary relief by crimping the role of the state. But much of the privatization drive in MEs during the past decade has been justified on ideological grounds (Swann 1988), basically the belief that freedom and liberty necessitate private ownership and the compression of the role of the state to the bare essentials. In several MEs, privatization was motivated by concerns about breaking up entrenched trade-union rights and privileges that inhibited resource reallocation (Heald 1988, pp. 31-32). This philosophy contrasts markedly with that prevailing in Eastern Europe.

The main motivation for privatization in the PETs has been a negative one, namely undercutting the power of the entrenched bureaucracy and getting even for the denial of nonstate property rights for such a long time. Economists are aware of the allocative implications, but these concerns, when expressed at all in these debates, as a rule receive short shrift. Other related motives may be to enhance freedom and hence the democratic process. For that, some critical minimum of property rights' reform may have to be quickly enacted, for a democracy without a solid ME is unthinkable. Yet, it bears to recall that there continues to be a considerable degree of egalitarian thinking in the PETs and a strong public sentiment for economic equality. This in spite of the fact that economic differentiation is bound to occur in marketizing these economies, even if at the start of privatization equality of share holding can be ensured (King 1990). All this certainly complicates the assessment of the results of privatization.

Although privatization of SOEs in MEs envisages the redistribution of property rights in an environment that differs in many respects from that of a PET, some useful lessons could be derived. But one must heed the political philosophy on ownership, the role of trade unions in the post-industrial society, and the social contract through which the policy was pursued. In that narrow perspective, privatization is by definition a success. But in some cases privatization had explicit economic and wealth intentions. Whether these objectives can be realized depends very much on restrictions imposed by economic structures and the obstacles encountered in implementing privatization schemes.

First of all, the outcome of privatization is contingent on the prevailing market structures. For markets to function properly, the PETs must re-create competition. The latter requires (Nuti 1990, pp. 18ff.) a sufficient number of autonomous and competitive firms capable of responding to market incentives, whose managers are chosen not for political merits but for their professional qualifications. To attain this, the monopoly power of large SOEs must be substantially reduced. This requires not only physically breaking up the monopolies but also, in case of natural monopoly, implementing a sufficient regulatory framework, including on antitrust and access to markets for new small and medium-sized enterprises. Above all, it necessitates breaking the link between the center and firms as regards managerial controls, incentives, and budget dependence.

Such demonopolization can be pursued by different means. One way of ensuring independence of SOEs from central tutelage is privatization. But there are evidently other avenues. The elimination of the "petty tutelage" exercised by ministerial bureaucracies, including the central planning agency, should not lead to the dissipation of state ownership. In the smaller PETs, even after breaking up the presently existing monopolies, there is unlikely to be sufficient competition that can be harnessed in the short run. Liberalizing the trade regime is the only way in which competitive pressure can gradually be brought to bear on the performance of domestic firms, especially in core industrial sectors.

Market structures are, then, key ingredients of the decision to go ahead with privatization. Once taken, many practical obstacles lie ahead. Key questions are how to evaluate the assets, whether a reservation price should be established, how and how quickly privatization should proceed, and for what purposes the proceeds should be earmarked. In most MEs, privatization has been enacted in an environment with overwhelming private ownership of the means of production, functioning markets for goods and capital, in most cases integrated capital markets, and with individuals having some culture as regards private enterprise and stockholding. None of these features is strong in any PET.

Has privatization in MEs been successful, for example, by leading to lower product prices, greater allocative efficiency, greater internal efficiency in privatized enterprises, better service, and other measures of enterprise performance? Even against this more limited canvas of economic discourse, it is difficult to provide a straightforward answer. Empirical studies of how public and private firms compare have led to ambivalent results. Although there is some support for the superiority of private enterprise, this claim depends critically on the degree of competition, the incentive structures in alternative organizational forms, and the degree of regulatory policies designed to correct market failures rather than ownership per se (Yarrow 1986, p. 333). Changes in ownership in the absence of competition and an adequate regulatory environment (Helm and Yarrow 1988) do not inevitably lead to improvements in performance (Heald 1988, pp. 33-35). Changes in ownership, particularly those accompanied by the creation of competitive conditions are likely to be beneficial. These studies illustrate that rarely are such divestments conducted simply on the basis of economic motives, say within a bold competitive approach. Results must therefore perforce be assessed against the broader backdrop of what originally motivated privatization. Those advocating privatization have often been guilty of oversimplification. Sensing the strength of their argument for removal of firms from the nonprivate sector, they have failed to work through the mechanics of the actual transfer. It is easy to advocate the sale of an SOE. It is much more difficult to specify how the sale should be conducted, to whom, for how much, and how best to allocate the proceeds.

6. Difficulties of privatizing state assets

As far as economic objectives are concerned, privatization should aim at improving the allocation of existing capital assets, maintaining the value of these assets, and ensuring that new capital is formed and utilized as efficiently as possible. Recall that privatization is neither necessary nor sufficient to guarantee improved static allocation of capital resources or the efficient formation of new capital. What is required is the recognition of the usefulness of the entire range of property forms, from outright private ownership all the way to communal property. The principle should therefore be accepted that the choice of one form over another follows, *ceteris paribus*, essentially from the least cost of coordinating the allocation of the service flows emanating from capital assets.

1. Divestment

To divest state assets properly, the real worth of capital assets should be assessed and be turned over to society, perhaps as a means of reducing some of its liabilities (such as amortizing the external and domestic debts or offsetting claims to social services, pension rights, and so on). That is to say, a "proper" price needs to be established. At all cost, reformers should avoid a sellout of existing firms, often through the intermediation of self-interested managers, at prices that deviate substantially from the intrinsic market value of assets.

This is by no means an easy task, given the problems of establishing a market value for assets that have never been priced in a competitive environment, however constrained, and cannot quickly be priced in that manner as prevailing prices are heavily distorted. Market evaluation can only begin once a certain volume of shares has been distributed. Each aspect gives rise to many questions that essentially focus on the starting conditions of the PET's reform. These include the legacies of central planning but also the potential incompetence, malevolence, or lack of control of reformers over rapidly changing societal arrangements.

a. Absence of capital markets. The key mechanism of capital formation and distribution in the planned economy is the state budget. In the absence of capital markets and with prevailing prices in the incipient PET not clearing markets, riddled as they are with all kinds of distortions, there is simply no easy way of establishing market value on the basis of the discounted value of the expected residual returns to capital over the lifetime of the assets. It must simply be accepted that determining asset values outside a competitive market environment is a hazardous proposition even under the most favorable circumstances. Of course, the problems get sharply compounded by the fact that the principals in the negotiations are rarely sufficiently scrupulous to avoid deliberately undervaluing assets so that they can eventually appropriate capital gains.

PETs have resorted to makeshift rules that in fact allow one group to appropriate part of its knowledge and transform it into a stake in the property. This has at times been strengthened by having some international accounting rules applied to such an SOE, even though it was clear that the firm in question would find it very difficult to have its profit-and-loss situation properly audited. This is perhaps the more egregious way in which society's wealth in some PETs has been alienated. Not all of this sale at bargain prices has been on account of malevolence or incompetence of those entrusted with privatization, however. The below-value sale stems also from inherent lack of transparency.

b. Absence of a capitalist class. This has several dimensions. The one of interest here is that there is insufficient indigenous savings available to purchase outright a sizable portion of state assets. In some cases, setting up proper financial institutions, such as independent pension funds, insurance schemes, commercial banks, and the like to whom state liabilities are "sold," as distinct alternatives to the institutional monopolies in place, can assist in the intermediation. But this cannot be a panacea.

Certainly, in some PETs there is a substantial monetary overhang. This could be soaked up in exchange for state assets, provided these funds originated from above-board activities. In most PETs, the monetary overhang has been eroded through inflation or it is very small. Remaining savings could be earmarked for the purchase of housing, small plots of land, small handicraft shops, or service firms. But it remains to be seen whether savers are interested in such purchases without there being first substantial other reforms, including the anchoring of a genuine wholesale trading system, macroeconomic stabilization, revamping of the fiscal system, and demonopolization of SOEs (Nuti 1990). There is, of course, a flipside to the absence of a capitalist segment, namely the propensity of savers to be risk-aversive and the societal nature of state assets. Apart from the uncertainty introduced in having share prices fluctuate, Eastern Europe has been accustomed to near certainty over jobs and basic income over the past fifty years. Although they may espouse the idea of an ME, bankruptcy with attendant fluctuations in fortunes may be more difficult to accept.

Whether it would be worthwhile to privatize SOEs piecemeal with part of the shares being "given" to workers at preferential prices is something to be carefully weighed. Perhaps auctions that are as transparent as circumstances permit, hopefully after rationalization of the SOEs so as not to encumber potential buyers, offer a solution. In the absence of widespread experience with such divestment, however, careful experimentation is warranted both in the methodology of organizing markets and in phasing in the privatization.

Inasmuch as society's assets have been built up essentially through forced savings allocated by the state, they belong to society and should be distributed with a considerable degree of egalitarianism. How to do this even if shares are given away poses numerous technical problems that may or may not be surmountable in the short run. A wide distribution of assets would avoid future resentment about giveaways to a favored class. It would also ensure support for the temporarily painful measures needed to make those assets more productive by reforming monetary policy, freeing prices, and ending subsidies. Above all, it would support democracy by greatly reducing the economic power of the *nomenklatura* and strengthen the economic power of the electorate.

c. Selloff to foreigners? In principle, it should not matter whether assets are sold to domestic or foreign agents, provided fair sales can be conducted and society is willing to accept a dilution of the country's economic sovereignty. There is little doubt that all PETs have been looking towards a significant influx of foreign capital, including through the formation of joint ventures and the outright sale of SOEs to foreign owners. This would furnish badly needed capital, but also managerial expertise, technology, marketing skills, an easier entry into established markets, and other benefits. But economic sovereignty matters, particularly in countries whose scope for autonomy was so narrowly circumscribed for so long by Soviet-type development precepts. The question, then, is less whether to sell assets to foreign owners as such than in what sectors, to what degree, and how will foreign ownership be regulated.

d. Weak layer of entrepreneurship. Exit and entry of firms in planned economies are generally decided at the apex of societal decision making, not in response to individual venturesomeness, thrift, and acquisitiveness. Furthermore, managers of SOEs are on the whole entrusted with priorities and rules that have little to do with their ability to enhance the firm's net worth. So even if the state and its appointed officials were to withdraw quickly from microeconomic decision making, who would take their place? Furthermore, will would-be managers and entrepreneurs successfully manage, or even protect, assets?

e. Incomparable accounting rules. SOEs in planned economies do not keep books according to transparent criteria that are internationally acceptable. Not only that: Accounts have for so long been shielded from public scrutiny for reasons that transcend the confidentiality that can legitimately be claimed for "commercial secrets." Excepting a few individuals imbued with the socialist ideals for a brief period of time, management certainly had no incentive to maximize the SOE's net worth on its own initiative.

f. Legal environment. Although the means of production in a planned economy are society's, in some countries it has for some time been unclear who is the legal owner of these assets, owing to the fact that assets were simply turned over to enterprise councils. To rectify this confusion, it would be desirable to transfer legal title to SOEs back to some societal trustee charged with divestment. Some technical agency subject to parliamentary scrutiny in the newly emerging democracies could go a long way.

2. Private exploitation of the usufruct

Several of the aforementioned hindrances are likely to be present also when ownership as such is separated from the usufruct, which is leased or contracted out to private entrepreneurs. The key obstacles rest firstly in the determination of the property rent to be paid to the state. As a first step, to provide some guidance to auctions, the state may start off the contracting process by offering assets at a rent set equal to its own expected rate of return and evaluation of assets. To foster marketization, it may well be instructive to let markets set the proper leasing fee with the option of owners to transfer their lease to others willing to outbid the former. Of course, some of these assets will be taken up for a song, while others will not find a bidder at all. Such an investment in marketization may yield a temporary loss on the revenue that government may eventually capture. Perhaps more difficult would be to enact insurance schemes to protect assets against the lessee's negligence or true misfortune and to institute measures that encourage management to upgrade them.

The problems of managerial abilities, fostering a competitive environment, and putting in place sufficiently comprehensive, yet not stultifying, regulatory mechanisms remain, of course. Some of these issues (such as managerial behavior, ensuring the emergence of a competitive environment, and putting in place the proper regulatory framework to induce enterprise management to behave like private owners in a competitive environment) are still present if the state retains control and enjoins enterprise management, for example, through management contracts, to behave as private entrepreneurs.

3. Operating privatized assets

It is often assumed that new owners of privatized state assets will by definition allocate their services more efficiently than state-appointed officials. But there is no guarantee that they will automatically begin to maximize the net worth of their assets. For one thing, it assumes that those acquiring state assets will be in a position to manage the assets better than their erstwhile state-appointed caretakers. This is a vastly unrealistic assumption as few individuals in PETs have had proper managerial experience because planners did not encourage the acquisition of such a culture. Managerial skills and experience cannot be acquired quickly in any MBA program, certainly not in an accelerated, compressed version that is at times proposed to PETs. Rather, such skills can be built up only "on the job," in good measure through trial and error.

Related to this is the assumption that individuals are interested in holding part of their wealth in the form of shares and in fact will exercise their ownership rights through managerial oversight. That is hardly realistic. In the planned economy, households were not at all encouraged to think in ways required for the operation of an ME. Stockholding is particularly alien to this mentality. Giving each individual a stake by distributing public assets would certainly help to create such a culture, but it would take time and mistakes are bound to be made. Not only that, most households in MEs do not hold a share of their wealth in the form of stocks and only some have bonds in their portfolio; there is no reason to believe that things would be very different in PETs. Even if individuals own shares, they rarely exercise the right to "vote" on management. Participation costs may be very high in some cases. But apathy toward monitoring management and "appointed" directors and "satisficing" of share owners by the management in place probably play a much more substantial role.

Third, it is often all to facilely assumed that the PETs will in due course be in a position to bring about fair competition in privatized markets. There is simply no guarantee for this. At the start of the reform, these countries are highly monopolized. Substituting private for state monopolies will not necessarily enhance allocative efficiency or increase the net worth of the firm as competitive bidding is virtually precluded in the process. Unless effective competition and regulation are introduced, the privatization of firms with market power brings about private ownership in precisely the circumstances where it has least to offer. The desire to privatize speedily, to widen share ownership quickly, and to raise short-term revenue should not stand in the way of devising adequate measures of competition and regulation for the industries concerned.

The existence of management that holds a monopoly on information, because of widely dispersed shareholders or of a market monopoly, leads to principal-agent problems that can potentially be quite serious. If the intensity with which management is monitored is low, managers have discretion to pursue their own objectives, rather than those held by owners. Monitoring problems are important in structuring incentives to make management behave according to the instructions of owners. The firm's monopoly of information must be broken and the regulator needs to be given independent access to detailed information bearing on, for example, the potential for cost reduction and the relative costs of services supplied by a multiproduct firm. Widespread ownership inevitably dilutes the monitoring role of owners and hence modifies the behavior of management so that it no longer maximizes the net worth of the firm's assets, a point that is often ignored in the zealous advocacy of privatization (see Feige 1990; Hemming and Mansoor 1988; Leipold 1983, 1988; Pejovich 1990; Schroeder 1988).

Fourth, two hundred years or so of experience with capitalism has made it clear that there are numerous market imperfections. At the same time, experiments with ways of allocating resources suggest that there is no alternative to embracing some market arrangement if the economy is to progress steadily. To avoid the worst side effects, yet enhance the positive features, of the market mechanism, a well-entrenched and adequate regulatory mechanism in the hands of an impartial body is absolute necessary. Only then can private interests be harmonized with those of society as a whole, including on monopoly rents.

Fifth, thriving competition must apply also to the acquisition and disposal of private assets. For that, it is necessary to have in place adequate capital markets, including the proper safeguards and regulatory mechanisms against abuses of stock-exchange provisions and the like.

Finally, a proper capital market can function only if the regulatory mechanisms are in place and there is sufficient transparency in the market. To attain the latter, firms must adhere to certain supervisory and accounting rules that foster competition among economic agents on the basis of expected returns.

7. Alternative forms of privatization

Privatization can take many different forms. I shall consider here spontaneous privatization, essentially giving away assets, selling assets, and seeking to divorce ownership from the usufruct of assets.

1. SPONTANEOUS PRIVATIZATION

This means that those being entrusted with state assets take possession of the assets and turn the SOE into a joint company, part of which can be transferred to clear owners. This was the route that Hungary initially chose to take because decision makers did not wish - or dare - to renationalize assets. This has not been a happy experience in view of economic, financial, political, and organizational problems (Lee and Nellis 1990). Financially, spontaneous privatization allows former management and possibly workers to become owners without paying a fair price and thus deprives the government from needed revenues to offset its liabilities.

Economically, there is no reason to believe that turning over assets to people who ran these facilities poorly when they were formally under state control will improve resource allocation. Being entrusted with assets may change the allegiance of management from Party dominance to that of true asset holders, but again there is no guarantee that this will emerge on a sufficiently large scale. It may be true that because of the incentives embedded in being owners the managers in place, called "entrepratchiks" by Bruszt (1989, p. 722), could behave very differently from how they made decisions as state employees. But there is no guarantee that they will potentially do better than other asset holders. Furthermore, free distribution may exacerbate already existing inflationary pressures on account of wealth effects (Nuti 1990, p. 20).

Politically, management in place has frequently been appointed under the *nomenklatura* rules. At the very least, conflict of interest laws should have been used to prevent managers from laundering state assets through dummy corporations that they created in the private sector (Lipton and Sachs 1990). There is also bound to be an equity problem. Worker ownership might be fine for those employed in profitable or potentially profitable operations, but not for those in persistent loss-making operations. Of course, those not employed in SOEs who involuntarily contributed to asset formation would be excluded altogether.

Finally, there is an organizational problem with worker management in the sense that those belonging to the former managerial group, who have the experience and know-how to supervise the firms, may be eliminated from the newly formed managerial base.

2. FREE DISTRIBUTION

Because state assets in place were obtained either through nationalization or public savings over which the population had little control and ideology emphasized that property belongs to "society" at large, a logical case can be built for embarking on privatization by distributing assets free of charge (Hinds 1990a). Several forms have been entertained. Most common has been worker self-management of SOEs, which is essentially an extension of labor-managed firms. The Yugoslav experience with the labor-managed firm has amply demonstrated that this "forced substitute" (Kornai 1990a) for private ownership or clear property rights does not encourage the long-run profit of the firm. This is likely to prevail even more when there is no capital market to enable the worker voluntarily to sell his share - the right to participate in future profit earnings - at a market valuation based on the firm's expected earnings. That is to say, worker management is insufficient to ensure efficiency; ownership and a market in which such property can be traded are also required (see Tardos 1989b). This can function properly only if individuals with no connections to the firm are allowed to acquire shares. In other words, there must eventually be the possibility of capitalist ownership. Dąbrowski (1989), however, argues that the rules of the labor-managed firms could be sufficiently revised to encourage greater productivity and maximization of asset value.

The second form is based on the argument that ownership in state firms should be transferred to existing workers, who are requested to improve the firm's profitability. The key assumption of such transfer is that property owners automatically improve the allocation process and thereby render the firm profitable. Such an assumption is fallacious and rather inequitable in any case. For one, the value of capital per worker in state firms varies a great deal for reasons that have nothing to do with the relative merits of the present labor force. Furthermore, free distribution of assets fails to provide funding for the government to free itself of some liabilities. Furthermore, it tends to favor reinvestment in existing types of activities under present management and to continue employment of the present labor force.

Whereas the labor-managed firms suffers from weak principles, some ESOP is worth considering, particularly if it can be coupled with promises to limit demands for monetary compensation, foster productivity, change work rules, and resort to other measures that give workers a material stake in their firm. Note, however, that this can be done without outrightly privatizing the SOE. All it requires is that the latter become a joint-stock company, whose performance incentives include obtaining a share in the firm's capitalized value.

Third, property can also be distributed to society at large. There are good reasons to do so as state assets have been accumulated through confiscation and forced savings. To ensure some measure of equity, rather than grant ownership rights to the labor force of existing SOEs, assets could be distributed to the population at large, either on an individual basis or by households. This form of divestment is also advocated in view of the inadequacies of capital markets and the shortage of domestic capital in PETs (Hinds 1990b).

Although such a free distribution of shares in SOEs is intuitively appealing, there are serious drawbacks of such divestment, apart from the wealth effects at a time of already significant inflationary pressures. First of all, there are potential losers as well as beneficiaries. Thus, the distribution of assets by states that are heavily indebted may diminish the prospects of repayment (Vaňous 1989, p. 6). To meet this objection, the state could guarantee repayment of borrowed funds, for example, by laying first claim to fiscal revenues from profits of the divested state firms. Second, the fiscal base of PETs is largely made up by corporate and indirect taxes. In the absence of a personal income tax, the already inadequate revenue-raising ability of the government would be further hampered by privatization as it deprives the government of the future stream of revenues from assets and should ideally be accompanied by the retirement of state obligations, either debt or other future obligations with financial implications. Privatization without revenue raising does not offer this possibility and makes the need for fiscal reform anchored to personal income taxation all the more necessary. Furthermore, if shares are distributed equitably, any one household would hold only a miniscule interest in any one. The distinction between the pre- and post-reform situation would be largely nominal. Greater concentration of ownership might come through the creation of several mutual funds randomly allocated (Feige 1990). But how to ensure that each household receives portfolios of approximately equal value, given serious asset-valuation problems in the PET, is a conundrum that needs to be resolved. Unquestionably the most serious shortcoming of this way of proceeding would be that privatization does not exert beneficial effects on management - normally, the principal focus of privatization. The population at large is unlikely soon to become sophisticated investors or attend Board meetings. Even mutual fund managers will not have the knowledge or incentive to assess managerial performances and promote takeovers when needed. There is therefore a potentially serious monitoring problem.

Numerous alternatives have been considered (Feige 1990; Hinds 1990a, b), including by the PETs themselves. Thus, one of the more imaginative and creative proposals has been formulated by Márton Tardos. He argues for entrusting state assets to a large number of public institutions funding pensions, stipends, insurance claims, research funds, and related expenditures. Consisting of shares in SOEs, these endowments would be managed so as to protect asset value while maximizing their return. The income stream thereby generated would then go not to private individuals, but into various funds from which institutions spent for their chartered purposes. Tardos's major objective is to detach from the government all kinds of socially necessary functions, yet to ensure that those entrusted with managing those assets will be concerned about net worth. Tardos allows individuals to purchase shares in these funds and trading in open markets. Enterprises in such a scheme would essentially be run in the form of the typical ME corporation. Thus, managerial functions would be detached from ownership functions. Furthermore, owners would steer management into maximizing net worth through various incentive schemes.

3. Distribution of user rights

Custodial rights over the use of social property could be traded in functioning capital markets. Can such a market for the usufruct of capital be entertained and, if feasible, can it lead to a more effective allocation of scarce resources than attained with traditional management of SOEs? An answer can usefully be formulated by first looking at the stationary state and then at one where there is positive growth of the capital stock.

With a stationary state, policy makers must impose proper charges and safeguards to ensure that capital users do not erode assets. In principle, it is entirely feasible to let economic agents place a fair bet on the right to access society's capital, to set up a mandatory insurance scheme to protect the capital stock, and to let firms fail when unable to pay the net charge for the usufruct.

In a growing economy, questions of how additions to the capital stock and its replacement are decided upon loom large. These problems include how best to facilitate exit and entry as well as how to ensure that there will be a steady upgrading of the capital stock. Both additions to and replacement of the existing capital stock could be handled through exit and entry by entrepreneurs bidding on access to future assets. This could be organized through full-fledged capital markets, including for forward transactions. Entrepreneurs would simply explore with commercially viable financial institutions how best to allocate society's savings, including amortization funds and state savings.

Given the complexity of organizing such efficient markets even in mature industrial MEs, however, it is hard to see how the reforming PET could institute fully functioning capital markets within a comparatively brief period of time at a tolerable transaction cost. In fact, multiple ownership forms in combination with the gradual emergence of capital markets for the bulk of society's capital based on technical economic grounds may well be the more desirable way of proceeding. The case for separating ownership from its usufruct justifies careful consideration of the merits of leasing and management contracts as ways of measurably improving capital allocation, however.

4. Sale of state-owned assets

The final form of privatization involves the outright sale of state assets through auctions or more discretionary channels, although how best to establish prices and what to do with the proceeds remain poignant questions. Apart from the fact that auction markets would have to be organized, the sale of state assets calls into question the availability of funding, given that private savings in these countries are highly limited, whether society would be prepared to put even these limited funds into company shares, and at what price the auction should be reserved.

To mitigate the lack of funds and to entice individuals into holding shares, one of the more appealing forms of selling off state assets is through debt-financed auctions. This form of divestment would essentially be anchored to making available generous financial resources to those willing to acquire state assets and able to manage them profitably. In essence, the state as lender would become a rentier while private sectors end up as debtors and capitalists (Lipton and Sachs 1990, p. 76). Clearly, the government would be in a position only to make such resources available from domestic means. Some agents would, however, be able to borrow funds abroad. But this option would most definitely *not* be open to all potential asset holders, and some regulation will therefore be required to avoid rigged bids.

Whereas it would in principle be possible to conduct auctions with reservation prices clearly established, the ambiance in which this would have to be carried out probably rules out the imposition of a realistic reservation price. That could be implemented much more safely through a discretionary divestment program. Determining a reasonable reservation price and ensuring that the discretionary sale would not infringe upon society's rights or extend favors that one was trying to rule out otherwise are no mean tasks. Regarding the determination of a reservation price, some carefully conducted research by custodians of property under the supervision of the newly formed parliamentary organs, perhaps with the assistance of outside accounting firms, should yield a plausible range of asset values. For most undertakings, there should be some positive price that can be realistically established with some good will on the part of all actors involved. To mitigate the room for conflicts of interest, custodians and trustees should be denied the right to acquire ownership rights

* * *

Fast and widespread privatization in the PETs may not be the most desirable transition. Whilst a number of benefits have been claimed for privatization, "many of its goals are better achieved by other policies and ... it is on its contributions to economic efficiency that privatization must ultimately be judged" (Yarrow 1986, p. 324). In the case of the PET, skepticism is warranted for all the reasons that are recited for MEs plus at least two others, namely the hold of Party and bureaucracy over economic affairs and the highly monopolized industrial structure. There are, however, alternative ways of achieving these objectives. On the basis of these propositions, undertaking a massive program of ill-prepared privatization in a hurry for ideological, political, or sentimental reasons may lead to "une économie de casino" (Vickers and Wright 1988, p. 25). This is an unjustified way for the state to divest itself of assets that it holds in trust for the nation, however badly these resources may be utilized now. Under no circumstance could privatization be considered to be a panacea for raising economic efficiency. That, in my view, depends critically on the creation of a competitive environment and the recognition in principle of the validity of all alternative property forms.

Implicit in the analysis of this chapter is a certain sequencing regarding privatization and the establishment of property rights in PETs. But this can be specified more clearly in the context of the ongoing broader transition toward the ME. I shall do so in the next chapter in connection with the streamlining of the western assistance effort.

8

East-west assistance and PETs

In Chapter 5, I examined the ongoing efforts by the DMEs to assist the PETs and came to the constatation that there is room for greater organization and streamlining of the entire assistance program. The main purpose of such resource transfers should be to maximize the benefits for PETs that could be derived from the limited resources available and minimize in the process any adverse repercussions on the trade and aid flows to other countries. Rather than recreate a Marshall Plan, as argued in Chapter 6, target assistance is required to buttress the incipient market orientation so that RPEs will in due course emerge and become genuinely self-supportive.

This chapter addresses some of the multiple issues involved in improving the efficiency of western assistance, both from the point of view of the individual and collective self-interest of DMEs as well as when placed in the context of the needs of Eastern Europe. Section 1 looks at the overall macroeconomic policy framework of reforming socialist societies. The key feature of PET-style reforms needed to operate an ME are explored next. The three components of the economic mechanism (macroeconomic policies, institutions, and policy instruments) are examined in the subsequent section. Whether there is a desirable sequencing of reforms in PETs and how this could be supported by DMEs are two questions addressed next. An analysis of whether the western effort can be improved concludes the chapter.

1. Macroeconomic policy framework

The critical features of the economic situation in the PETs have been the key trigger that led notably Hungary and Poland to request economic assistance from the DMEs. These motives in turn are being used to justify budgetary appropriations in some form for PETs. The features that should be taken into account in designing an effective assistance program as an integral component of the transition toward genuine economic and other reforms in the process get less attention than warranted.

Recent economic performance of the PETs has been symptomatic of the more general situation throughout Eastern Europe. This is characterized by substantial macroeconomic imbalances, which in some countries are being translated into open price inflation, whether measured in official statistics or not. In others, centrally managed administrative pricing systems have thus far succeeded in repressing inflationary pressures. Price modifications are the normal way for MEs to work off short-term imbalances. Quantum adjustments from one planning cycle to the next would have been the ideal way of ridding the CPE or MPE of substantial divergences between aggregate demand and supply or palpable imbalances in their principal components. In the very short run, say less than the annual planning cycle, involuntary savings or forced substitution of second-best goods and services for the first-best ones that are not available in sufficient quantity would necessarily emerge.

In addition to inflation, macroeconomic imbalances throughout Eastern Europe and the Soviet Union have also manifested themselves in the form of and have indeed been caused by sizable budget deficits that get monitized, in part for lack of a sufficiently flexible financial infrastructure. Part of the monetization results only after the *de facto* insolvency of the banking sector, which thus far has acted as a treasury of the government, has become recognized (Brainard 1990). The precise magnitude of these financial imbalances has often been disclosed only after the political core of the traditional CPE or MPE regime has been unseated. Furthermore, the domestic disequilibria have found a counterpart in external imbalances. Unexpected or poorly anticipated disturbances in foreign sectors have imparted undesirable perturbations to the domestic economy for quite some time now. This has occurred even though in some countries this transmission is not at all organized through the direct linking of domestic and foreign prices (see Chapter 4).

An endemic problem of the CPE and MPE has been very slow change in economic structures once the first outbursts of revolutionary fervor waned and the war-ravaged ME had been turned into a CPE. Part of this phenomenon is connected with the exceedingly cumbersome transmission of achievements of science and technology into the production process for organizational reasons. It also stems from significant biases built into the microeconomic planning framework that tend to work against innovation and structural adaptations in firms. Unless the central budget actively supports technical progress, usually in the form of "extensive" development (that is, the construction of new production facilities rather than the renovation and modernization of existing ones), the firm as such has little incentive to innovate.

Almost from the very beginning of central planning, these countries have run into a foreign exchange constraint. Under strict planning, this could be held in check through direct trade controls. The MFT was very successful in suppressing the adverse effects of this chronic excess demand for imports. Once the most rigid aspects and implications of the MFT were relaxed and foreign trade had to be managed more and more through the indirect instruments and institutions, however, the pressure of excess demand for imports began to result in chronic balance-of-payments problems. These had to be cut to size or suppressed altogether through periodic central rationing of foreign exchange, in spite of the goals of economic policy enshrined in the central plan.

A counterpart of the chronic tendency toward deficit has been poor export performance. This applies both to the east-west framework as well as to CMEA trade, albeit for very different reasons. Regarding east-west trade, where the foreign exchange constraint has been more pervasive by the nature of how this trade is conducted, export performance during the past two decades has been singularly unimpressive. Certainly, the CPEs and MPEs had bouts of strong export performance. For the former, this was achieved largely through the marketing of primary goods, including Soviet oil exported directly or indirectly to DMEs. For the MPE, the strong export performance emanated by and large from the "storming" of foreign markets at a time when the degree of freedom in imports was on the whole delimited by the choice between domestic stagnation or worse and finding the means to procure essential imports from convertible currency markets.

The combined result of these developments has been sizable external debts in several CMEA countries. Czechoslovakia and Rumania are the two exceptions. The latter wiped out its debt as a result of quixotic "denial" policy, which was a compulsive streak of Ceauşescu's singlemindedness. The former managed to avoid debt because of the deliberate choice not to borrow from abroad, a stance that was aided by shifting a substantial portion of Czechoslovakia's east-west trade toward the CMEA, the Soviet Union in the first instance, after "normalization" in 1968-1969.

Poor performances of CPEs, and even more of MPEs, have also materialized as a result of the inadequate policy-making infrastructure. This applies to the macroeconomic, the enterprise, and the household spheres. On the macro level, the poorly developed institutions and policy instruments for conducting genuine monetary and fiscal policies, or income and price policies for that matter, left a vacuum with respect to the coordination of decision making and ensuring that microeconomic behavior would on the whole dovetail with the expectations of central policy makers. In the MPE, it was difficult to ensure this synchronization in the absence of a "constitutional" framework for the conduct of decentralized decisions. These include legal frameworks on property and commercial codes, a fully developed infrastructure to intermediate, flexibility in labor markets, fostering voluntary wealth accumulation, establishing genuine wholesale trading and autonomy of firms, and other expertise required for obtaining functioning markets for goods, services, labor, and capital.

Overall, one central aim of the western assistance effort, aside from alleviating emergency needs out of humanitarian or related concerns, is the promotion of more effective resource allocation. This priority is being reflected in the conditionality and monitoring provisions attached to the bulk of the new credits and the types of support being offered. Little doubt is left about the entire scheme revolving around the IMF's central role in allocating standby credit facilities in exchange for adjustment programs, especially proper monetary and fiscal policies. Earmarking bilateral and multilateral bank loans for project financing directly guarantees that resources are channeled into ventures that the western lender has deemed to be productive. Likewise for direct investment flows and the financing of training programs to enhance the capacity of the élites in PETs to grasp the intricacies of the market and its inherent adaptations with respect to new and reconstituted resource allocation.

There are broadly two risks involved in this western strategy. One is that most of the financial flows are being extended on the basis of bank lending and will thus worsen the external debt. Whether the PETs will be able to cope better with this larger debt by promoting exports, the ostensible purpose for which many of these loans are being arranged, than the way in which they failed to manage properly a smaller debt incurred mainly during the 1970s, remains to be seen. This assessment concerns not only to ability of the PET to transform economic processes, but also the determination of DME governments to smooth market access for the PETs. If these loans are properly coordinated with the visions of the PETs themselves, barring untoward circumstances, they will have a fair chance of reaching their goal. Whether this will materialize in the most effective way is a matter of the application, administration, control, and supervision of the financed projects. However, when these loans do not fit in well within the overall policy framework envisioned by the PETs, even in the best of circumstances, they are almost from the start bound to fail in ensuring greater productive efficiency and improving the allocation of resources.

Finally, as already intimated in Chapter 5, the western assistance program is somewhat of a misnomer. Though the Commission of the EC was requested to elaborate a comprehensive program in close cooperation with other international agencies, little genuine coordination has thus far emerged. Clearly, there have been numerous formal and informal contacts among the many agencies involved. But there is as yet no rump blueprint of precisely what could be done most effectively to keep the process of change in the PETs moving along at an affordable socioeconomic cost. This criticism applies not only to the safeguarding of turf that is the traditional hallmark of World Bank and IMF operations, the latter two frequently not even dovetailed in spite of these institutions being physically located across from each other. It would appear to be so too of the EC itself. Devising a coherent program has elicited greater interest in allocating the "management overhead, responsibilities, and travel programs" than in ensuring that the maximum impact of the given assistance fund is being extracted for the PETs themselves with minimal adverse repercussions for other countries.

On the face of it, there would, therefore, appear to be considerable room for greater harmonization of efforts, both with respect to the priorities of the PETs in moving toward the RPE variant they covet and with regard to the internal synchronization of the western efforts themselves. Too many ill-prepared missions are currently overwhelming the absorptive capacity of the Eastern European top-heavy bureaucratic and fleeting political structures in place. In addition to the sheer claim on physical and human resources, considerable problems have also arisen in consequence of conflicting advice being offered. This often stems from different ideological precepts within the various organizations involved in some aspect of the assistance programs.

I have two main other criticisms of the western efforts. One is the question of the role and function of the CMEA for the PETs and whether there is room at all for pursuing regional integration, possibly with active western support. This may in the end require a degree of explicit discrimination against trade with the DMEs or perhaps also DEs, at least in the short run and as a precondition for creating the necessary structures to engage soon fully in the global multilateral trading and financial worlds. That issue does not yet seem to have been addressed. I shall devote Chapter 9 to this entire topic. The other is that the current leadership of most PETs appears to be imbued with the spirit of the ME as it may have been heralded at one point by its most optimistic textbook proponents; some may even have sworn by it in the 19th century. Even worse is the ostensible commitment to liberalism and democracy, two weaselwords *par excellence* that mean quite different things to the many actors involved in this grand remaking of Eastern Europe. Rare have been suggestions that full-fledged democratic decision making may well not be the most desirable - read effective - path to laying the foundations of solid export-oriented economic reform (Amsden 1990). No effort is being made to temper this apparent naiveté or to reach a clear consensus on what must be done as a minimum and what in addition would be desirable to facilitate east-west integration regarding the for now unshakable belief in the ME. MEs have a long history of coming to terms with the benefits as well as the drawbacks of markets. Without a proper institutional framework, including on regulatory powers to ensure legal standing and protect against market failures, an essential component of the transmission of knowledge seems to be missing.

Certainly no less important a consideration is that the PET is characterized by substantial rigidities that pervade the economic framework, especially the supply side of the market equation. It is not very helpful to shift relative prices overnight in the expectation that there will be a very quick supply response. Of course, there will be a reaction to the monetary squeeze because SOEs will no longer be able to honor their commitments and, as a result, will be forced into some *de facto* default. Formal bankruptcy may be a desirable outcome for some of the more inefficient SOEs that should not survive the restructuring effort. However, to accomplish that goal by undermining the viability of substantial portions of the economy that would otherwise thrive, however modestly, is not a commendable way to proceed. Though the process of selecting which SOE is viable and which is not will in the end require some arbitrary choices, that choice issue need not be tackled until the trade-off becomes unclear for lack of transparent, market-determined scarcity indicators. I suggest that the PETs in their present cloak are still very far from that stage and should have at their disposal more positive criteria to guide firms into bankruptcy and others into market-conform behavior. Disappointment with market-oriented reforms in PETs is almost preordained, if not on the part of the leadership, certainly among wide layers of the population. The example of quixotic privatization at all cost and under just about any circumstance, whose negative features were examined in Chapter 7, suffices in this regard.

2. On the creation of a market

As sketched in Chapter 4, the prospects for genuine market-oriented reform in the former CPEs or MPEs are at this juncture rather favorable, certainly more promising than they ever were in the postwar period. The reason is partly political. With the near-collapse of the Communist Parties and the emasculation of their erstwhile all-overpowering role in social life, including economic affairs, there is presently a fair chance of working toward a better-defined separation of technical economic affairs and social precepts on property build-up and uses. The latter include the distribution of incomes so as to ensure some modicum of social equality that reflects societal preference, ascertained now through a much more democratic way of decision making. The purpose of distinguishing between technical economics and other matters would be to improve the efficiency of resource allocation and at the same time fulfill tasks that the market will not take care of under normal circumstances. For example, the market fails notoriously in allocating resources to those not now contributing to the production process either as workers or by placing their assets at the disposal of users at some positive rent.

A market is almost tautologically concerned with resource allocation. It is thought to be the most effective way of ensuring the efficient exploitation of resources under most circumstances (Lavoie 1990). The latter do, of course, require some interference by central powers to mitigate market failures. Note that the market system as such has little to say about the distribution and possible abuses of ownership, regardless of the great emphasis placed on this element by the neo-Austrian school (Shand 1984). Especially its more libertarian exponents (Leipold 1983, 1988; Pejovich 1987, 1989) have derived their claims primarily from liberal commitments rather than solid economics.

Inasmuch as a market is concerned with resource allocation, its logical address must target both input and output structures. Regarding inputs, there is ultimately capital and labor, and of course land and other natural resources. On the output side, there is essentially wholesale and retail trade of goods and services, the distribution of incomes between consumption and accumulation, and the distribution of working time between leisure and work; whether the output on the resource ledger is negative or nominally constant is a matter that society should decide upon because the market's failure in this respect is notorious, partly in view of the short-range outlook of private agents.

There is currently little dispute about the need to entrust the entire gamut of wholesale and retail trading operations for both goods and services to instances other than allocation through the central planning mechanism, specifically the material-technical supply system. In the case of wholesale trading, it will of necessity have to emerge by firms interacting with one another strictly on the basis of economic interests and profitability. Similarly in the case of retail trade. It will need to be increasingly geared by small firms of a private and cooperative nature trying to improve upon the rather dismal record of state retail outlets.

There is likewise little dispute about the choice between work and leisure. Excepting a few years of overly ambitious regulation, this aspect of the allocation process has always been dominated by sovereign decision making, subject, however, to more or less rigid, at times even all-embracing sociopolitical rules on shirking and idleness. There is little doubt that trading off leisure against labor income is now largely a matter up to the individual, certainly within institutional arrangements that can be flaunted only by becoming an independent contractor or business operator - both alternatives now distinct possibilities. Inasmuch as the labor allocation process cannot be left completely to free-market operations, however, there is a need to come to some arrangement on labor representation and how best to resolve disputes. The formation or activation of genuine trade unions on the pattern of Western Europe's may be required to guarantee that labor rights are respected yet not abused for whimsical reasons. A labor-management dispute-settlements procedure may have to be worked out as part of the social consensus.

The key outstanding market issue is that of capital allocation, not ownership per se.[1] It is a paramount issue, if only because one of the structural pillars of socialism has been public ownership of the means of production, which was seen as the *sine qua non* for avoiding alienation and exploitation of labor, neither of which was achieved under real-existing socialism, however. Allocating capital resources is essentially a matter of how best to organize capital markets in the sense that some ownership forms are better suited to allocate capital services at a smaller cost than others.

The key question that faces PETs at this juncture is what to do with publicly owned capital now that the state has decided in principle to withdraw from exercising direct ownership functions. It is a vexing issue with all kinds of colorations, some more disquieting than others, that are being shaded depending upon the ideological bent of the individual commentator. The battle cry of the most liberal reformers in the PETs, with the active support of many international organizations and more privately organized interest groups, has been the widespread privatization of state assets by selling off or giving them away. In some cases, this may be warranted. If the coordination tasks involved in improving the optimal use of capital assets can be accomplished at lesser cost, other things being equal, than through a formal market process, then obviously private property would be the answer. But even under those conditions it does not necessarily follow that privatization should be enacted quickly and below fair market value.

Perhaps the most critical task in organizing the capital market can be tackled best after recognizing two facts. One is that neither private nor public ownership of the means of production guarantees the most efficient use of capital resources. Hence, from an economic perspective, it would seem justified to throw ideological bonds over board and put in place as neutral an environment for property forms to emerge as possible (Szénási 1989, p. 169). The simple acceptance of the proposition that what matters is the allocation of the user rights to capital is at stake. By disjoining, at least conceptually, ownership from ownership rights (all property rights minus alienation of the assets), one could start thinking about the proper technical issues involved. In that context, second, it would be extremely important to recognize without inhibition that in a PET any kind of property form may exist because there will be at least one productive endeavor for which each of the possible forms that can be imagined (private, cooperative, corporate, public, and various mixes) will be best suited.

Regardless of how the capital market is organized, a critical element on the agenda should be the regulation of entry and exit. If that right is not available to whomever is able, and willing, to accumulate wealth or entitled to bid on the user rights to wealth at whatever personal risk involved in the chosen venture, it is hard to envisage how the capital allocation process can be organized efficiently. Even if existing capital assets are kept in public hands directly or

[1] There is a marvelous, if admittedly "personal utopia," expressed by the present president of Czechoslovakia, Mr. Václav Havel (1989, pp. 17-22). In spite of its utopian character, I think he is absolutely correct in arguing (pp. 17-18) that the real problem of a socialist society is not ownership but rather how to ensure that individuals can realize themselves - can avoid getting alienated - throughout the production process by having an interest in their work.

indirectly, exit and entry should be ensured both for the formation and utilization of new capital. It should also apply in competing for the user rights to existing, publicly owned assets. That, to my mind, can best be organized through some form of competitive bidding.

Whereas with the recognition of exit and entry, new capital formation will occur according to whatever suits the best allocation of resources subject to regulatory powers where there are palpable market failures, this cannot be anticipated for the publicly owned capital stock at the outset of the movement toward the status of a PET. The answers to the key questions of privatization and property rights' reform of existing assets, then, should revolve around the allocation of capital services, that is, the usufruct of capital assets and guaranteeing that it does not erode or misappropriate capital assets for "private" purposes. This applies with some minor modifications also to the use of natural resources, most of which cannot be privatized for one reason or another. There are, of course, other issues that concern entry, capital formation, innovation, and expansion of existing assets.

The leaderships of the new Eastern Europe have been much preoccupied with the creation of full-fledged capital markets. In setting for themselves such an ambitious agenda, it is frequently forgotten that there is room in the global economy for only a few efficiently organized full-fledged capital markets. These are essentially London, New York, and Tokyo, and perhaps Frankfurt and Zurich. Only in these centers is there a critical minimum to institute the entire gamut of financial-sector activities, from the ordinary commercial, merchant, and investment banks to all kinds of insurance companies, an effective money market with open-market operations and public financing of enterprises, and indeed to a widely organized public stock exchange. Not only that, these centers have become what they are only after a protracted, at times painful, evolution. This conjecture not only recognizes realities. Portfolio theory suggests that the best way for a new firm to finance itself initially is not through a public issue of stock, but through other financial channels revolving around bank intermediation (Brainard 1990). Once the venture succeeds and its capital needs are too large to be financed through other channels, the merits of a public stock offering can be entertained. Moreover, being constantly concerned about how one's stock is faring on public exchanges is not necessarily the most effective way to ensure medium- to long-term capital efficiency.

3. Macroeconomic policies

Following the approaches known as constitutional (Grosfeld 1990, Moser 1989) and institutional (Ickes 1990, Kanel 1974) economics, social interaction among individuals, corporations, and government agencies are conditioned by two broad sets of constraints. One is a physical one, arising from the limit on resources. In addition, behavior in society is also influenced by rules or institutional arrangements that govern the choices of individual actors (Pommerehne 1990). Rules essentially define the framework within which these ordinary choices are made. Because they shape the structure of incentives, they have an important bearing on outcomes. The postulates of constitutional economics imply that if the limits to individual behavior are well defined and the rights are recognized and accepted, social interaction will proceed in an orderly fashion. That is to say, an order will emerge within which the interdependent behavior of individually motivated agents is reconciled with the gradual pattern of outcomes that are tolerable to participants (Kanel 1974).

In the context of reconstituting countries, fundamental are the issues of control and coordination measures required not only to keep the reform on track but especially to guide the transition through the PET phase to that of the RPE. Very often, as amply demonstrated by the many MPE variants (see Chapter 3), the macroeconomic infrastructure in a CPE or MPE embarking on yet another reform is either that of the inherited model or ambivalent replacements are installed that are clearly not up to the mark (Kaletsky 1990). There are several ways to pursue the reform process. Some are feasible in theory and others may be set as an objective for practical action. The range of alternatives is determined by two extremes. One could be seeking measurable structural change in the CPE through full-fledged market mechanisms, except perhaps in some spheres in which the prerogatives of socialism remain very strong. Substantive structural change could also be sought as the outcome of an adaptive process. This would seek gradualism in introducing changes in economic structures with two purposes: (1) to cushion palpable social and economic costs associated with structural adaptations over time and (2) to ensure that the costs are distributed equitably, by some standard of measurement.

Whichever way decision makers opt to go, progress with economic reform will almost inevitably be conditioned by and anchored to incremental changes in development strategy and, more important, in the economic model in place. As discussed in Chapter 4, this raises questions about how best to coordinate policies and their underlying institutions and instruments, to substitute market coordination for the organizing principle embodied in central planning. Although critical, how to ensure proper coordination of decentralized decisions has rarely been examined comprehensively. This is regrettable for with the adoption of more democratic decision making in part through market relations the role of the government as coordinator shifts but it certainly does not vanish. There are two reasons for this. One derives from the role of government in the transformed societies as mandated by the electorate. The other is the need to maintain order in decentralized decision making. To discharge these functions, it is critical that those managing the transition toward an RPE institute comprehensive monetary and fiscal policies to steer the behavior of individual agents and satisfy social preferences. Instituting coherent macroeconomic policies in lieu of traditional central planning is an exceedingly complex assignment if only because the traditional CPE or MPE has not been very much concerned about this particular macroeconomic infrastructure.

To make headway in creating the macroeconomic infrastructure that will eventually be required to steer a sustainable RPE environment, key building blocks are the financial and monetary spheres, the legal protection of property rights and economic activity, and an adequate regulatory framework to ensure that market failures are taken care of. Arguably the most important issues to be taken up as soon as possible in the PET are those revolving around macroeconomic stabilization and encouraging private initiative as necessary conditions for bringing about the required transformation of the supply structure.

As discussed in Chapter 4, at the outset of the reform CPEs and MPEs suffer from three types of imbalances, namely those inherited from past macroeconomic policies, those emanating from current macroeconomic policies that entail monetary and fiscal imbalances, and those that result from restructuring relative prices and imposing a different, market-conform incentive structure on economic agents, especially by revising relative scarcity indicators - prices in the broad sense. Introducing market-conform behavior in an environment with a palpable monetary overhang or marked current macroeconomic imbalances (either because the fiscal base of government expenditures is being eroded or monetary discipline cannot be enforced upon SOEs) would seem to be the key to making a good start with market orientation. For that, monetary discipline is required. This can be achieved only if there is a monetary authority, such as a central bank, that can regulate and supervise monetary policy independently of government instructions, especially as regards the financing of government deficits (including of SOEs). Sound money and financial discipline can be attained only by separating government from monetary policy, once overall socioeconomic objectives are set through some concertation (Wolf 1990). Without this, any movement in the direction of entrusting autonomy to SOEs is bound to be undermined by the unenforceability of financial discipline. In the case of the CPE or MPE, such a shift toward monetary tightening in SOEs must necessarily be accompanied by provisions regarding exit and entry for otherwise it will prove impossible to enforce financial discipline. Furthermore, that institution should divest itself of its commercial banking activities by devolving those tasks increasingly to an emerging commercial banking network.

Setting up a comprehensive financial infrastructure is an urgent matter because it will be nearly impossible to induce greater flexibiliity in the use of resources without putting in place the means to promote effective financial intermediation. For many years to come, the PET and even the RPE will have to ensure that savings be earmarked in the most rewarding manner through ordinary financial institutions rather than through a full-fledged capital market. Critical components of such a financial infrastructure will most likely be commercial banks, perhaps patterned after those of continental Europe. That is to say, the independent banks should take on the character of commercial and investment banks, and perhaps even be involved in the monitoring of enterprises, whether privatized or not.

In most MPEs, commercial banks have been created by government, usually by simply detaching operational branches of the central bank, even though they may have had a nominally independent legal status, and investing them with an own statute. That has led to disappointing results. This was in fact programmed with the foolhardy decision to set up these institutions by simply assigning the loan portfolio of the erstwhile monobank and its affiliates to the newly created commercial banks. Inasmuch as that loan portfolio is of questionable financial merit, many loans extended to unprofitable SOEs in fact being worthless, endowing the new banks with questionable assets is not conducive to fostering rational, market-conform decisions.

What is required is the creation of financial institutions that have a fair chance of starting off with a clean slate. For that, the government will in fact have to separate bad from good loans in its portfolio and protect the newly created financial infrastructure from the consequences of unwise financial policies particularly during the MPE phase. There are various ways of recapitalizing these banks, including by opening up the domestic market to financial management imported from DMEs or to the establishment of foreign banks, possibly in the form of joint ventures with domestic institutions. Only then can these institutions be held responsible for their own decisions, for mobilizing fresh financial resources on the part of enterprises and households, and for lending money to those with a fair chance of succeeding.

Inasmuch as competition is a *sine qua non* for enforcing market discipline, although it is not a sufficient condition to ensure the best allocation of resources, the authorities in the PET must make headway with breaking up monopolies, encouraging foreign competition, and inducing economic agents into setting up ventures that can wage effective competition with the structures in place. The latter can be done by different means, including raising their own capital, through funds loaned from banks or central agencies at preferential rates, sales of state assets, managerial contracts for SOEs, and leasing of state assets.

Perhaps next in importance is coming to grips with the overmonopolized situation, a key legacy of the CPE and MPE environment. For that some degree of privatization may have to be pursued, which may furthermore help in enforcing the necessary monetary discipline. In addition, it will be necessary to ensure a reasonable degree of entry and exit, including for foreign capital. Whether the latter should be confined to joint ventures is an issue to be carefully weighed. Given the unbalanced situation at the start of the transition, it may well be advisable to move forward cautiously with attracting foreign capital at terms that, in retrospect, may turn out to have been quite onerous.

Putting in place an adequate competitive environment takes time, even under the most favorable of circumstances regarding the availability of capital funds and the awakening and nurturing of entrepreneurial and managerial cultures. It is, then, of the utmost importance to open up the economy to foreign competition as soon as circumstances permit. Of course, this will only be useful once the domestic economic situation exhibits a semblance of stability and headway can be made in adjusting relative prices, including the setting of an effective exchange rate. In this, policy makers may aim at making the local currency convertible for current account transactions. But the first step should be making foreign exchange available on an equitable basis to all legitimate commercial undertakings, perhaps through formal auctions of the type discussed in Chapter 4. Customs duties should take the place of the price-equalization mechanisms so typical of the CPE and MPE. BTPAs should be replaced by direct interenterprise negotiations as soon as feasible. This may not be possible in relations with CMEA members that have not yet opted for market orientation. Because such trade cannot be compressed overnight, as discussed at length in the next chapter, special arrangements may have to be explored to protect emerging domestic markets against dysfunctional signals emanating from such trading relations. The PET may also explore the usefulness of entering into formal arrangements with partner countries on the creation of a customs union with a view to fostering foreign competition and thereby promoting market-conform behavior. PETs finding themselves in similar situations may usefully explore joint actions of such a nature.

Part and parcel of economic stability is the financing of the government budget according to criteria approved by the parliamentary organs in place and in line with sound macroeconomic policy. Whether aggregate budget deficits can be tolerated depends very much on the social consensus and the ability of government to reform its fiscal stance. But simply running the printing press must be avoided. Instead, deficits must be financed in competition with other claimants on loans, which may lead to crowding out. An overhaul of the fiscal infrastructure is an urgent necessity. As SOEs are increasingly required to base their decisions on financial autonomy and own profitability through leases, management contracts, privatization, and suchlike divestments, the government will have to find substitutes for the earnings of SOEs to finance its outlays. Similarly, there is an urgent need to revamp the indirect tax system so as to minimize the distortions in scarcity indicators that the fiscal system in the past has introduced. Perhaps most important is that the government will have to implement its social mandate through income tax systems that do not discourage economic agents, yet ensure that the mandated income redistribution and funding of state expenditures can be implemented without having recourse to massive borrowing, which would crowd out private investment, or resorting to the printing press, which would only fuel inflation and depreciate the currency.

Although initially the government may not be overly concerned with inequities introduced through markets and hence the opportunities that become available to some economic agents, possibly at the expense of others, eventually some minimum market regulation will need to be instituted. Perhaps most critical in this respect is to foster monetary discipline for SOEs and setting in train a regulatory infrastructure that enjoins management of these firms to behave as in a private undertaking. There are various ways of doing so, as examined in Chapter 7. Most urgent is undoubtedly the strict enforcement of monetary discipline and having a commercial banking sector base its lending policy on the commercial viability of SOEs.

Perhaps the most glaring weakness of the CPE or MPE consisted in firms being managed by people experienced in administering firms in a highly bureaucratic fashion who had earned their spurs in Party politics and administration. Few of these people would have been able to succeed as managers in an environment where a premium is placed on economic profitability and enhancing the net worth of the firm. There is simply no way in which these layers can be replaced all at once. Furthermore, management in place embodies useful knowledge that cannot smoothly, if at all, be passed on to other individuals. That is to say, there is a need to retrain a vast layer of administrators, including from the ministries as well as enterprises so that they can become effective regulators, fiscal administrators, or successful managers. This could be achieved by changing training methods so that the next generation will be much better equipped for the task faced in a market environment. Unfortunately, it would be a tragedy if painful adjustments and the manifold nonmarket policy errors and interferences with the market were to have to be dragged out until the next generations can assume the proper mantle.

Inasmuch as the CPE and MPE provided security to the population, including through lifetime job guarantees, assured pensions, social security, low-cost necessities, and so on, the government of a PET should be concerned about mitigating the most adverse impacts of its economic and social restructuring on the weakest layers of society. This calls for putting in place an adequate social safety net. Whereas it will not be possible to maintain the all-embracing kind of overprotective social security typical of the *ancien régime*, it would be sociopolitical suicide to usher into such socialistic societies the destabilizing vagaries of raw capitalism.

From a technical point of view, one core maxim of market orientation should be "getting prices right." Without having in place instruments that ensure that relative prices reflect real relative scarcities, it will be impossible to coordinate decentralized decisions and ensure the best allocation of scarce resources. Prices in incipient PETs are heavily distorted through all kinds of mechanisms. Not the least are price-formation rules derived from an exceedingly antiquated average-cost rule justified vaguely on the labor theory of value (Brabant 1987b). Furthermore, the intrasectoral redistribution of profits thus mandated has brought about its own dysfunctional influences on enterprise decision making. Perhaps most detrimental has been the systemwide application of all kinds of government subsidies and taxes to preserve a good deal of domestic price autonomy, either for social welfare reasons or for what was thought to be required to ensure plan stability in the short to medium run.

Where to start with price revisions poses intricate problems. Rather than leave it up to as yet unexisting markets to generate *ex post* equilibrium prices, there would seem to be some room for government to provide minimum guidance. A useful intervention in fostering shifts in relative prices, especially for a small economy, would be to take WMPs of key inputs - including fuels and critical raw materials - and translating them at an estimated equilibrium exchange rate that is deemed to be real. I have no illusion that the latter can be spotted easily. But some fair estimate of the shadow cost of importing critical inputs can be prepared; even in economies that are net exporters of such goods, the opportunity cost of trading should be derived from WMPs. Once set, the authorities should be in a position to free up domestic price determination by setting a "fair" exchange rate. There may be a residual need for regulating pricing including of monopolies that have not yet been "corrected" and those that cannot be "corrected" for various reasons well known from the market context (see Chapter 7). Finally, market conform behavior requires a drastic change in behavior on the part of *all* economic agents. This includes households as consumers and providers of labor services. The required adaptations here will be less severe, chiefly in the case of reconfiguring the trade-off between work and leisure on the one hand and between consumption and savings on the other, than those needed to bring about new entrepreneurial and managerial cultures.

That is to say, the initial steps of the transition model should endeavor to get prices right for the microeconomic sphere or to move decisively in that direction. As a counterpart of the initial macroeconomic action, steps can be taken to change the gross direction of relative prices. Rather than leaving this up to the free play of market forces, by introducing the so-called "big bang," an alternative for countries that wish to move more gradually could be initiated by recalculating administratively set prices. Two traditional pitfalls of orthodox price reforms should be avoided: comprehensiveness and the desire to maintain domestic price autonomy.

4. On the sequencing of reforms

As argued earlier, transforming CPEs and MPEs into RPEs is a task fraught with hazards and uncertainty, if only because there are few experiences upon which managers of such a wholesale mutation or their advisers can rely for guidance and inspiration. Nonetheless, the transition needs to be molded in a comprehensive fashion and be carried out speedily. The order in which the various reform components are introduced is not, of course, a random matter at all. An ideal sequencing can be put forward only on the basis of successful experiments. Nonetheless, implicit in the above analysis is a certain kind of reform sequencing. One could consider basically four phases. The first one would be concerned with getting rid of chronic imbalances inherited from past mismanagement. To do so, room must be created to divert pent-up demand either to new goods made available to the domestic market or to new financial instruments; monetary reform in some cases cannot be avoided. State assets may have to be renationalized to establish clear property rights. In this phase it may already be useful to recognize the full scale of property rights and to allow the gradual buildup of new property structures from gross state, corporate, and private savings. To help blot up excess money balances, a start should be made with the privatization of small-scale undertakings (such as retail and service outlets), handicrafts, and housing. Also broadly based land reform, perhaps along the "China theorem" (Hewett 1989), may be required so that farmers can obtain access to the residual profit of their efforts to maintain and improve the land and work it as effectively as they know how to.

The next phase of the reform program should be concerned with reestablishing macroeconomic balance in current monetary and fiscal policies. This should be directed in the first instance at regaining domestic balance (Nuti 1990), but with the gradual shift of resources so as to reestablish external balance in due course as well. For that, a tight monetary policy will be needed and fiscal reforms will have to be sought to ensure that the government budget does not become the chronic source of inflation. Big monopolies should be quickly broken up into meaningful autonomous units. Other remaining assets (including housing, handicrafts, small service centers, and land) should be privatized quickly through bidding procedures open to all. If savings have been wiped out through inflation, generous financing at a realistic interest rate may be desirable because private property in this case is the most effective way of coordinating the service flow of these capital assets. At the start, prices are likely to be volatile. A trustee appointed with the support of parliament, to which responsibility is owed, should organize such auctions. Of course, experimentation and publicity may initially be required to overcome entrenched skepticism and inertia about state auctions. Regarding land, a bold move forward with *de facto* land reform would seem to commend itself. Finally, all SOEs (excepting perhaps for some strategic goods and public utilities) should be turned into joint-stock companies and placed under the supervision of an impartial, professional body that may have to purchase some state liabilities in exchange for acquiring these assets. Again, the trustee should supervise such transfers. At the same time, full property rights have to be established to encourage the formation of new capital from private sources. To foster also competition the Government may even consider enacting financial inducements, for example, by making loans available from amortization funds as well as new savings at favorable interest rates or with fiscal incentives.

The next logical step would seem to call for enforcing competitive behavior by creating a regulatory environment and an incentive scheme that will ease the principal-agent problem in SOEs. Gradually, such assets should be allocated through competitive bidding for leases or management contracts, with the supervisory authority being charged with maximizing the return on assets and seeing to it that sufficient insurance schemes are put in place to minimize abuses. At the same time, the government should continue with comprehensive stabilization, fiscal reform, and demonopolization. It should vigorously foster market-type pricing, perhaps by first anchoring key input prices to WMPs at a realistic exchange rate and changing relative prices in a "gross sense" (Hewett 1989). The determination of wholesale and retail prices of consumer goods and services could be deferred to markets. At the same time, progress can be made with other wholesale prices provided the material-technical supply system is in essence replaced by wholesale trade.

Once the former SOEs are behaving like competitive firms, and the most urgent structural adjustments have been completed, their privatization through outright sale should get under way at a measured pace. This should take the form of feeding the budding domestic stock market or opening to bids for domestic and foreign capitalists.

5. Is western assistance in need of reform?

A comparison between what should ideally be embraced in western assistance efforts, on the basis of what reformers hope to accomplish, as analyzed here and in the preceding chapter, and are most in need of and western governments find it worth supporting, given their own interests as analyzed in Chapter 5, suggests that there remains ample room for improvement. Donor countries may become frustrated very quickly, and recipient countries - and especially their population at large - disillusioned beyond recourse unless the reform package is quickly streamlined from two points of view. One is the purely institutional parts of western assistance. There is a need to improve coordination among the various reform efforts of bilateral, multilateral, governmental, and private agencies. In addition, there is presently no coherent view of how the at times conflicting calls for speed, comprehensivenss, and sequencing of reforms can best be harmonized.

Perhaps more important is the technique of assistance. Formulating a support program that dovetails best with the reform ambitions envisioned in PETs is in the first instance a technical economic issue, namely how to obtain maximum benefit from limited resources. As argued earlier, the most desirable forms of assistance are for emergency purposes; for building the technical (private as well as public) institutional, financial, and legal infrastructures; and the training of cadres in economic policy formulation, management, capital market participation, and what is required to ensure public scrutiny according to commonly accepted criteria.

An example may illustrate my case. Economists in CPEs and MPEs are trained in the political-economy thinking of Marxism-Leninism. That contains quite a bit of sound long-term macroeconomic policy, especially on the steady-state growth environment and long-term equilibrium. It has very little to say, however, by way of short-term stabilization policies or price-related, market-oriented decision making because these were not the topics uppermost on the inquisitive mind of Karl Marx and indeed in some aspects of economic policy formulation as well, has always been stronger in the more committed CPEs (such as Bulgaria, the GDR, and the Soviet Union) than in the more reform-flagellated Eastern European countries. Nonetheless, the Marxist frame of reference, however useful in other contexts, is not quite appropriate to either micro- or macroeconomic policy making in an economy bent on quickly reestablishing markets and indirect economic coordination. These countries could, of course, gradually train their own cadres. But that would take at least a generation. Time is perhaps the commodity in greatest scarcity in the reform process.

Some assistance from the west may come in very handy here, although it is hard to imagine that such help could be designed wholly without imparting an ideological or cultural bias. This is particularly the case for assistance provided through educational and cultural exchanges. Educational systems inevitably pass on values held by the societies that have nurtured them. Thus, for those reforming economies that strive to enlarge the private sector and to move all but completely to the free market environment, given that the United Kingdom has spent the past decade moving drastically away from an increasingly government-managed economy, a stint at a U.K. institution of higher learning could be very rewarding. Furthermore, the U.K. economy is at its strongest in precisely those areas where the Eastern European economies are at their weakest: from financial services through the media to supermarkets. And British business might be favorably disposed toward putting up the kitty required to finance such scholarships, rather than to leave the assistance entirely up to governments or international organizations, in either case financed from the public purse. Likewise, as far as fundamental and applied research is concerned, a study tour in Japanese and North American schools could be very rewarding.

Similar caution is in order when a rapid pace of privatization is proposed. Western experience stresses the crucial importance of competition in the relevant sector in order for the potential gains in efficiency to be realized (Yarrow 1986). A change in ownership may simply transform a public monopoly into a private one, although the private managers will probably be better paid than when they were in the public sector. Because there are major problems in establishing correct estimates of net worth in the PETs, there is considerable risk that social assets will be sold off at prices that would imply large transfers of wealth to the old managers and to former members of the *nomenklatura*.

The rush to attract foreign investment into Eastern Europe may also be premature if a competitive market framework is still far from completion. It is a mistake to believe that all foreign firms require a competitive ME in which to operate. As long as they have security of title to their assets and guarantees of profit repatriation, foreign enterprises, like most musicians, will be happy to play according to whatever the baton of the orchestra's conductor calls for. However, if the framework ensures that the market will be at least reasonably competitive, foreign firms can play an important role in maintaining and increasing competition, as well as in transferring technology, modern management techniques, capital, and the wherewithal of what is required to broach convertible currency markets.

It is worth recalling here also that many of the supply-side policies adopted by the MEs in the 1970s were aimed at deregulation and facilitating competition. There is a variety of experience among the MEs which increases the chance of individual PETs finding policies and techniques that are in line with their own particular preferences and situation. There is also considerable expertise on these matters as well as knowledge about the structures in place in incipient PETs, both in official (national and international), academic, and private institutions on which PETs could easily draw. A technical assistance program could easily be set up for the PETs to obtain expert advice in this area. It will not be expensive and the long-run returns could be very beneficial indeed.

Such specialists are, moreover, familiar with the nature and causes of market failure in the MEs, issues that are not often enough emphasized in the public discussions of the possibilities of creating markets in Eastern Europe. Efficiency gains of a decentralized market system depend on the degree of competition in product, capital, and labor markets.[2] Since real world markets are usually far from satisfying the optimality conditions of perfect competition, because of monopolies, externalities, or public goods, government intervention to try to improve the efficiency of markets can never be excluded on *a priori* grounds. There is nearly 200 years of experience with government intervention to come to grips with market failure, from nationalization to competition policy, as well as pervasive efforts to seek to make markets more competitive.

Technical assistance will also be needed to set up a variety of financial institutions (commercial and investment banks, insurance companies, pension funds, and so forth) vital for the efficient working of an ME. There is an abundance of specialized technical expertise in all these areas in DMEs, upon which the PETs may easily draw. Because the possibilities are numerous, it might be wise to use first the more general advisers mentioned in the previous paragraphs to obtain guidance as to the types of institutions and financial expertise that are likely to be best suited to the particular needs and circumstances of individual PETs as they evolve toward RPE status.

Another area that should be given high priority, because of its importance to the efficient functioning of an ME is the collection, processing, and dissemi-

[2] The Austrian school's case for the market rests more on its superiority as a coordinating mechanism in a situation of uncertainty and imperfect information. As represented by Hayek, the school's case for markets also rests on libertarian value judgements.

nation of quantitative and qualitative information about the economy and society as a whole. In this regard, the deleterious state of statistics of CPEs and MPEs has recently been the subject of ample - in some cases devastating - comment. Much of this criticism has focused on the poor coverage or inaccuracy of the published data. The precise extent to which this is due to biases in the reporting systems, to defective methodologies, or to deliberate falsification is difficult to ascertain. But there is no dispute that official statistics exhibit major deficiencies.

An efficient economy needs not only accurate statistics but different types of quantitative and qualitative information from that required in a CPE or MPE. In the first place, macroeconomic policy in an ME relies mainly on various instruments of fiscal and monetary policy, rather than direct controls. As such, it requires a different information base than that of a central planner. Some of these statistics, particularly in the monetary field, will only be generated, of course, after certain institutional and behavioral changes have occurred. Second, the provision of reliable economic and commercial information becomes essential to efficient decision making in individual firms as they move from a command system to one where they must themselves choose inputs, outputs, and investment in response to market signals. It is also a public good that can make a crucial contribution to the efficient working of an ME. The PETs also require statistics to monitor their progress and to track adjustments in economic behavior to the new incentive systems. Such data will be necessary for the effective fine-tuning of particular policies. They may also be required by foreign donors of financial aid and technical assistance. In this context the institution of business surveys, as conducted by business organizations or research institutes in the west, could make a useful contribution.

Statistics in the broad sense is thus another priority area where a technical assistance program could be speedily effective in helping to meet the requirements of the evolving PET. Most reforming countries already have competent statistical offices and this should ensure that effective programs can be drawn up fairly quickly and soon yield tangible results. Once the requirements for assistance are clear, a well-defined program of financial assistance in this area, for example for computers and target software, could easily follow.

The radical reforms under way in the PETs will obviously need to address a considerable number of the factors behind the deteriorating export performance of these economies. The collection and use of market intelligence and the whole range of skills required to compete effectively in world markets are areas that have been neglected for many years but are crucial for improving export performance. Not only that: Most PETs must come to grips with a burdensome external debt and will need to broaden market access to gain entry abroad and anchor export-led growth by dismantling the MFT in favor of instituting a full-fledged commercial policy. This may be quite protective on a transitory basis. The gradual adjustment of restrictions on imports not only reflects an element of the postwar Marshall Plan but is well-founded in the classical tradition of MEs. Especially the EC has made the removal of import quotas and related restrictions subject to continued progress in economic and political reform. If such progress were to stop, the restoration of quotas might very well be amplified by what happens after 1992. Clearly, if all PETs embark on roughly the same path of radical reform, approximately the same concessions will have to be granted to all. This could lead to adjustment problems in the EC. It might therefore be necessary either to set a timetable for the gradual elimination of all restrictions or to increase the available funds for restructuring and/or regional assistance, something that seems useful in any case, given that the supply responses in PETs are not likely to be very rapid. The elimination of restrictions would have to be precise and strictly adhered to in order to avoid endless postponements being obtained by special interest groups. This provides then another area for technical assistance.

The creation of internationally competitive firms is a slow process, and the PETs will have to do this at a time when the competitive pressures in Western Europe will be increasing as the Single Market act is being put into place by late 1992. Moreover, the process is complicated by the need for such a large number of interrelated reforms in the economic systems in which firms from PETs currently operate. As noted in Chapters 1 and 2, the CMEA has not led to a high degree of production specialization and has failed to meet many of its original objectives regarding stimulating growth in its member countries. Relations among the CMEA members are strained at present because of problems in clearing intragroup trade. In part, these stem from increasing divergence in the pace and extent of the various reform programs. Some PETs appear to be turning away from the CMEA altogether. But it is worth considering whether some reform could provide an intermediate but temporary stage between the rigid bilateralism of the traditional CMEA and full integration in a world economy through multilateralism and free trade. Again, some lessons can be drawn from the postwar reconstruction of Western Europe and the way in which it was funded and administered with foreign assistance (see Chapter 9).

* * *

The manifold problems being faced by the PETs, and those Eastern European countries currently moving toward that status, are daunting. No ready recipe is available. Imaginative policy making will be required not only to see the process through at a tolerable social and political cost, but also to ensure that the adjustment burden incurred will not have been in vain. Much of that burden can only be borne by these societies themselves. But to the degree that third countries are willing to come to their assistance, the magnitude of the adjustment cost can be alleviated and the process of transition accelerated.

On the strength of the arguments developed here, there would seem to be room to further curb the adjustment burden and its duration without necessarily appropriating more resources than the DMEs and some newly industrializing economies (NIEs) have already committed. Some streamlining both in the organization of the assistance effort and in targeting it more precisely at what the PETs want and need to accomplish would seem to be required. As suggested, high priority should be accorded to providing technical assistance in a wide area of activities, including public finance, monetary policy, commercial bank intermediation, regulatory and competition policies, adequate public information, enterprise management, public administration, all kinds of legal codes, and integration in global markets. Since the requisite information is readily available in DMEs and such a package would not be very expensive, this type of assistance could be very cost-effective and yield substantial results in a short period of time. In addition, much useful knowledge can be transferred that would enable the PET to succeed in international markets, provided the countries will undertake painful restructuring and foster FDI, including importantly by TNCs. Most of the capital required to assist in the industrial restructuring of the PETs should be mobilized privately, including through FDI and portfolio choices reached on the basis of commercial decisions. Governments may wish to enhance the environment within which private investors make their decisions with respect to the PETs. Some investment guarantee schemes and dissemination of information about investment opportunities and the way to go about taking advantage of them would be exceedingly important. Again, this should be quite cost-effective in the short run.

The above call for allocating priority attention to technical assistance does not, of course, obviate the need for sizable financial transfers. Apart from emergency requirements, capital transfers will be needed to come to grips with the external debt and debt-service obligations of the PETs and to assist these countries in opening up their economies through moving resolutely toward currency convertibility, at least for current account transactions. A fund in support of efforts to make the Eastern European currencies convertible, provided the countries involved were to be willing to promote market orientation and monetary and fiscal stability, would be an exceedingly constructive way of assisting the mutation processes in the PETs and facilitating their integration into the world economy and the global concert of nations.

There is presently no single instance that can coordinate all of these efforts to the benefit of the PETs. Perhaps the newly created EBRD could play a pivotal role in this transmission process. For that to occur, however, its founding members should put in place firm policies as regards the kind of projects that the bank will support in conjunction with specific policies to be promoted. If, as expected, the bank will simply emulate the traditional adjustment packages of the Fund or World Bank, it cannot succeed in generating the greatest bang for the bucks that donor countries have been willing to make available to PETs. The creation of a new institution from the ground up provides a unique opportunity for putting in place an imaginative policy with respect to assisting the economic restructuring of emerging democracies. It would be tragic if this opportunity were squandered because of ideological and political bickering about how individual countries can best assist the transformation processes in Eastern Europe, including the Soviet Union.

Assistance to the reform in PETs can also be provided by these countries collaborating with each other with a view to alleviating unnecessary burdens arising from the disintegration of their habitual economic cooperation in the context of the CMEA. How this could best be done is the subject of the next chapter.

9

Remaking the CMEA and east-west assistance

As argued in Chapter 1, most participants in the debates on remaking Europe in general and Eastern Europe in particular have simply written off the CMEA. Inasmuch as this decision appears to be motivated by looking at several cloaks of the CMEA that are not at the core of the current debate, the pivotal trade and payments problems of the reforming CMEA members, and the available room for cooperation on economic grounds, this assessment is incomplete at best. This chapter argues the case for remaking the CMEA, if necessary under a different name, while at the same time facilitating the further integration of the PETs and other reforming CMEA countries into global trade, financial, and monetary relations. This integration should be looked at in the context of the organized global economic framework as well as from the point of view of less formal, but no less important, private relationships in the global economy. The repercussions of remaking Eastern Europe and, in the end, Europe are many. Some of the economic aspects thereof point in the direction of the need to reformulate the postwar global economic framework in more than one respect, an issue that I shall take up in more detail in the last chapter.

In Section 1, I paint the general background against which the multiple issues invoked by thinking about the remaking of Eastern Europe could best be placed. The case for remaking the CMEA is the subject of the next section. What can be accomplished in terms of trade and payments regimes is discussed in the next two sections. The potential western contribution to the emergence of that state of affairs is sketched in Section 5 together with how the German monetary union may inhibit - at any rate slow down - the emergence of such desirable east-west cooperation. The final section looks at the usefulness of creating a constitutional framework for revamping the CMEA.

1. General backdrop to Eastern European integration

As emphasized in Chapters 5 and 6, there are several similarities between the plight of much of Eastern Europe, including the Soviet Union, at this stage and the economic and political situation in Western Europe, including the United Kingdom, after World War II. In fact, there is a host of parallels even between the crisis atmosphere of 1947, which was aggravated most notably by the abrupt failure of sterling convertibility, and the current imbalances in Eastern Europe. But it needs to be recognized too that for PETs to move decisively forward with economic restructuring and growth, measures are called for that are of an entirely different scale, given the background against which this evolution needs to be seen and the mechanisms needed to sustain the successful revolutions of late 1989 and early 1990.

There are undoubtedly many individuals in east and west who feel strongly about the political gains reached against the interests of the Soviet Union and the need to weld the newly won democracies into the liberal economic, social, and political frameworks of Western Europe. This may be a very desirable option to aim at in the medium to long run. For the time being, however, the PETs are not ready to assume the incumbent responsibilities. They could therefore become, perhaps chronically, dependent on western assistance.

When looking at the international economic relations of these countries, one area that deserves priority attention in the gamut of assistance efforts is rebuilding their international trade and payments regimes as quickly as possible. In many respect, it should aim at erecting an environment that functions as easily and successfully as the one that was slowly regained in Western Europe after World War II, with a considerable degree of U.S. financial, political, and moral support, persuasion, and indeed cajoling. I launch this argument simply from the point of view of the situation of the Eastern European countries themselves, regardless of the position taken by some new-fangled politicians in the area. The experience of Western Europe after World War II, given the presence of the United States, the recalcitrance of the United Kingdom and its imperial preference, and the lingering doubts about French-German reconciliation, is extremely instructive for at least two reasons. Perhaps most important, it helps to make, what I hope is, a persuasive case for greater economic cooperation among the Eastern European countries themselves - the PETs in the first instance - as a precondition for constructing a solid buttress upon the basis of which these countries will be able to gradually strengthen their eventual fuller integration into the all-European framework. I believe it also renders a cogent case for providing active Western European financial as well as other support. This cooperation should preferably be channeled into areas where the need of the Eastern European countries is greatest and the inflow of nonprivate funds from abroad, including for FDI and portfolio investment, would in all likelihood face the least amount of distortions. This may, perhaps paradoxically, require that the west temporarily accepts discriminatory treatment in trading relations, even in violation of international commitments, such as those of the General Agreement.

Several propositions and suggestions for action can be built on the strength of the arguments launched in connection with the daunting tasks of PETs making a successful transition to RPE status (see Chapter 4) and the, in some respects, poorly conceived and inadequately coordinated, if undoubtedly well-meant, western assistance efforts (see Chapters 5 to 8). Inasmuch as PETs have committed themselves to pursuing greater integration in the world economy through a wholesale restructuring of their trading sectors and the pursuit of export-led growth policies, the paramount task of economic policy is arguably ensuring that these countries can participate fully in international trade. This cannot be done quickly, given the various constraints faced by these PETs in their trade and payments relations with respect to both the TR and the convertible currency area. Certainly, declaring a convertible currency with a flexible exchange rate could provide a sufficient condition for fusing PETs into the world economy. It would be sufficient in the sense that a relentless depreciation of the currency would eventually enable the country to balance its external accounts, abstracting for the moment from the existing foreign debt. However, in the process, resources might be decommissioned that, under normal competitive conditions, would have been warranted in the sense that they could have been operated at a positive rate of return to assets exceeding the required rate. Adjusting to the external environment without some transition mechanism could possibly occur at a level of living well below what appears needed to sustain the transition process and hold together the social fabric of these countries. Such an eventuality would therefore be self-defeating both for the present leadership of the PETs as well as for the west, given its self-interest in seeing the democratization and marketization processes succeed in Eastern Europe.

The existing and budding PETS face similar problems in their external trade and current payments relations. There is generally speaking at best weak prospect of genuinely rationalizing trade with the TR region through direct interfirm relations that determine prices and quantities of traded goods, subject to clear rules on foreign exchange policy. How can the trading and payments mechanisms of these countries be rebuilt while maintaining at least modest growth and keeping the structural adjustment process on track? Part of the answer is predetermined by what these countries want to accomplish themselves. Another part needs to be formulated on the basis of the facilities that the PETs will receive to carry out in particular the foreign aspects of the envisaged reform blueprints. Some can be made operational from within their primary trading regime, and these issues are discussed here. Others depend on how these countries will ultimately be integrated in the world economy, which is the subject of the next chapter.

2. The case for remaking the CMEA

Because of the breathtaking pace of changes in Eastern Europe, the CMEA has *de facto* been disintegrating; at the very least, it has been immobilized in a number of respects, as set forth in Chapter 1. This outcome was partly unanticipated. But it owes a good deal to the malaise of SEI since the late 1970s (see Chapter 2). Because of the severe difficulties in their regional cooperation efforts over the past decade or so, CMEA members have been pondering reforms of their regional cooperation infrastructure for a long time, so far largely in vain (Brabant 1987c; 1989a, f; 1990c, j). The sequence of official deliberations about CMEA reform is very tedious. Especially with the failure of the 45th Council Session (Sofia, 9-10 January 1990) to enact incisive reforms, the question whether the CMEA is, in fact, defunct has arisen with increasing frequency; its counterpart, namely whether serious efforts should be initiated to ensure its survival at all, has also been posed. It is clear that all attributes of that integration process painstakingly founded on the socialist qualifiers should now be considered null and void. But regional integration remains something worth pondering. Finding solutions to the issues underlying the debates of the 1980s is, of course, a task yet to be fully addressed.

Recent policy deliberations in Eastern Europe have left little doubt about the fact that the proposals regarding CMEA reform soon to be tabled focus on three developments. One concerns the very *raison d'être* of the CMEA, and several members of the present reform commission (see Chapter 2) have indicated their preference for changing both the name and the constitution of the CMEA and transforming the organization essentially into a regional secretariat comparable to the OECD for DMEs. Second, conventional arrangements for trade and payments, both within the framework of BTPAs and within the comparable CMEA-wide trade and payments arrangements, are bound to be abolished and replaced by purely bilateral arrangements. Prices in intragroup trade will be attuned much closer to WMPs, trade will be conducted primarily by autonomous firms on the basis of their own profit motives and settlements will be arranged through convertible currency clearing and, eventually, payments in convertible currency at exchange rates that approximate the real resource cost of trading with alternative markets. Finally, the new organization to be constituted should assist the member countries in their quest to become more fully integrated in the global economic framework. The multilateral cooperation principles of the CMEA worked out especially during the 1960s and 1970s are no longer acceptable. Intragroup integration efforts, in the sense of interlinking several economies through positive policy action, will no longer be on the agenda of policy discussions at the groupwide level. Greater emphasis on bilateral cooperation, and trade and payments negotiations, where possible with the support of the CMEA's successor organization, will be fostered.

The realignment of national and regional economic structures along precepts that have some economic rationale is bound to affect the level, geographical direction, and commodity composition of trade in ways that in time can only benefit global trade. The current trade allocation is by no means optimal in the sense that resources can be reallocated without harming any partner country. Greater orientation along comparative advantage lines cannot but improve these countries' welfare - and in the end also the world's. It would be desirable to find ways and means to buttress maintenance of buoyant trade flows among the reforming countries themselves, while enacting major structural changes. Suggestions in this direction have included the creation of a customs union and a settlements mechanism comparable to that used after World War II to assist Western Europe with a return to convertibility and an open trading system.

There are many reasons that plead for reinforcing the CMEA as the regional organization called upon to forge meaningful integration ties in Eastern Europe and for those linking up into the world. These can be divided into three group: (1) the existing dependencies in Eastern Europe, (2) the lack of a flexible trade and payments system that would enable quick switching of markets at a tolerable socioeconomic and political cost, and (3) the exploitation of static and dynamic comparative advantages some of which derive from there being an active CMEA. By elucidating these features, a good case can be made for at least taking a closer look at what can be done with the CMEA.

First of all, there can be no dispute that the CMEA countries depend on each other for a large share of their trade, although one may quibble about precisely how large that share in reality is. This is true in the exchange of regular commerce as detailed in Chapter 1. It is even more so in the case of primary factor supplies. Foremost is that the available capital stock cannot be scrapped outright and that the labor force cannot be retrained overnight. Far from it being replaceable in the short run, the existing capital stock will have to be utilized for years to come, in spite of its relative obsolescence when measured in terms of world standards. Similarly, the structure of labor skills fits the existing capital stock. This implies that for several years these countries will have little choice but to produce goods with technical characteristics that continue to be accepted in the CMEA, but not, or only partially, in world markets. Inasmuch as a substantial proportion of the existing capital stock, particularly of the machine park, is of CMEA origin, there will continue to be a demand for spare parts, components, maintenance, and servicing that can be provided only from within the CMEA. In fact, improving the processes whereby these goods and services are furnished can contribute measurably to raising the level of capital efficiency.

Neither should it be forgotten that for the most important traded products and services, the CMEA countries are strongly tied together through a common transportation and transmission infrastructure. This holds in the first instance for oil and gas pipelines. It also applies to the evening out of peak electricity usage across the CMEA group. Other transportation infrastructure, including the common wagon pool; the facilities for transshipment of river barges onto motherships for long distance shipment to the Indian Ocean; regulations on rail, road, and air transshipment; and many similar forms of regional cooperation forged in the past, is still in place. As such, it inevitably imparts advantages to the countries willing and able to improve the efficiency of this trade, while making use of the available infrastructure.

Any attempt to jettison the infrastructure in place (for example, by trying to substitute oil imports from the Middle East for shipments through the *Druzhba* pipeline system) is to founder quickly onto two reefs. One is that PETs have so far gathered little experience with fluctuating prices and quantities in spot markets. The other is that the capacity in place (such as crude oil unloading facilities in Poland) does not allow the quick switching of sources of supply at minimal cost. This capacity may be emplaced in a comparatively short period of time but the cost is likely to be very considerable indeed. Whether it is affordable and should be afforded at this stage, given the many other claims on scarce resources, are questions that policy makers should weigh very carefully.

Second, as examined at length in Chapter 3, the CMEA economies suffer from not having a convertible currency and from having anchored their external relations within the CMEA context to detailed BTPAs negotiated at a high governmental level. The PETs may try to change these features as quickly as circumstances permit. Regardless of policy makers' intentions and aspirations, however, such transformations can realistically be sought only over time even if PETs could afford to do so without trading with poorly reconstructed MPEs. Not only that, serious steps need to be set to buttress the emergence of a convertible currency in the near future. The lack of a convertible currency constrains the scope of the PETs for purchases of all kinds of western goods, including fuels and technology, required for maintaining economic growth and redirecting it to fostering modernization. It also limits the ability of these countries to purchase many other products that are currently procured from within the TR regime.

But the outlook for jointly enacting technical change in the trade and payments regimes specifically in support of the transformation sought by PETs is not altogether dim. Whereas it may be difficult - and counterproductive - to aim at the quick realization of convertibility, enacting meaningful changes in trade and payments practices is not. In Sections 5 and 6, I shall outline ways in which the PETs could streamline their payments regime, preferably in support of intragroup integration, while pursuing vigorously their other changes and making solid strides in the direction of laying the foundations for moving toward currency convertibility that they can support.

Finally, even if the PETs had a more solid financial capacity for importing products from outside the CMEA, a wide range of goods and services would continue to be traded within the CMEA because of satisfactory quality, geographical proximity, tradition, comparative marketing advantages, and so other. There are many measurable benefits of reinforcing trade ties within the CMEA, especially if these commercial relations could be placed on a more businesslike, rather than administrative, last. Clearly, if some CMEA members do not wish to embark on broad-based marketization, this would shrink the opportunities for reciprocal trade, but it would not eliminate them altogether. It is ironic that most observers applaud the present rush of western firms into CMEA markets. They obviously perceive a substantial potential for profitable trade, although that gamble may pay off only in the medium to long run. If the CMEA members were to succeed in enacting a much greater degree of marketization in their economies, they should be in a position by and large to emulate the postwar experience of Western Europe.

Basic market-oriented reforms should improve factor productivity and hence the competitiveness of the output of PETs. By more fully engaging in international commerce, including in intra-industry trade, these countries should be able to reap considerable scale economies from specialization. This would include the harmonization of the three different markets (domestic, CMEA, and west) for which these countries have been operating for so many years in a highly compartmentalized fashion. Once marketing conditions in east and west exhibit greater uniformity, the PETs should find themselves poised to switch markets according to prevailing economic conditions on the strength of competitiveness that eastern manufactures now lack. It would also facilitate integration into western markets on a more "regular" basis than the extraordinary conditions that are currently being explored. The creation of the Single Market in the EC, and perhaps the European Economic Space, would only reinforce this attractiveness. Larger and freer international markets would tend to lessen the power of domestic monopolistic elements, thereby strengthening reform of domestic market structures.

This broader framework within which reforms of the PETs should be seen has other benefits too. It would certainly assuage growing concern in the west about the ability quickly to absorb a substantial diversion of CMEA trade to the west. It would strengthen economic and political stability in the eastern area as such. Furthermore, it would tend to place competition between PETs and DEs on a more even keel, whose cutting edge should be the truly competitive position of the agents confronting each other on roughly comparable terms rather than through discriminatory trade-facilitation schemes.

As discussed in Chapter 1, economic relations among the CMEA members have recently been complicated by several negative developments, including obstacles in clearing agreed-upon trade volumes and divergences in reforms. CMEA members that seek to anchor their economy more and more through indirect economic coordination and market-oriented decisions encounter problems in dealing with countries that, by and large, still act through detailed central planning. Progress with gradually reserving ampler room for microeconomic decision making within a comprehensive macroeconomic control framework can occur only if CMEA relations are placed on a solid economic footing as well. Pending incisive reforms in trade and payments regimes, regional trade is being needlessly compressed and its harmonization with the newly emerging interests of the reforming economies impeded. For that reason, some of the reforming economies have expressed a preference to veer away from such extensive dependence on CMEA relations as quickly as possible. This sentiment is being buttressed in the context of the policy advice being offered by IEOs, most notably the Commission of the EC, the World Bank, and the IMF. This invokes two propositions. One concerns how to accomplish this trade diversion. In the short run, it would be very costly to do so, given that these countries are tightly interlinked in their trade. Even if a drastic change in the geographical distribution of trade, and the factor supply upon which such commerce has been predicated, were to be a policy objective in its own right, the paramount technical issue of how to accommodate the CMEA relations that cannot be suppressed in the short run, until either the integration mechanism can be reformed or the reforming members can redirect a substantial part of their trade to MEs, remains to be addressed.

The other proposition is much more fundamental and rests on the ineluctable existence of static comparative advantages within the region, which is a truism, and the potential for building up dynamic comparative advantages as well, if only because of growth through broad-based, market-oriented national economic reforms. From a technical economic point of view, then, these opportunities should be fully exploited. For that, the appropriate institutions, trade policies, and commercial policy instruments are urgently required.

To reconcile the orthodox trade and payments regimes of the CMEA as they operate today with the aspirations of the reforming economies, gradual accommodation of economic structures and processes through economic discipline is required. On that basis, productive processes that are really not warranted on economic grounds, as distinct from their *raison d'être* from the engineering point of view, for example, must be phased out as quickly as circumstances permit. Others that ought to be fostered to exploit true static and dynamic comparative advantages are in need of more suitable accommodation than has thus far been possible or even considered.

3. Reforming the trade regime

The essence of the CMEA's trade regime (see Chapter 1) is the accommodation at the regional level of the BTPAs that the members negotiate. For that to work, the CMEA set a policy regarding the conclusion of TRPs, it adopted rules and regulations on how to advance production specialization, and it continued to endorse that trade negotiations be conducted at comparatively high administrative levels under the supervision of the Ministry of Foreign Trade. In that sense, the trade regime has been intimately bound up with the existence of the MFT in each member economy, the desire of each member to separate its domestic transactions from its engagements with outside partners, and the preference for considerable domestic policy autonomy, including in price formation and income distribution. Inasmuch as this system has been extant since the end of World War II, and in a sense since the 1930s, it cannot be an easy matter to disengage from it quickly. If only for that reason, a gradual, three-phased approach could usefully be considered by PETs.

At the core stands the question of how best to ensure that domestic economic decisions, especially in the microeconomic sphere, are not overburdened by the irrational prices and administrative regulations so pervasive in the CMEA. Central authorities that have signed away commitments in formal BTPAs, including on production specialization and STC, may feel impelled to discharge these obligations for now. To do so, *ex post* subsidies and taxes need to be instituted to ensure that the transition in domestic pricing and entrepreneurial decisions based on competition, including WMP signals, is not obstructed or hollowed out from below. Differences between TRPs and domestic prices, or prices that are geared toward WMPs, must be absorbed through taxes and subsidies by the central budget. That trade yields a net fiscal revenue or expenditure, very much like the price-equalization account used to operate in the CPE and even MPE (see Brabant 1989a, pp. 229-45).

The second step should ensure that the next sequence of BTPAs is negotiated as much as possible on the basis of the microeconomic efficiency guidelines that are developing in the PET. Practical reasons may necessitate that also these agreements be negotiated bilaterally at a high-level rather than by the firms that will eventually be assigned to discharge those trade obligations. Even so, these negotiations need to be guided as much as possible by the emerging parameters of a more rational allocation pattern. Those adopted for "reasons of state" should be subsidized from the general state budget or, as the case may be, subjected to a levy that accrues to the general budget. Regarding the bulk of trade, however, government negotiators must ensure that the commitments for which they draft their economic agents are synchronized as much as possible with the direct interests of enterprises in trading with CMEA markets.

The final step consists in actively pursuing reform of the CMEA trade and payments regimes. This can take on several forms. One would be outright replacement of the orthodox administrative SEI mechanism with one anchored closely to economic efficiency indicators. Another would be to take advantage from within of the growing sentiment for CMEA reform. This applies even to countries whose economy continues to be steered overwhelmingly through non-scarcity instruments and bureaucratic institutions. Thus, direct enterprise relations across national frontiers should be encouraged. It is important that profitable microeconomic operations, except those of an illegal (such as weapons) or harmful (such as drugs) character, not be interdicted outright. Instead, such relations need to be steered through economic policy instruments. If firms from a reforming economy can take advantage of the nonscarcity pricing incentives administratively maintained in partner countries, there is no reason why such exchange should be discouraged by the reforming economy. Microeconomic rationality dictates that the firm has identified a temporary niche that yields arbitrage or other economic benefits; it should not be discouraged from exploiting such opportunities. On the other hand, if such activities have side effects that cannot be properly priced, then the government should try to capture them through economic instruments. Thus, it may be necessary if firms overexpand toward the ruble area to revalue the ruble so as to take the wind out of the sails of the few companies that have not so far shown serious interest in procuring imports from the ruble area and steering exports to the convertible currency area.

Very little attention at this stage is being paid, either by the PETs or those not yet in a position to enact swift changes, to the possibilities of pursuing genuine CMEA reform, that is, creating institutions, instruments, and policies that enable CMEA partners to exploit their real static and dynamic comparative advantages. The efforts made in the 1980s to reform the CMEA from within have unquestionably reached an unbridgeable impasse (Brabant 1990c). Instead, the Central European countries and the Soviet Union are reinforcing their bilateral relations through *ad hoc* solutions that fall short, at least for now, of placing their reciprocal exchanges on a convertible currency footing. Especially the reforming Central European economies covet placing their trade on a full-fledged convertible currency basis. In relations with the Soviet Union, however, the drift of the discussion and recent events appears to be replacing the TR regime with convertible currency clearing of transactions evaluated at "imputed" WMPs rather than prices that firms can profitably support.

Little thought appears to have been given to endowing the CMEA framework with a full-fledged constitution similar, for example, to the Rome Treaties that have been so important in the case of the EC. By separating judicial, legislative, and executive aspects of CMEA integration through an overall constitutional framework, the boundaries within which individual members can advance their own cause would be clearly demarcated. A fairly flexible arrangement would then enable some countries ready and willing to move forward with integration more rapidly than others to do so without harming the latter's interests (Brabant 1989f; 1990g, j). In this connection, it is worth pondering what can be done by the countries of Central Europe that have wedded themselves to radical market reform. Their mutual trade could increasingly be based on simple market relations, provided a solution can be found for the prevailing imbalances and those likely to emerge during the transition toward full-fledged marketization. Especially these countries would stand to gain considerably from actively pursuing their integration, perhaps through a customs union. Finding the proper ways and means of exploiting their comparative advantages would seem to constitute one key ambition of domestic reform. But pursuit of this goal is presently chiefly motivated by concerns about quickly boosting trade and integration with DMEs.

Among the proper ways and means, negotiations about quantities and prices of tradable goods, in most cases, can best be left at the discretion of the economic agents most directly concerned in cross-border transactions provided they are held responsible for their actions. If guidance is needed, relative WMPs could be adopted as the starting point for negotiations. But in due course, some divergences that suit local demand and supply relations could emerge and there is no good reason to try and suppress this phenomenon. Settlement of such transactions and how to come to grips with imbalances, however, are matters for which central authorities must assume full responsibility. If enterprises, for example, were to decide to trade at WMPs in convertible currency, the question of the exchange rate would be purely a domestic affair. By definition, there would be no technical problem of what to do with imbalances.

Rather than leave foreign trade reform to each PET in isolation and the exploration of profitable trade to firms, given the rather primitive trade and payments regimes, there would seem to be a marked economic merit (perhaps as distinct from current foreign policy considerations) in contemplating a Central European Economic Union (CEEU). Such an concept is not new, of course (see Brabant 1976, 1989a; Wandycz 1970). But earlier advocacies of some economic union in Central Europe were anchored to the central planning framework of MPEs.

The identified countries trade among each other essentially manufactured goods. Previously, CMEA countries with a tariff regime had a three-column approach, with the zero column applicable primarily to socialist partners. The lower of the two other tariff columns was for imports from countries that abide by MFN treatment, including in the GATT context (see Brabant 1990a). This is now being reversed. MFN tariffs on this trade, certainly as newly applied by Poland, are fairly high (on average some 20 to 25 percent). Czechoslovakia is already contemplating a high tariff during the transition phase. Relations with the GDR after economic union are subject to the EC's external tariff, which on average is low but not for many export products of direct interest to Central Europe. Finally, the Hungarian tariff, which is fairly high, is now also applied to CMEA trade. All this is placing incremental restrictions on the traditional commerce among Czechoslovakia, the GDR, Hungary, and Poland even though these countries have highly interdependent machine parks.

There is plenty of room for building up scale economies, albeit in products that for now are difficult to market in the west, but not solely because of their inferior quality. Such effective regional specialization would enable these countries to maintain fairly buoyant levels of trade while they are forcefully restructuring their economies in part to reflect intragroup needs but also world demand. There might be room to consider how best to provide the financial support and supervisory discipline to guide this process, which is the subject of another option, on which more in Section 4, that is not now being considered by these countries.

On the grounds of normal customs union considerations, a CEEU would primarily be trade creating, possibly after a brief contraction to reconfigure profitable trade structures, because the underlying economic processes of these countries are mostly competitive rather than complementary, and their trade with each other and outside markets has been heavily constrained for systemic reasons. These countries would therefore stand to reap substantial economies of scale. In addition, a CEEU would strengthen the market orientation of the PETs and enable them to enact structural adjustments in a somewhat more orderly fashion and at a lower short-term sociopolitical cost than if they were to be forced upon them through direct competition in world markets.

Perhaps even more important, greater subregional cooperation would in all likelihood elicit considerable Western European support for two reasons. On the one hand, it would postpone the diversion of substantial volumes of trade from CMEA to western markets. This is difficult to accommodate in the short run, given the EC's other priorities and its reluctance to compound the already sizable adjustment burdens on account of realizing the unified market. Also, in this way it might be easier to enact the changes in economic structures required to be fully integrated as an ME into the EC, as coveted by most Central European countries. Second, because of the time gained, orderly accession deliberations could be scheduled. It would in any case be unrealistic to expect such to get under way before late into the decade. For one, the EC is completing its Single Market. Carrying out the multiple and ambitious tasks of "1992" at the same time as coming to grips with the absorption of the GDR is claiming the full attention of EC officials. Furthermore, the assimilation of Greece, Portugal, and Spain is yet to be completed. Also, Austria, Cyprus, and Turkey are already queuing for entry negotiations. Next in line are the other EFTA countries, excepting perhaps Switzerland. In other words, the CEEU should not be seen as an alternative to joining "Europe." Quite the contrary: I look upon it essentially as a temporary stage to facilitate the transition phase, both in terms of the time required and the costs incurred in the process, toward eventually becoming fully integrated members of a united Europe, perhaps early into the next century.

4. Toward reform of the payments system

The critical intragroup trade problem presently confronting the PETs is twofold. One is the chronic shortage of convertible currency. Likewise, external pressures are such that these countries are quite reluctant to earmark this limited foreign exchange for defraying payments that used to be denominated in TRs and cleared in some fashion through the IBEC's settlements mechanism. As a result, the absence of a convertible currency payments facilities is sharply constraining the traditional trade patterns of the PETs and thus putting pressure on these countries to divert trade or contract domestic economic activity - neither of which offers the most propitious opportunity for orderly restructuring these economies. Short of introducing resolutely a CMEA-wide "big bang" approach, it might be useful to rethink the experiences of Western Europe after World War II. The main architects of postwar recovery and prosperity had committed themselves, in some cases for purely ideological and political reasons, to pursue domestic stability and gradually regain full-fledged market relations through policy measures.

After the war, trade among the Western European countries was severely hampered by inconvertible currencies and a network of bilateral agreements. To conserve hard currency each country applied a range of quotas and other direct controls on trade, but the liberalization of trade required a reform of the payments system. After two earlier schemes with mixed success, the EPU was set up in 1950. Within the union, bilateral surpluses and deficits were offset. Only net positions came up for settlement with the central clearing authority, which was backed by Marshall Plan funds. The scheme minimized members' payments in gold and convertible currency and effectively made all member currencies mutually convertible within the Union, although surpluses could not necessarily be used outside the union without impunity. This, as well as the provision of automatic credit facilities up to certain limits, helped to encourage the removal of quantitative restrictions on trade among the members of the Union. In fact, trade liberalization was an indispensable corollary to the multilateralization of payments because there is no point in freeing payments without freeing transactions (Triffin 1957).

As a result of EPU, competition and trade were stimulated within Western Europe and the allocation of resources could be more closely adapted to the underlying patterns of comparative advantage. By 1958, most of these countries had regained nonresident current-account convertibility. During the transition period the EPU gave some protection to members against dollar imports and encouraged the reconstruction of firms capable of producing substitutes for dollar imports. Considerable and rapid progress was made in liberalizing intra-European trade.

Could a similar arrangement perform a constructive role for the PETs? I firmly believe that the creation of a Central European Payments Union (CEPU) as an intermediate stage in the transition toward a fully multilateral system of trade and payments would be very desirable and could be set up at a small cost in seed capital from the west. Of course, such assistance would only minimally interfere in the emerging structure of market-based incentives in these countries.

In suggesting such an institution two considerations are especially relevant. As argued in Section 2, one is the need to maintain CMEA trade while at the same time fostering brisk structural change. Another reason is that reforming the present system of intra-CMEA trade relations is a much more arduous task than simply removing obstacles to trade. What is required is fundamental reform in the microeconomic foundations of that trade so that its level, composition, and market structures are changed in line with comparative advantages assessed at efficient market prices. To achieve all this in circumstances of foreign exchange penury is a tall order. Convertibility could be introduced suddenly - the "big bang" approach - but this assumes that the various structural adjustments would occur quickly and that the "supply responses" would be large and rapid. Most PETs are skeptical as to the possibility of such rapid responses and are clearly in favor of gradual adjustment. A CEPU would meet the demands for gradualism while at the same time providing a central authority with the means to ensure that gradualism does not undermine progress toward the ultimate objective of full convertibility and broader-based integration into the world economy. The precise modalities of a CEPU would have to be explored in much greater detail by specialized working groups. A CEPU offers the possibility of gradual but disciplined adjustment in the trade and payments of the reforming countries and, as such, could make a significant contribution to the success of the various programs of reform.

Membership of a CEPU might at first be attractive only to those advocating genuine market-oriented reform, even though pursued at different speeds. At this juncture, these comprise Czechoslovakia, the GDR, Hungary, and Poland. Other Eastern European countries could easily join later once they embarked on genuine market orientation. Also the Soviet Union could eventually be brought into the clearing schemes, though because of its size and trading structure key provisions of the CEPU might then have to be adjusted. One complication arises from present CMEA relations with the GDR (Section 5).

The purpose of such a clearing union would be quite similar to the EPU's, namely to ease the foreign exchange constraints through a mechanism that compels the participating countries to adjust to each other and reach convertibility. To make this attractive, intragroup payments must increasingly be effected in fungible assets managed through the CEPU, but biased in favor of creditor countries. To support such asymmetry in the mix of convertible currency and claims on the union, a starting capital fund is required. This could usefully be supported in the context of the assistance efforts coordinated by the EC (see Section 5).

The key features of the CMEA payments regime suggest that the central task of alleviating the constraints on intra-CMEA trade is slightly different from what was the root economic motivation of the EPU. The core short-run objective is not so much bolstering the opportunities for trade as mobilizing support for revamping within-group trade relations. This renewal needs to be anchored to principles and mechanisms that are on the whole in line with economic rationality in the microeconomic sphere. The latter itself must be subject to coordination according to explicit macroeconomic policies, aided by appropriate institutions and policy instruments.

Whereas the main task of the EPU and CEPU is, therefore, slightly different, the mechanisms by which these objectives can be fostered exhibit considerable commonality. The central technique is to accommodate bilateral imbalances by transforming them into multilateral ones and ensuring that the net surpluses or deficits *vis-à-vis* the participating group as a whole remain manageable. Manageable in this context means that the clearing agency should have sufficient funds to finance the imbalances and ample supervisory clout to guide partners into mutually reinforcing behavior. At the same time, it should be conceived in such a way that the relative magnitude of funding needs decreases over time as a steadily rising share of the cumulative imbalances is being paid in convertible currency.

Having a capital fund to support the asymmetric settlement of imbalances is critical in two respects. It would enable these countries to run larger imbalances than can be accommodated on an *ad hoc* basis. Also, it is important to make the scheme sufficiently attractive to encourage countries to aim at a surplus with the clearing agency. Such a fund could be constituted by outsiders, as discussed in the next section, or by the members themselves. In the latter case, it probably would be hopeless to expect the PETs to put together a sufficiently large fund to enable them to effect clearing in payments as well as claims on the union. If the own fund were to be small, it might be useful initially to let surplus countries acquire convertible currency loans to be repaid to the fund. Deficit countries would then provide the additional funding after meeting certain agreed-upon rules on deadlines and magnitudes of tolerable imbalances. Such a way of proceeding would not be the most attractive, however, as discussed later.

How long could it take to reach convertibility? What conditions need to be met to ensure that the clearing agency can operate in a stable environment? What should be done with the fund's capital base when convertibility is reached? These are some of the many questions to be addressed. Regarding the duration of the clearing mechanism, everything depends on how quickly these countries will be able to move over toward complete convertible currency trading. This may be more difficult than was the case for Western Europe in the 1950s, owing to the fact that these countries not only need to introduce market-oriented reforms but also to restructure their external trade and payments over wide segments. The task of maintaining trade volumes, while at the same time effecting major changes in the commodity composition thereof, and perhaps in the geographical distribution as well, in line with comparative advantage indicators, is a daunting one. When it is realized that the latter can proceed only by revising the traditional pricing structures, particularly TRPs, and ensuring that the necessary shifts occur by knitting meaningful linkages between domestic and trade sectors, the tasks ahead become more complex still, even under very favorable developments of both the domestic economy and international trade and payments. It might take as much as a decade to cement in the foundations of these tasks.

Regarding technical aspects of the clearing fund and what needs to be safeguarded against to prevent its premature demise, ample experience is available from earlier clearing schemes, including the EPU, the French franc zone, the sterling zone, the Belgian-Luxemburg monetary union, and others. Perhaps foremost is the constatation that any clearing scheme suffers from a fundamental theoretical weakness. To require in principle that all countries balance their current accounts within the clearing system is tantamount to assuming that they balance at the same time their accounts with countries that remain outside the system. Without this, participants may be tempted to utilize their surplus with clearing partners to offset their deficits elsewhere; because of a fundamental asymmetry, countries in deficit *vis-à-vis* clearing partners will not want to repatriate their surpluses with outsiders.

In the case of the EPU, this temptation was on the whole not very significant for several reasons. One was the size of intragroup trade. Most participants conducted the bulk of their external commerce among themselves once the process of solid economic recovery was well on its way. Furthermore, these countries had a great degree of political trust in each other. They were moreover on the whole imbued by the confidence that all stood to gain from observing the rules. As a result, each was willing to pay some price for making the EPU and the transition toward currency convertibility work. Some, as the Benelux countries, had indeed already earlier embarked on erecting an enviable degree of regional economic and political cohesion, which helped in formulating consensual solutions for otherwise intractable technical problems. Also, trade and payments with the nonparticipating countries were overwhelmingly with the United States, hence in the vehicle currency. This country had been one of the main sponsors of the EPU to begin with and consequently had little interest in draining its own currency from the fund.

It is not at all clear that one could count on comparable conditions prevailing for the PETs at this juncture. Given the present disarray in the CMEA, it is difficult to envisage these countries as a group being imbued with a great deal of trust and confidence. Such a feeling may emerge once the uncertainty dissipates about where they, including the USSR, may desire to go from here. This lack of confidence is much less pronounced for some of the smaller countries, however. Thus, a clearing agency for the Central European countries, perhaps to be joined later by other reforming countries, would reflect similar political interests and commitments "to making it work." Lingering social and political revendications even in that subregion could be overcome through concerted policy action.

There is no panacea at hand. But a solution can be constructed gradually, in the first instance by recognizing the potential obstacles arising from other technical issues. One concerns the currency unit of the CEPU. Another revolves around the exchange rates to be used in the process. There is no readily identifiable optimal solution, given that convertible currency exchange rates are flexible, that the present currencies of the CMEA countries are inconvertible, and that there is simply no ideal - let alone fixed - exchange rate that could be selected for the CEPU members. A pragmatic proposition could be studied. This could place, for example, the ECU at the heart of the CEPU scheme. The ECU is attractive because it is increasingly used as the invoicing currency of Eastern Europe's trade with Western Europe. It is also more stable than most other currencies, including the dollar. Furthermore, it is a currency unit that does not depend on any country's national monetary policy.

The members themselves would have to take care, for the time being, of managing the rates at which their external trade gets translated into domestic currencies. This solution would not only invite the CEPU members gradually to manage their foreign exchange regime in tandem with that of the European Monetary System (EMS). It would also subject them to the latter's discipline. Of course, such a choice would invite the EC to assume a major role in bankrolling the CEPU and seeing to its success over a protracted period of time.

The severe payments problems especially of Hungary and Poland may undermine the scheme from the very beginning. To avoid this, it would be useful to find a way to permit these countries, at least for now, to focus on current trade, while the seemingly intractable problems of their inherited external debts are resolved through other means.

Even so, the major flows of these countries would chiefly be with third countries. On the one hand, the key partner in the CMEA is the Soviet Union, with whom trade is soon to be conducted at imputed WMPs that are not based on true scarcities. On the other hand, Western Europe constitutes the key western partner and that trade is conducted in convertible currency. This might tempt participants to erode the clearing fund's base by appropriating surpluses to pay for convertible currency deficits.

5. East-west economic assistance and the CEPU

The prospect of German unification ushers in its own problems. Inasmuch as the GDR has been a very important partner in the CMEA, German economic and monetary union is bound to exert palpable impacts on that grouping as well. Because these economies are not comprehensively interlinked, the transmission belts of the implications will be essentially the trade and payments regimes that still form the mainstay of CMEA economic relations. Regarding trade, the implicit preferences extended to the CMEA would disappear as the commercial regime in the eastern part of Germany would necessarily have to be abolished and replaced by the mainstream commercial policy of the FRG. Most CMEA countries have MFN status in the FRG and the EC. But that might nonetheless complicate their traditional exports to the eastern part of Germany of foodstuffs and agricultural products, let alone manufactured products (clothing, textiles, footwear, metals, chemicals, and others) whose imports are restricted in the context of the EC. They are also subject to fairly high tariffs, altogether a new phenomenon in CMEA trade.

Much more serious, however, are the two monetary effects: the replacement of TRPs by WMPs and the need to effect payments in convertible currency. Given the tight external payments situation of most CMEA countries, the room for simply placing trade with the GDR on a convertible currency footing is presently non-existent. Inasmuch as the bulk of Soviet exports to the GDR consists of goods that can be easily marketed at WMPs without entailing substantial terms-of-trade losses, the problem of maintaining levels of Soviet trade with the eastern part of Germany is not as acute as it is for Eastern Europe; the FRG is in any case anxious to assuage Soviet concerns about German unification and to placate it into endorsing complete submergence of the GDR into the FRG through trade and finance. In the short run, this would necessarily lead to a shrinkage in trade and complicate the provisioning of a substantial part of the Eastern European machine park with spare parts, components, maintenance, and the like.

The GDR has been the second largest trade partner of most CMEA members. Its industrial prowess, while perhaps lagging significantly behind that of most DMEs, is nonetheless intimately linked to the requirements of CMEA partners, including Central Europe. At the very least, the latter will continue to need parts, components, maintenance, and so on of the existing machine park, and this can be guaranteed only if the submergence of the GDR will preclude such trading relations from being abruptly eroded. If only for that reason, it would be very important to ensure that part of the trade of a united Germany be temporarily conducted through the CEPU, for the CMEA members will probably find it difficult, for economic and psychological reasons, to place their trade with the former GDR *de facto* on a convertible currency basis in the short run. Under the circumstances, it might be useful to devise means whereby the trade of the GDR with the CMEA countries can be maintained through some clearing arrangement. The creation of a CEPU would meet these concerns, at least for the more reform-oriented CMEA members.

In the context of the east-west assistance effort it might be useful to explore the possibilities of setting up a capital base from which the Central European countries could find support for moving in a relatively short period of time toward convertibility. The sums involved are not terribly large. Intragroup trade of the European CMEA countries (measured before the recent changes in data and exchange rates as new bilateral data are not yet available) amounted to some $75 billion in 1989, with half of the absolute sum of bilateral imbalances totaling some $5 billion, largely on account of the sizable deficit incurred by the Soviet Union for unusual circumstances. If the scheme were to be mounted initially for the most reform-oriented countries, the volume of trade among Czechoslovakia, the GDR, Hungary, and Poland in 1989 was roughly $7.7 billion with half of the absolute imbalances *vis-à-vis* the group amounting to $288 million. The imbalances actually to be financed would be even smaller, owing to offsetting service imbalances and other factors. True, the lifting of bilateral constraints on trade among these countries would in all likelihood initially lead to greater intragroup imbalances, but not necessarily larger absolute claims on the clearing region, hence the magnitude of finance to be placed at the disposal of the clearing union by the EC.

Earmarking some of the assistance, say, less than a quarter, already committed through the multilateral financial institutions and the Group of Twenty-Four for the purpose of reinforcing the trade relations of the reforming countries would be ample. Not only would it support the national and CMEA reform trends from within and strengthen intragroup trade and payments relations for which there is sufficient economic justification. It would also transfer assistance in a form that would least interfere with the emerging economic incentives for economic agents and the market-oriented macroeconomic framework being elaborated.

Such earmarking of western assistance could be very beneficial in other respects as well. For one thing, it would get Western Europe directly involved in the transition process, thereby presumably giving the PETs another, concrete measure of confidence in their ability eventually to join "Europe" once the transition toward RPE status is well under way (*The Banker*, 1990:5, p. 4). Arguably more significant would be the leverage this scheme provides over policy adjustment for CEPU members exceeding their assigned quota. Holding CEPU members to EMS-like discipline will presumably ensure that the adjustment process is being increasingly firmed up by proper macroeconomic policies. Indeed to make the CEPU work, concerted action on the part of the major convertible currency partners initially financing the clearing scheme could help to stem that tide.

Active western assistance with moving toward genuine currency convertibility would provide some impetus to coming to grips with the substantial debt problems of key potential CEPU members. Certainly, the experience of dealing with severe debt issues during the 1980s in the DEs is not particularly encouraging in this regard. However, the east-west assistance efforts coming to fruition under the EC's aegis may well embody a greater degree of political capital and potential commercial interest in ensuring the separability of the stock of debt from current payments for trade and services other than debt service.

The easiest problem to resolve if such east-west assistance were to crystallize is what could usefully be done with the capital fund when the clearing agency loses its *raison d'être*. In the case of the EPU, once the outstanding clearing credits and debits were transformed into long-term loans, the capital fund was appropriated for development loans and grants to the less developed countries of southern Europe. Something similar could be envisaged, for example, for the CEPU. Thus the remaining capital could be allocated to debt retirement, to combat the severe environmental problems on the continent, or to come to the aid of the DEs. This might provide one instance in which the anxiety of DEs about financial flows being diverted to Eastern Europe (see Chapter 10) could be alleviated, albeit not in the short run.

6. Toward a new CMEA constitution

As argued in Chapter 6, Western Europe's recovery after World War II owed a good deal to the fortitude of the countries themselves, but also to the economic, financial, and political support obtained in the process. Thus Marshall Plan aid was pivotal. Also, the support mobilized from within Western Europe and the blessings received from the United States as the then dominant power to forge ahead rapidly with economic integration were of singular importance to the successful enterprise of Western European economic integration. The EC's experience has demonstrated how difficult it is to avoid retrenchment into national chauvinism during the transition without there being a political agreement on unification. The critical role of the Treaty of Rome in holding together the EC at various stages of its evolution should be underlined here.

There is nothing even closely comparable in the CMEA's statute. The latter has two principal features. One is a sequence of mostly exhortatory declarations regarding the advantages of international socialism, solidarity, and fraternal assistance. The other deals with the concrete organization of the CMEA and its various administrative and "policy-making" bodies, and the rules whereby the member countries in principle commit themselves to fostering integration. There is really no vision as to what the CMEA could or should accomplish by way of staging economic integration. Under the circumstances, and in the context of the ongoing efforts to formulate incisive reforms, it might be worthwhile to consider redrafting the CMEA's charter along constitutional lines that compare favorably with those adopted in the Treaty of Rome. The rules need not be identical, of course. But they should offer an adequate legal, organizational, and institutional framework within which the cause of regional economic integration can be advanced on its own merits. Certainly, states are bound to interfere at some point with what seems eminently logical and justified from an economic point of view. That may be troublesome at times. With a comprehensive, yet pragmatic, framework firmly in place, such state interference is not likely to last long as, under normal circumstances, the institutional infrastructure will protect against wild aberrations from either the left or the right.

What is required, then, is what I have elsewhere (Brabant 1989a, pp. 411ff.; 1989f; 1990c, g, j) called a constitutional framework. Its need derives from several considerations. One is that changes in the CMEA are likely to emerge from the sheer impact of reform in weighty CMEA members. But it can be eased and facilitated through positive policy action. Unless national economic reforms explicitly aim at diverting trade and economic cooperation toward non-CMEA partners on a large scale for its own sake, which I feel is undesirable, the idea of promoting positive economic integration holds promise also because it will get considerable support from the external reverberations of national economic reforms. Thus, to the extent that genuine wholesale trade and flexible pricing emerge in PETs, the pressure to modify significantly the orthodox way of doing business in the CMEA cannot but mount.

Working out such a reformed framework for CMEA integration would not necessarily force all members to adopt the same type of economic reforms, including on macroeconomic policies and their associated institutions and instruments. But it should not hinder those ready to move swiftly with reform from doing so without being stymied by partners who prefer to move more cautiously and perhaps to do so through a good deal of planning. Of the utmost importance is "rule certainty" for all agents. This presupposes that the room for lower-level decisions be unambiguously delineated and the interests of economic agents reflected in the criteria by which these decisions can be reached.

A critical feature to be heeded in constructing feasible reform is clear-cut economic criteria of choice. Even if countries choose to render development assistance or to promote factor transfers for reasons other than strict material gain, the economic calculus needs to be embraced vigorously so that the direct and indirect costs of political decisions can be placed in their proper perspective. The economic benefits and losses of decisions for the self-accounting of firms cannot be obfuscated with impunity. At the very least, the economic calculus needs to be refined as a technical tool to distinguish more clearly between resource appropriations and output results, to weed out what is not up to par, and to foster profitable processes as measured by strictly economic yardsticks.

* * *

On the strength of these arguments, there would seem to be sufficient cause for focusing on CMEA reform as a means to envigorate the support that the organization and what it stands for can provide to national reform efforts. In that light, the real kernel of the debate on CMEA reform should be to formulate answers to the following two critical questions of economy policy. First, to what extent do the CMEA members consciously opt to safeguard their regional economic organization and their national independence in economic affairs against effective competition from outside the group? Second, in view of the fact that this preference must entail a cost in terms of economic efficiency forgone, as measured by productivity standards that these countries avowedly wish to emulate, who will be asked to shoulder this cost and according to which rules will the inefficiency burden be parceled out? In other words, also at the regional level a "social compact" needs to be worked out that ensures, perhaps through a CEEU and CEPU, that eventual fuller integration into the world economy will be entirely feasible.

10

PETs and the global economic system

One of the greatest challenges facing the global community at this juncture is the management of economic, political, and security changes taking place throughout Eastern Europe. In laying this claim, I do not wish to underplay the importance of other problems besetting the world such as poverty, regional military conflicts, AIDS, and the environment. However, inasmuch as the postwar global framework has been dominated to a large extent by the divisive relationship between east and west, the revolutions in Eastern Europe are yielding unprecedented opportunities for better managing our globe.

Remaking global relations is not just a task for diplomatists, as argued, for example, by Ludlow (1989, p. 168); neither is it something that can be entrusted only to the "west," meaning essentially the key hegemon or pseudo hegemon of what remains of the postwar global security system. It requires, in fact, the comprehensive readjustment of the global economic framework to conditions that prevail today and are likely to be with us in the years to come. Certainly, hegemons may play a pivotal role in this process. Without proper adaptations of international regimes and their associated institutions, however, it is difficult to envision how a more harmonious world could be constructed by making hay of the historic chance emanating from the Eastern European revolutions.

This chapter addresses in particular some of the manifold opportunities of remaking Eastern Europe and facilitating the further fusion of Eastern Europe into global trading, financial, and monetary relations. Section 1 restates the case for positive reform in the CMEA as an essential ingredient of an orderly transition in Eastern Europe and indeed in European economic relations. Next, I look at the narrower area of the consequences of the east-west assistance particularly for DEs and how the international community could come to grips with these legitimate concerns. The following three sections examine the implications of Eastern European events for the monetary, financial, and trading regimes in place and the redesigned role that the PETs could play in the associated institutions. The chapter concludes with a brief dissertation on the implications for European integration.

1. Remaking the CMEA and the global economy

Unlike most participants in the debates on remaking Europe, who have written off the CMEA, I have tried to offer cogent arguments why this may well turn out to be a costly and unnecessary policy error. There are basically two sets of reasons for this. One is that the PETs enjoy, or could benefit from, static and comparative advantages *vis-à-vis* Eastern Europe. To exploit them, proper institutions, policy instruments, and policies must be designed. In my view, outright trade cancellation or explicit trade denial is definitely *not* a desirable response. Also, the Eastern European countries will have to pass through a wrenching stabilization phase. For that funds are required to refashion their capital stock, transportation infrastructure in the wide sense, and human skills. The main purpose of these transfers would be to enable these countries to produce goods and services that are competitive in global markets. It would be useful if this transition phase could be forged quickly, allowing these countries to gain a degree of competitiveness on a scale that will permit them to maintain nearly full employment and steady per capita income growth. If in the process trade needs to be diverted from the CMEA to other parts of the global economy, more than casual thought should be allocated to the proper forms in which such trade could best be accommodated and what needs to be done to allow these countries to work out such a more productive relationship with the world economy. The repercussions of remaking Eastern Europe and, in the end, the European economy are many. Some point in the direction of the need to reformulate the postwar global economic framework in more than one respect. Especially critical is how the PETs fit into it and how their position could prospectively be enhanced through reforms of the financial, monetary, or trade regimes singly or in combination.

There are several similarities between the plight of much of the European CMEA countries, and indeed former and other planned economies, at this stage and the economic and political situation in Western Europe after World War II. In fact, there are several parallels between the crisis atmosphere of 1947 and the realization of the PETs that moving decisively forward with economic restructuring and embarking on a "new" growth path call for measures that are of an entirely different order of magnitude than what enabled these countries to undertake a successful revolution in late 1989 and early 1990 against considerable odds.

Although one cannot expect governments to lose sight of politics, and hence the political "gains" reached by the "west" *vis-à-vis* the Soviet Union cannot be completed ignored by the economist, a dispassionate analysis of the feasible and desirable should take cognizance of the fact that the new democracies cannot quickly be brought into the "liberal" economic, social, and political framework of Western Europe. Whereas moving resolutely toward a united Europe based on democratic principles may be a highly desirable medium to long-run objective, for the time being the eastern countries are not ready to assume fully the responsibilities associated with playing their "rightful" role in the concert of nations and the western partners are not quite ready to absorb the adjustment costs required to accommodate the east quickly.

What needs to be stressed at this stage, in my view, is the concentration of national, regional, and international efforts on rebuilding a method of conducting international trade and payments that would function as easily and successfully as the one that was slowly regained in Western Europe after World War II. Certainly, part of the east-west ambiance stems from cultural, political, religious, and other noneconomic overtones. But there are also economic implications. In the broad sense, the PET phenomenon begs the question of reforming the global economic framework and its main institutional pillars in the postwar period. More on the practical side of things, the renaissance in economic thinking in the PETs is bound to have serious implications for trade and payments relations, both in the CMEA context and the east-west domain. Because flexibility in the west appears to be available, the repercussions of reforms in Eastern Europe are likely to be pronounced. In this context, one can pose the question of whether the potential impacts on east-west trade, payments, economic cooperation, and integration plans should be dealt with in a comprehensive framework, of which rendering east-west assistance should be one principal component? Or would it be more productive to let markets take care of most of the east-west repercussions if only to minimize interference with budding markets in Eastern Europe? There is something to be said for either position. I would favor the first one on the ground that the greatest support for the PET phenomenon should be mustered from the resource at hand. These include domestic resources, the potential for fruitful commercial interaction, as well as the economic assistance being provided.

Regardless of what avenue the PETs choose, a major structural shift in the postwar global economic framework is bound to ensue. It will occur in international monetary affairs, now that the former planned economies no longer insist on having their own international currency and are willing to work positively toward international monetary reform. Similarly with respect to international financial relations. These countries will need considerable balance-of-payments and structural adjustment support - not just in terms of financial transfers - to put in place the proper mechanisms, instruments, institutions, and policies to function as normal market-based economies. Finally, by throwing over board the major aspects of the MFT that have to do with market insulation through price equalization, they will now be in a position to grant effective reciprocity. Their foreign exchange regime and the management of external accounts will increasingly come to resemble the postwar path trodden by most DMEs. A brief look at each of these three areas may yield food for thought on how best to reconstruct the global economic framework. Before doing so, however, the likely repercussions for DEs need to be placed in the perspective of the opportunities they offer to redesign global economic management.

2. East-west economic assistance and the DEs

DEs individually and as a group have repeatedly aired their anxiety about the ramification of the unprecedented attention in the west for events in the east. Their fears fall into three distinct, though interrelated, categories. On the one hand, they are concerned that greater association of the east in particular with the EC and EFTA may curtail their own ability to compete in western markets, as well as eastern markets though they have been more reticent in that respect, as the east can expect to obtain a discriminatory advantage over the DEs through trade concessions and possibly an association agreement with the EC. In addition, there is great concern about the diversion of ODA to the PETs.

The reasoning is simple: Aid budgets are such that, politically speaking, it is very difficult to increase total commitments; any diversion of aid to PETs must cut into the amounts left for DEs. Finally, the DEs fear that the marketization of Eastern Europe will open up attractive investment opportunities for TNCs and hence, given global savings, possibly divert capital flows from DEs to the PETs.

Are these fears warranted? A distinction needs to be made between the DEs that have been favored partners of the CMEA countries and others. Regarding the former group, it is important to underline the impact of changes in the CMEA in general and individual PETs in particular on the position of the three DE members of the CMEA and the eight DE cooperants as enumerated in the introduction. Also the preferential arrangements with some other DEs with a strong interest in enhancing the state sector within the context of socialist leanings are under review. The *de facto* disintegration of the CMEA and the transformation of PETs cannot but have important consequences for these countries, including through trade volumes, the terms on which that trade is cleared, ODA and other forms of foreign assistance, labor migration, and scientific-technical assistance. Perhaps most important will be the elimination of substantial economic assistance embedded in, and transmitted through, the peculiar trade and payments regimes (especially prices and tariffs, but also in the ability of DEs to maintain deficits with respect to the CMEA) typical of the CMEA countries. For some of them, notably Vietnam, worker remittances from the European CMEA have constituted a significant prop in servicing TR debts. With the commercialization of economic decisions in the European CMEA members, the real cost of ODA extended to DEs, especially the non-European CMEA members and the cooperants, is henceforth going to be carefully scrutinized. At a time of palpable internal and external economic imbalances, chances of holding assistance levels at present levels, let alone of raising them, are not at all promising.

Looking at DEs more generally, it is useful to distinguish the potential impacts of the western assistance effort on commercial, financial, and monetary relations.

1. Impacts on trade and the international trading regime

Expectations that the various processes of structural change in Eastern Europe would exert positive effects on the trading opportunities of DEs are yet to materialize. There are, however, several reasons that would now make it reasonably certain that the restructuring process will be trade creating for several reasons. One source of export growth is going to be through the strengthening of the competitive position of exports from DEs as the PETs shift their economic structures to reflect underlying relative scarcities. The other impulse will come through the abolition of the MFT, which has for so long so incisively complicated access to these markets in the absence of broad intergovernmental agreements. But some ingenuity will be required to establish positions in these markets for some time to come.

On the other hand, the PETs in particular are likely to become more formidable competitors of DEs, particularly in Western Europe. Owing in part to low labor costs and proximity to markets, they are likely to wage competition especially with many products of the NIEs, at least in the short to medium run. If the reforming countries were to obtain preferential access to markets in Western Europe, over and beyond the elimination of discriminatory quantitative restrictions maintained in particular by the EC, the negative effects of this increased competition for DEs might be quite sizable in the short run.

Preferential access to western markets might be arranged under various guises. One can distinguish among the removal of discriminatory quantitative restrictions, the easement or removal of quantitative restrictions for Eastern Europe but not for other countries, and various types of tariff concessions, including those that would be arranged under some type of association agreement with either the EC or EFTA (see Chapter 5). The removal of the EC's discriminatory quantitative restrictions, which may on the margin temporarily disadvantage some DEs, should be welcomed in the context of the international trading regime in place, including efforts being made to streamline it in the context of the Uruguay Round. The easement of generally applicable quantitative restrictions, provided they would not discriminate against other countries, should also be welcomed by themselves and in the context of the trade liberalization sought under the Uruguay Round.

The easement of quantitative restrictions or the granting of preferential tariff arrangements in favor of the PETs would be undesirable for as long as east-west relations cannot be firmly embedded within the context of a strict interpretation of article XXIV (on customs unions and free trade areas) of the General Agreement. The more complete merging of the PETs under the discipline of the General Agreement should be welcomed, not only in the context of potential discriminatory trade access for Eastern Europe being considered by some DMEs, but also in terms of the impetus such moves impart to strengthening the GATT framework.

Although there may initially be negative trade effects ensuing from the reforms in PETs, once radical marketization gets firmly under way a major impetus to global trade and finance is likely to ensue, including to the benefit of DEs. If the PETs succeed in quickly transforming their economic structures, rapid changes in wage and income levels are likely to occur, thereby creating additional room for DEs to gain a competitive position in Eastern Europe, as well as in strengthening their position in the markets of many DMEs as the competitive position of the PETs based on low wages is being rapidly replaced by skill-intensive, hence higher-cost, goods.

2. Reforms in PETs and the international monetary regime

The disintegration of the TR regime has led several countries to seek to strengthen their participation in the international monetary regime. Any substantial further relaxation in the international political and security climate will probably exert a favorable impetus so that also the Soviet Union will be permitted to take part in the Washington financial institutions, if not on a full accession basis at least for all practical purposes. In this context, three issues are worth considering. One is the adjustment discipline of the Fund. Another is movement toward currency convertibility, although this is not a requirement of

Fund membership; but it is a high priority item on the policy agenda of the PETs. Finally, there is the question of the debt burden, which is substantial for several PETs. They will lay claim on some Fund resources. But these are unlikely to be so large that they would inhibit the Fund from financing balance-of-payments requirements of other members. However, if substantial structural adjustment loans were to be forthcoming, active competition for Fund resources might well come to the fore. On the other hand, bringing Eastern Europe under the Fund's current-account discipline should be very desirable. For one thing, movement toward currency convertibility cannot but facilitate capitalizing on the competitive position of MEs.

In the context of the unprecedented assistance efforts to Eastern Europe, a resolution of the chronic debt problem of some of the PETs may be in the offing. If such a constructive step were to crystallize, motivated by the desire to buttress flow activity and set aside the burden of stocks inherited from past mismanagement or domestic and external adversities, it could presage similar moves to the benefit of DEs.

3. Reforms and international resource flows

The impacts of east-west developments on global financial flows are likely to differ when one considers ODA, official bilateral and multilateral assistance flows, FDI, and portfolio investment. In this equation, the role of German monetary and economic union needs to be borne in mind for its potentially adverse impacts through inflationary, exchange rate, and interest rate effects, which will depend on how the union is implemented (see UNECE 1990, pp. 224-6).

Regarding ODA, it is now fairly clear that most DMEs will not divert funds earmarked for DEs to PETs. Instead, such funds will be appropriated in addition to ODA budgets. That does, of course, imply that these increments could have been allocated to DEs and are not now. On the other hand, without the extraordinary events in Eastern Europe, there would probably not have been sufficient political support in donor countries for measurably raising ODA appropriations. So on that score, the outcome of the assistance effort to Eastern Europe tends to be neutral.

As regards other than ODA official financial transfers from bilateral and multilateral agencies, there seems to be little doubt that Eastern Europe has been competing with similar flows to DEs, basically because budgets of national and international organs that deal with external assistance programs are entrusted with Eastern European issues as well, and so nearly fixed budgets will have to be spread around further. Although there may be some room for revising national budget appropriations of substantial donors to Eastern Europe, the budgets of the multilateral agencies, the World Bank in particular, have not been raised sufficiently to maintain their potential and desirable level of lending to DEs while at the same time raising appropriations for Eastern Europe. Until support can be mustered for a substantial increase in World Bank resources, available funds will have to be spread more thinly. This is true at least until the EBRD can take over the mantle from the World Bank.

One factor that is often overlooked but should not, particularly in the medium to long run, is the beneficial effect of a sharp reduction in military budgets and ancillary expenses that have for so long been justified by the Cold War. Whereas the peace dividend of converting military facilities to civilian uses, while not completely superfluous, is generally small and certainly far less than widely anticipated in the popular press, the savings on expenditures that would otherwise have had to be earmarked will in time offer a very significant margin of flexibility. Of course, such a reduction in expenditures will in the first instance be deflationary, especially in those countries where it will be utilized to better balance the budget. Nonetheless, either lower taxes or less crowding out in financial markets cannot but exert a beneficial effect from lower expenditures on military budgets. Such an event may furthermore strengthen the environment for regular commercial interchange on a global basis.

That leaves the question of the impact of reforms in Eastern Europe and the Soviet Union on FDI and portfolio investment. Given the prevailing uncertainty about the course to be taken by PETs, excepting the GDR, the inflow of FDI and portfolio investments is likely to remain small, certainly in comparison with total available global savings. Even if that process were to accelerate quickly to what Eastern Europe could usefully absorb from the point of view of relative factor proportions, the size of the total amount of capital being diverted from potential allocation to DEs is likely to remain rather small.

In this connection, it bears to recall that capital flows into the DEs in the 1980s have been heavily concentrated in a select few. The vast majority of the DEs have not really participated in the global reallocation of corporate savings of the TNCs. But there is a distinct possibility, particularly in the case of the FRG, that funds that would otherwise be available for investment in the NIEs will now be earmarked for eastern Germany for reasons examined below. However, even such a substantial shift is likely to be gradual rather than abruptly massive as the impetus for FDI emanating from widely differentiated rates of return on capital in the GDR will likely be a rather short-run phenomenon.

4. Are concerns warranted?

To the extent that the anxieties of DEs are not warranted, an effort should be made by the international community to dispel such concerns. And to the degree that adverse repercussions are likely to come to the fore, every effort should be made by the international community to minimize their size, particularly for the least fortunate among the DEs. That is to say, discriminatory trading arrangements in favor of PETs should be confined to rolling back discriminatory commercial policy measures traditionally maintained against the planned economies and to putting in place trade-creating association agreements.

Perhaps most attention should be devoted to the potential positive aspects of the marketization of the east. Here is a very substantial market with considerable resources that have not thus far been sufficiently and efficiently tapped. The opportunities for trade expansion, for increasing the level of welfare in the area with its beneficial ramifications for trade and welfare levels attainable by other countries, need to be seen in a medium- to long-term perspective. If PETs succeed in becoming RPEs, their trade should grow very rapidly under impact of the process of structural change that is bound to ensue. In which directions the dynamic comparative advantages need to be identified is hard to say at this stage. But there surely are comparative advantages to be exploited to the benefit of the global economy at large, if not necessarily for each and every individual component thereof.

3. PETs and the international monetary regime

Prior to the revolutions in Eastern Europe, about half of the socialist countries were members of the Fund and the Bank. Membership was held by China, Hungary, Laos, Poland, Rumania, Vietnam, and Yugoslavia (Brabant 1990a, p. 112); that is to say, six out of fifteen countries that belong to the socialist world economic system and three out of the seven active European CMEA countries. Arguably the most important actors of both groupings, including the Soviet Union and the other more developed partners of the European CMEA (Czechoslovakia and the GDR), were not members. With the revolutions of late 1989, this situation is bound to be altered fairly soon. Bulgaria and Czechoslovakia have already applied for normal accession and are expected to obtain that status in the fall of 1990. The Soviet Union has left little doubt that it is fundamentally interested in following suit; the GDR's accession will in fact be through German union.

In pondering the future relations between Eastern Europe and the Fund, it is instructive to recall the conditions upon which the socialist countries have traditionally participated in the Fund. First of all, none of the countries has thus far introduced a convertible currency, opting to remain in the Fund under the "temporarily exceptional" circumstances regulated by article XIV of the Articles of Agreement. Furthermore, none of these countries fitted in fully with the international monetary regime in place or the standard approach taken by the Fund as the institution entrusted with the application of that regime. Perhaps the only exception to this generalization was Yugoslavia, basically because it had earlier jettisoned central planning. But its problems in the international monetary regime resembled very much those accounting for the uneasy relationship between the Fund and many DEs. Furthermore, the politics of macroeconomic control in post-Tito Yugoslavia did not improve matters at all (Tyson, Robinson, and Woods 1988). As a result, all CPEs or MPEs have had strained relations, particularly with the Fund (Brabant 1990a, pp. 126-35).

Part of the problem of associating planned economies with the Fund has been on account of the Fund applying by and large its standard current-account adjustment policy package designed essentially for MEs with fully integrated, flexible markets. True, by the time the Fund was asked to come to grips with the macroeconomic problems of CPEs and MPEs in the 1980s, it had slightly expanded its arsenal of policy tools particularly in the direction of making positive efforts to alleviate the burden of adjustment by restructuring supply to some degree. Unless such policies were firmly embedded in the planning environment of the targeted socialist country, of course, the adjustment program tended to be watered down. Also, conditionality conditions that were not fully predicated on the country-designed adjustment program tended to entail serious political conflict, including over the issue of reform and structural adjustment.

The tasks ahead in PETs now are vastly more complex than simply managing the current account. There are also opportunities for cooperation about suitable adjustment policies, the sequencing of marketization, and the desirable speed of this process. At the present time, the potential for political conflict over policy autonomy is much less acute or worrisome for that matter, than the need to redesign primarily purely technical issues. But other matters should certainly not be underestimated, given the fragility of the political process in the emerging democracies.

Nonetheless, the technical angles of adjustment are of most interest here. These stem on the one hand from the unusual situation in which the PETs find themselves. Technical issues also arise in connection with the way in which the international monetary regime has been managed since the breakdown of the fixed-par system. Although one frequently hears complaints about the fact that it has been allowed to disintegrate and efforts to rebuild it have thus far foundered (Black 1985, Williamson 1983), the Fund has demonstrated its ability to evolve and provide critical components of what could be construed as global economic management. But many problems of international demand management can be attributed to, at times bewildering, macroeconomic policies in key participants in the world economy. Certainly, these issues need to be addressed primarily by national authorities in light of how they decide to manage their economy. But it would stand to reason to argue that there is perhaps something to be gained from greater coordination, at least among the vehicle members of the global economy (Bourguinat 1988, Cooper 1985).

The Fund needs to expand its appreciation of the economic, institutional, political, and social constraints under which policy is pursued in individual countries (Bird 1983). This raises the lid of Pandora's box regarding collective management. It is certainly wishful thinking to proceed on the assumption that the international monetary arrangements can be rolled back to the 1950s. There has in the meantime been too much politicization of the monetary issues and much greater diffusion of economic power to make this a feasible proposition. Nonetheless, it would undoubtedly be useful to strengthen collective management exercised through the Fund or its successor institution, rather than proceed with solutions that result from *ad hoc* crisis management. To reach such greater coordination with a view to strengthening international economic security, improved international organization and a redesigned international monetary regime may well be key supports for enhancing economic stability or security in the global economy. Can this task be facilitated by reconstituting the international monetary regime with a view to taking into account the issues facing the PETs now and in the near term?

In forging a relationship between the Fund and the PETs, it would seem useful to agree on three preliminary issues. One is the need for greater awareness of the desirability of looking at a broad array of domestic policies. Also, it needs to be recognized that the issues involved are politically sensitive and cannot just be dealt with like any other ME. It would seem particularly important to avoid the Fund getting embroiled in the domestic fight over the concrete design and stepwise implementation of the transition in its broad sociopolitical setting as distinct from purely technical matters. Finally, it must be recognized that the transition cannot be pursued without heeding the exceptionally dense interconnectedness of national and international issues.

In this connection, it would seem useful to recall that the problems between the Fund and the CPEs or MPEs in the past (see Brabant 1990a, pp. 208ff.) had little to do with how these countries fit into the global economic framework or over the technical matters of whether or not to pursue adjustment when the current account became imbalanced. There were instead two angles of the politics of international relations. One stemmed from strenuous opposition on the part of key actors - the United States in the first place - to admitting political and military rivals, particularly the Soviet Union. By proceeding with measures that were aiming at the selective dismemberment of what was once referred to as the "Soviet bloc," domestic precepts on foreign policy strategy got confounded with economic expediency. Once admitted into the regime, however, the critical issue of a harmonious relationship, or lack thereof, revolved around the degree to which the CPE or MPE insisted upon domestic policy autonomy, especially in economic matters. These included domestic price autonomy, the separation of domestic and foreign markets through the MFT, the dichotomized foreign trading markets with the CMEA and east-west relations, and indeed the entire national and regional planning frameworks as such.

A better relationship between the PETs and the Fund must fundamentally be based on a mutual respect for different social and political systems, while building upon shared economic and monetary goals. Issues such as influence over policy making, access to liquidity and Fund resources, a reshaped policy on surveillance and stabilization measures administered by the Fund, greater control over exchange rate movements, dampening exchange rate volatility, coordinating monetary and other macroeconomic policies of the PETs are all essential ingredients of the debate. Furthermore, there is no doubt that the Fund has and will continue to exert a determinant role in the design and maintenance of the "proper" structure and functioning of financial institutions, the adequacy of money and capital markets, the actual and potential capacity of countries to generate domestic savings, the financial exploration of development programs in the context of the country's current external financial position, more general foreign debt problems, and related matters. These concerns need to be recognized and tackled in the context of prevailing and emerging conditions.

Such a technical rapprochement could, in my view, be built up on the strength of reciprocal advantages. The shared economic interests consist of the PETs' need for macroeconomic policy control; assistance with redesigning their monetary and financial systems; and how best to promote the importation of technology, managerial expertise, and capital resources without exacerbating external balances. Many of these resources will have to be attracted through private channels, including most importantly FDI and commercial borrowing. However, private capitalists and commercial banks cannot be held responsible for ensuring that the public good of the international monetary regime is maintained (Helleiner 1983, pp. 47ff.) and adjusted to accommodate the needs of the PETs in particular. In this connection, it bears to restate that, though the international monetary regime should not itself be responsible for formulating, managing, and modifying the global resource-transfer mechanism, it has a vital function to play in seeing to it that the international financial regime and its basic institution - the World Bank and its various regional counterparts - can function smoothly.

4. PETs and the international financial regime

Prior to the revolutions in Eastern Europe, the World Bank counted among its members the same CPEs or MPEs that are in the Fund (see Section 3). The commentary that could be formulated with respect to the planned economies that do not yet participate in the international financial regime and the shifting stances in recent years of countries that are not yet PETs on becoming associated with the World Bank in one way or another should be almost identical with the positions described earlier as regards the international monetary regime.

The conditions under which the CPEs or MPEs have traditionally been able to take part in the World Bank depended in part on their strained position within the Fund. However, because the nature of the international financial system differs in many substantive respects from the Fund's, the Eastern European countries, as well as other CPEs, have been able to participate somewhat less onerously in the World Bank than in the Fund (Assetto 1988). This pertains in particular to their ability to attract loans from and to participate in competitive bidding on projects financed by the World Bank or its affiliates. Nonetheless, it is useful to recall that these countries did not, in fact, fit in well or easily with the international financial regime in place or the standard approach taken by the institution entrusted with the application of that regime. This was perhaps less so at a time that the World Bank was mainly concerned about project financing than about lending for structural adjustment purposes embraced since the late 1970s. When economies being subjected to adjustment policies are not really fully market oriented, the key assumptions underlying the standard structural adjustment approach of the World Bank, just as the Fund's, cannot be applied indiscriminately, if at all. In this connection, it is not expenditure reduction and switching that are in doubt. Rather, it is the methods used to accomplish those tasks, both technically and politically, that differ measurably for countries that by and large adhere to substantial nonmarket methods of policy formulation and implementation. Of course, in the case of planned economies per se, the questions of policy autonomy and the ways in which international surveillance can be exercised should not be disregarded.

As a result of the shift away in lending policy from project financing to supporting structural adjustment programs, a particular development philosophy has been crystallizing around the World Bank's propagation of lending in DEs (Sengupta 1987). Instead of supplementing private project finance as its main *raison d'être*, the Bank has come to view its mission more and more as stimulating structural change in DEs through loans, perhaps on concessional terms, in the hope of alleviating eventually the severity of external constraints on sustainable development. Furthermore, such shifts have become increasingly motivated by a pronounced advocacy of private enterprise, market-type economic activity, thereby affecting the obligations of loan recipients. These have become heavily tilted in favor of dismantling institutions, policy instruments, macroeconomic policies, and behavioral guidelines that are perceived to hinder market-inspired entrepreneurial activity, whether of domestic or foreign origin. These shifts have also affected the decision-making mechanisms of the World Bank. Note that many of these issues share the policy concerns prevailing in PETs. Can those shared concerns be met through the standard World Bank policies on fostering market orientation?

Given the sorry state of the development process in general and what is required to pull the PETs out of their current quagmire in particular, I see no need to argue at length that considerable international resource transfers are required in the years ahead and that radical new approaches are called for to ensure that such flows emerge. The issues range from management of the global resource transfer mechanism, given the unequal opportunity to access financial markets; to responsibility of the global system as such for equitable and sustainable growth throughout the world, and thus the need to heed differential requirements for external finance; and to sectoral management of resource needs, for example, to raise food and energy output.

The resource-transfer mechanism is a public good just as the monetary and trading regimes offer public goods (Camps 1981, pp. 202-3). The regime's functions in that respect fall essentially into three categories: (1) the amounts, terms, and productivity of ODA; (2) the criteria for making choices about the countries and activities to be given priority in resource allocation; and (3) coordination among varied bi- and multilateral assistance programs that are extant. The prevailing divergent views owe much to political issues such as questions regarding how much autonomy is to be permitted, who decides, who manages, who pays, and who benefits.

The increased capacity of the World Bank to channel development funds to PETs too should accrue largely from multilateralizing development assistance to ensure that more of the available resources for development go to countries that need them most. Furthermore, multilateralizing concessional assistance and consolidating some of the related multilateral funds and programs would reduce the burden of beneficiaries having to comply with a myriad of policies propagated by different agencies. Regaining control over the global management of savings should be at the core of policies in the World Bank and the Fund. What the PETs need essentially is efficient resource transfers that enhance FDI based on domestic and foreign savings. That is not to deny that commercial sources of finance, such as in Euromarkets, have been important in lending for development purposes. But private banks seek profits and thus have an incentive to lend when prospects look favorable and to pull out when they look bad (Bird 1983, p. 13). The concern of private bankers pure and simple is to generate revenues that yield profit in the interest of protecting stockholders and depositors. In other words, their activities exacerbate cyclicality. This entails economic inefficiencies and inequities from the point of view of desirable global economic performance.

The ability of the international financial regime to mobilize global excess savings that would otherwise not be channeled from primary savers to potential users of funds for lack of a proper transmission mechanism in an interdependent global economy is in large measure predicated on a safe framework. That can exist only if responsibility for that framework is not divided among too many different and scattered institutions. The newly created EBRD offers opportunities for formulating such a harmonized approach to stimulating economic development in Eastern Europe. Unfortunately, the resources placed at the disposal of the bank and the restrictions on the degree to which the bank can supplement its subscribed capital with borrowed funds are such that the harmonization policies that can be pursued under the bank's aegis depend considerably on the goodwill of other agencies to take their cue from bank policies. This places a considerable burden on bank management to overcome reluctance and political interference in economic decision making. Certainly, not every issue of development finance for Eastern Europe could or should be entrusted to one organization, such as the EBRD. Nevertheless, a solid argument against further proliferation of resource-transfer institutions can be justified to ensure more transparent coordination and management at the global level with a view to fostering steady and reliable resource transfers, thus moving away from today's rather discretionary disbursements.

Now that the PETs have jettisoned traditional precepts on development strategies and participation in global economic affairs, there will presumably emerge a shift in the way in which these countries have looked upon development finance and especially extending ODA (Brabant 1990a). On the other hand, even with the best of intentions, these countries cannot quickly raise their own ODA efforts (Brabant 1990d). This, then, provides another opportunity for averting short-term conflicts in east-west development assistance that may sour the environment for reconstructing the global financial system.

One of the ways in which such conflicts can be mitigated is by letting the PETs and emerging PETs participate fully in the international financial regime. That applies also to the Soviet Union. Soviet policy makers could derive considerable knowledge from the structural adjustment policies and investment project analysis typically undertaken by the World Bank. It could also learn enormously - as well as derive valuable export revenues - from participating in World Bank projects. Gathering new experience in markets that will be vital to the envisaged expansion of Soviet exports of manufactures in the years to come is exceedingly important (Hough 1986, p. 493).

5. PETs and the international trading regime

Prior to the political revolutions in Eastern Europe, the CPEs and MPEs maintained a rather strained relationship with the international trading regime in general and the GATT in particular. On technical grounds, one can defend the argument that it is utterly meaningless to seek to associate the orthodox CPE or even the MPE with a trading regime specifically designed for DMEs. Such planned economies can at best only partially comply with the traditional trade-off of tariffs and other trade barriers. For that reason, all kinds of *ad hoc* arrangements had to be contrived to associate CPEs and MPEs with the GATT to some degree. These approaches fell essentially into four different kinds of association (Brabant 1990a, pp. 179-93), with the provisions enacted for Hungary coming closest to full Contracting Party status; some countries, including the Soviet Union until it was granted observership in May 1990, were in fact kept out of the GATT altogether and others were inhibited from transforming their observership into full Contracting Party status. But important derogations of the General Agreement were kept in place especially as a result of the decision of the United States to regulate its relations with so-called state-trading countries on an *ad hoc* basis and the discretionary authority of key DMEs, especially the EC members, to maintain discriminatory quantitative restrictions and safeguard measures against planned economies.

Whereas before, association of CPEs or MPEs could be arranged only by compromising on core foundations of the trading system, the market orientation of the PETs presents an opportunity for creative thinking about how more comprehensive association with the GATT could facilitate the transition process. At the same time, it needs to be recognized that several potential applicants, most notably the Soviet Union but in many respects also China, are nowhere near anchoring resolute market orientation at this juncture. The questions that crop up in an analysis of whether it would be worth seeking an entrance for those countries as well remain unanswered for now (Brabant 1990l).

These are not just rhetorical issues. If accession of reforming CPEs can help these countries to strengthen the foundations of the transition toward decentralization and the determination of policy makers to pursue this goal, it would seem useful to explore alternative ways of facilitating this process. This all the more when reforms can be expected in time to lead to new export markets for Contracting Parties. The "in time" qualification is crucial as countries cannot immediately abandon their trade regime without introducing severe instability. An acceptable proposal for meaningful association could usefully be tailored to present needs of these countries without overly infringing on the interests of Contracting Parties.

In spite of ambiguities about how reciprocity should be interpreted (Keohane 1986), countries have continued to emphasize gaining export markets while losing less in domestic production as a result of the strengthened import competition likely to emanate from reciprocal tariff and related concessions. This trade-off was difficult to enforce for CPEs and MPEs, in part because they pursued domestic policy autonomy. How can one determine nearly balanced concessions when domestic prices are not really the terms at which alternatives are offered? There is simply no adequate basis for determining reciprocity other than by estimating the export effect for the planned economy of a tariff reduction by Contracting Parties and enforcing a compensatory import effect through the central planning machinery. Agreeing on computational methodology and accepting the results of such technically complex estimates are bound to be no mean feat, given the evolving process of shifts in the global economy, the buoyancy of development, and policy objectives of the CPEs and MPEs.

With the emergence of PETs an entirely new situation is crystallizing. This as well as other reasons justify exploring ways of bringing even CPEs or MPEs only weakly committed to market orientation into the process by modifying the traditional trading arrangements and taking into account the potential needs of the countries that still seek domestic policy autonomy (Brabant 1988; 1989g; 1990a, l). Perhaps most important would be taking some aspects of the potentially acrimonious east-west relations out of the purely national political realm and placing it under rather more international surveillance. It would be most constructive to do so while providing maneuvering room for multilateral discussions of the manifold problems of how to bridge differences in economic organization and their implications for other countries (Brabant 1990d).

There is wide consensus in the profession that the prevailing international trade regime has become less and less universal and multilateral. There are many reasons that help to explain this situation. To some degree, it stems from the failure to transform the wayward station of the GATT into the third pillar of the world economic system on an equal footing with the IMF and World Bank. This would have yielded the necessary institutional tools to anticipate, identify, and address trading problems in the broad sense and to lay the groundwork for systematic negotiations of the many issues at stake. In this connection, it would have been possible to modify the trading regime in light of new and emerging circumstances and to come to grips with the issues arising from the nature of the international trade regime as a public good and the opportunities for free riding (Artis and Ostry 1986, p. 75). Among these issues are the problems of the NIEs; the role of DEs in the trade regime more generally (Dyumilen 1984, Koekkoek 1988); how best to foster structural change throughout the global economy with a minimum of adverse, even if localized, dislocations; graduation rules for countries that presently enjoy preferences stemming from the inability of the DMEs to address development issues head-on in the context of the GATT; the competitive export of unemployment; agricultural protectionism and the role of national security therein (Runge 1988); the proliferation of discriminatory restrictions beyond those condoned by the General Agreement; east-west economic issues (Paszyński 1988); and so forth. These multiple problems can be adequately addressed through persuasion and mutual accommodation that in time may lead to proper codification.

A concerted effort to improve the institutional mechanism for decision making, rule development, dispute settlement, enforcement, and the coordination of national policies affecting trade might ultimately prove to be a prerequisite to regaining full multilateralism at as global a level as feasible. At the same time, one should harbor no illusion that the immense impediments to such multilateral collaboration could be easily overcome. It is all the more urgent, then, with a view to enhancing welfare and fostering international security, that countries jointly attempt to prevent world trade from regressing to a situation where it might become still more precarious and restricted than in the 1930s.

It is doubtful that such a transformation is feasible within the present trading regime, certainly if it were to be embedded within the GATT context (Brabant 1990a, pp. 219-31), in whose legalistic framework countries other than DMEs do not fit comfortably (Camps 1981, p. 147). The world needs an institution that can reflect and cater to the interests of all participants in a multilateral trading system. For want of a better name, I earlier christened such an institution the Reconceived International Trade Organization (see Brabant 1990a, l). The purpose of such an organ derives from the fact that the world as a whole stands to benefit from an improved institutional mechanism within which trade issues can be addressed systematically and comprehensively.

Until recently, it was difficult to explore a reconstitution of the trading regime because major trading partners were not favorably inclined to do so comprehensively. The realignment of global economic forces, in part under impulse of the ongoing transformations in Eastern Europe, may offer a new opportunity for such a reexamination of fair trading practices and how to ensure that they are observed and adapted as a result of changes in the global economy. This could perhaps lead to investing an international organization with the task of coming to grips with the fundamental requirements of a fair trading world. Its institutional and organizational requirements are certainly not insuperable.

6. Remaking Europe

The eventual fusion of eastern and western Europe into one United States of Europe is, of course, not simply an economic matter. It is an eminently political act that may materialize after centuries of divisiveness on the continent. But a united Europe has economic facets as well, and it may be instructive to ponder some of their main implications for they set the tone for the kind of society that can be brought into the European community of nations. The tests to pass muster are at this stage by no means defined hard and fast. But it may just as well be instructive to speculate a bit about what might be minimum features to be strived for to facilitate the merger of east and west.

There are at least four criteria that could usefully be considered. First, the supremacy of the rule of law needs to be constitutionally recognized. Especially after the protracted recent experience with bureaucratic and Party-dominated interference in people's lives, it is now necessary to adopt legal codes that are squarely in the mainstream of the *Rechtsstaat* typical of most DMEs, especially in Western Europe. That is not to say that these countries should simply take over, say, the Napoleontic code lock, stock, and barrel. It does mean, though, that the principles upon which the legal codes are to be drafted should not deviate too much from the core of the juridical system of Western European countries. To ensure this, a constitution enforcing basic principles on human rights, the separation of powers, the prerogatives of the various powers, property relations, the role of political parties and free elections, the democratic process more generally, and many other items need to be worked out as expeditiously as circumstances permit.

Second, in view of the postwar history of Eastern Europe especially important is the unconditional guarantee of human rights even prior to the formulation of a new constitution. It would seem to be a minimum requirement for the PETs to tolerate the right to free expression in whatever form acceptable to society, to entitle citizens to travel and migrate, to profess their religious beliefs without interference, and in the end to recognize the inviolability of personal freedom. This may be circumscribed by communal needs identified in the social compact and eventually enshrined in a new constitution.

Third, a transition to a democratically elected government with a separation of powers among the executive, legislative, and juridical branches is highly desirable. That presupposes the recognition of the validity of multiple parties and the holding of regular elections to be fairly contested by all parties. It is essentially up to each country to determine what kind of parties will be able to survive the electoral process and in what form these parties will be represented in the parliamentary organs to be endowed with greater powers than ever before. The example of the western democracies may be just that. But they do not offer a patent recipe that the eastern countries can apply without experimentation and, possibly, reconfiguration "to taste."

Finally, there is a need to recognize that the precepts of economies with orthodox central planning are difficult to reconcile with the interests of MEs. It is therefore necessary that the former liberalize their economies in major respects. That is not to say that they need to throw out the child with the bathwater, and forego all planning. On the contrary, planning needs to be given a much more confined, but at the same time very powerful, role in the formulation and implementation of the government's macroeconomic policies and perhaps also in its precepts on social welfare and equity as supported through the democratic process. As far as the microeconomy is concerned, the PETs must constitutionally guarantee the validity of all property forms. To break the back of the entrenched positions of the former Party, *nomenklatura*, and managerial bureaucracy in economic affairs and to whittle the importance of monopolies some measure of privatization as well as antitrust legislation needs to be enacted as soon as feasible. But this process is strewn with pitfalls and will therefore have to be pursued with considerable caution (see Chapter 7).

Conclusions

There is little doubt that at the time of writing history is being made not only in Eastern Europe, but in Europe as a whole. This cannot but yield repercussions for the management of the global system. Whether the mutations under way in and for Eastern Europe add up to the best outcome among the feasible alternatives has been the subject of this book. Four broad sets of questions have been introduced. I shall briefly summarize the salient points drawn from the analyses that could usefully be borne in mind in further refining the east-west cooperation effort.

1. Consequences of the radical reforms

Because the economic revolutions that are being embraced by the PETs and those that may yet come to fruition elsewhere in Eastern Europe are indeed unprecedented and irreversible, their economic and other consequences need to be carefully evaluated. They offer a unique - historic, if you wish - opportunity for remaking Europe out of the postwar divisions and divisiveness.

There are many differences among the individual country reforms and the circumstances under which they are being conceived and implemented. This holds even if the discourse is confined to the PETs as defined in this book. Nonetheless, the "basic" reform program implicit in the various discussions is one that seeks to replace central planning through administrative means from the roots up with a decentralized ME geared by coherent macroeconomic policies, institutions, and instruments. Ultimate economic sovereignty in such an environment rests with economic agents themselves. Naturally, central authorities there are responsible for stabilization and coordination through the imaginative use of macroeconomic policies. That includes, where desirable, the steering of the economy in a particular direction of structural change that is deemed of strategic benefit in the longer term.

In many reforming countries, this feature of economic sovereignty, especially insofar as the reflection of individual preferences in societywide policy making is concerned, is resulting increasingly from a political process that gives rise to a social contract or understanding so that the responsibilities for macroeconomic steering as defined above will be entrusted by the electorate to its designated representatives. These will as a rule channel this mandate through some variant of a parliamentary democracy, with actual policy formulation and implementation being entrusted to the executive arm of government. The latter, by its nature, will be separate from the legislative and judicial branches.

What these countries hope to achieve is a divorce of the technical aspects of economics from its more normative features, including vital questions pertaining to unemployment levels, income distribution, social stability, and other preferences that as a rule can be heeded only through state intervention, not necessarily the government assuming these functions to the hilt. At the same time, precisely because they are unprecedented, these transformations are ushering into these countries an unusual degree of instability that may severely test the strength and cohesiveness of their newly emerging sociopolitical fabric.

2. Forms and sequencing of reforms

An underlying theme of the book has been that the transformation of planned economies into market-oriented societies is a daunting task, certainly far more complex than the reconversion of Western Europe from wartime controls. The nuts and bolts of the basic structures of the ME have to be largely created in Eastern Europe from first principles. Efficient markets do not simply spring to life on the retreat of central planners and bureaucratic controls. Among others, they require a complex infrastructure of laws, financial systems, adequate information that is widely disseminated, and the gradual development of certain habits of economic behavior that arise slowly under impulse of competition, risk taking, financial probity, and other features of operating within a regulated market context. Furthermore, to be competitive and encourage innovation and structural change in line with shifting comparative advantages, markets require a certain size distribution of firms, a degree of openness to the world economy, and a regulatory infrastructure.

It is because so many of these and related features of an ME are available in the PETs at best only in very rudimentary form that one must doubt the ability of these countries to transform themselves quickly into fully functioning MEs capable of absorbing immediately large amounts of financial resources in whatever form, regardless of the prevailing factor productivity gaps. That includes resources from domestic as well as foreign origin. This suggests that there must be ways in which the order of priority in policy actions, including those that find support abroad, can be set, however inaccurately, and that relative magnitudes of kinds of assistance from abroad can be pinpointed.

Since changes in structure and economic behavior can materialize only with some delay, the arguments presented point to a more evolutionary approach to the reform process than the rapid, shock treatment suggested by some observers. In addition to the logic behind this assertion, there are other considerations that weigh. One is that those advocating a rapid reform pace appear to be quite optimistic about the speed with which competitive markets can be erected. If this assumption is correct, there would be little point for any kind of broad-based foreign assistance program. Those subscribing to a more evolutionary approach not only see the establishment of competitive markets as a difficult process requiring time and careful intervention by governments, but they are also concerned about the consequences of the market optimists being proved wrong. Expectations of the population at large are invariably raised by reform promises. To add to this the prospect of rapid fulfillment is to risk an explosive social situation if the optimism proves ill-founded. From this point of view it is less costly to adopt the evolutionary approach and be wrong.

Second, the argument over whether reform should be rapid or gradual is sometimes obscured by the mixing up of macro- and microeconomic considerations and of long-run structural changes with macroeconomic stabilization issues. All PETs and those aspiring to that status need to implement sound macroeconomic policies, based on monetary and fiscal instruments. Persistent macroeconomic imbalances cannot but hasten the reversal of microeconomic reform, rendering it ineffective. PETs with high rates of inflation or pent-up imbalances and large external deficits must clearly move quickly to contain and correct these disequilibria. But that is a different matter from implementing a program of rapid structural transformation. Structural reform in countries with high rates of inflation will anyway prove to be difficult because uncertainty about real yields on capital investment tends to strengthen with growing inflationary expectations. Furthermore, stabilization in most PETs will have to factor in obdurate supply-side problems for some years to come. In this situation western assistance could be especially helpful in allowing these countries to concentrate on their structural problems by easing external payments pressures, particularly the constraints emanating from the inherited foreign debt.

Probably one of the most important determinants of success in reforms is whether the government is able to create and maintain credibility in its program. Economic reforms and liberalization measures usually generate political resistance because the population sees the immediate costs of the changes more clearly than the long-run benefits. This is even more so when reforms are extensive and interrelated. It is particularly true for the PETs whose latest reforms are moving into the *terra incognita* of transition from one economic and social system to another.

In most PETs, the new political landscape has only just begun to crystallize. Under the circumstances, there is presently a great deal of mistrust and suspicion on the part of broad layers of the population about government that will have to be overcome. Popular elections may help, but cannot be a panacea in the short run, given the fragility of the emerging political process. Credibility is not simply a matter of providing information or making propaganda about the ultimate benefits of certain reform intentions, but of presenting a coherent reform program, including its credible sequencing. If economic agents expect a reversal of reform policy they will act accordingly and undermine the policy before the government has an opportunity for second thoughts. There is, however, no simple formula of how governments can best secure credibility for their programs. In the end, the agenda for reform will in good measure be set pragmatically, including by *ad hoc* considerations. Because of the importance of gaining credibility, sustained support for radical structural reform is required, and this might be a crucial instance for western assistance to be assembled in such a way as to reinforce the coherence and proper sequencing of reforms. The preparation of such coherent reform programs is perhaps another area where technical assistance from western macroeconomists, especially those with knowledge of the eastern systems, could make a useful contribution.

Once a reform program gains credibility, the question of gradualist versus shock or "big bang" approaches becomes secondary. In practice, given the range and scale of the structural problems faced by the PETs, progress is likely to be difficult and gradual. But that may not matter very much so long as progress does not markedly diverge from the rising expectations of the population.

3. Adequacy and consistency of western assistance

If only because of the assistance these countries deserve, as judged on the basis of a wide variety of criteria, strategic and power-political not being the least of them, I inquired into the unprecedented efforts on the part of the MEs to come to the assistance of Eastern Europe in general and the PETs in particular. I have detailed and appraised the various assistance efforts undertaken from the point of view of their contribution to the stabilization of the PETs, the longer-term aims of moving toward a more market-oriented environment, the internal consistency of these programs, and the likelihood that they will maximize the benefits obtainable by the PETs and, at the same time, to minimize the drawbacks for other countries. Instead of putting in place a Marshall Plan for Eastern Europe, in the sense of repeating the exercise undertaken for Western Europe after World War II, I have advocated several instances in which the west might render more effective support to the various reform endeavors of the PETs. Inasmuch as I have identified some of the main priorities in assisting generic PETs rather than what could best be undertaken given the detailed circumstances of individual countries, the concrete forms of the assistance would in any case have to be molded according to prevailing circumstances.

In this context, the example of the Marshall Plan is often alleged to provide an appropriate model for formulating and implementing large-scale assistance to the east. However, a careful examination of the similarities and differences between the situation of Western Europe after World War II and the situation of Eastern Europe at this juncture suggests that the Marshall Plan is not an appropriate framework within which large-scale assistance can be most effectively provided to Eastern Europe.

Although a repeat of the Marshall Plan would not be appropriate, given the marked differences in basic economic structures in Western Europe after World War II and Eastern Europe now, experiences with the Marshall Plan provide a number of valuable lessons that could be put to good use. Given the nature of the structural problems of the PETs, the assistance effort should in the first instance be aimed at helping the PETs overcome their structural obstacles to a well-functioning ME (Prowse 1990). The argument that the institutional, legal, and financial infrastructures of MEs must be put in place before markets can perform as expected, suggests that the order in which reforms are introduced may be more important than the pace of reforms. Encouraging large inflows of foreign investment, for example, while there are still considerable distortions in domestic markets may entail serious misallocation of investment (Kaletsky 1990). It may also impart upward pressure on the real exchange rate when the opposite might be more appropriate.

The individual constituents of a technical assistance program to one PET or another depend on the particular circumstances at hand. Nonetheless, it is important to bear in mind the priority to be given to a number of elements that play such a critical role in creating credibility in the reform programs. They also help to modify the expectations of economic agents according to what appears to be a realistic pace of structural reform. Among the many priorities that could usefully be considered, I have argued the absolute need to ensure technical assistance for the creation of the legal, financial, and institutional framework that is so essential for the operation of a competitive market system. The same applies to the provision of comprehensive and reliable statistical and economic information services for both government and firms to enhance their decision-making roles in an ME environment. Essential to operating in a market is the acquisition of various marketing skills required for effectively expanding exports to world markets and seeing to it that the competitive environment does not get frustrated by the panoply of qualitative and quantitative import barriers. Changes in commercial policy in east and west alike can help to encourage and maintain such improvements. Some measures, such as the elimination of quotas and other discriminatory quantitative restrictions, are already included in the assistance programs on the books. But more could be done.

The above-mentioned priorities do not, of course, exclude the need for financial assistance, particularly in support of currency stabilization and the current account. It may also play a constructive role in breaking well-defined bottlenecks to establishing efficient markets. It is essential that such financial assistance be in the form of grants rather than additions to already high debt levels in many PETs. It should also avoid repeating the mistake of the 1970s, when commercial lending was rapidly increased without proper appreciation of the microeconomic distortions and inefficiences embedded in the CPEs and MPEs. Any financial assistance, other than for emergency purposes, should have as central focus the removal of domestic market distortions, which are still very substantial. This applies also for the proposed CEPU which has been conceived as one further instrument to making foreign trading more transparent, including in its links to the domestic economy. The CEPU is there essentially as a guarantee for enterprises to be concerned primarily about prices and quantities of goods for which they feel they can earn a profit; exchange rate and settlements matters would be left to the central policy makers, including through the CEPU. In this context, a major transformation of the CMEA and making it into an effective integration organization has been advocated. For the more adventurous CMEA members, I have argued the need to envisage regional integration in multiple stages, with the most ambitious ones taking the form of a CEEU that would be supported through a multilateral clearing scheme - the CEPU.

To obtain maximum benefit from western assistance, it would be useful if a medium-term assistance program were to be drawn up by the recipient countries themselves on the basis of a needs' assessment, in which they show how they intend to reach their structural adjustment objectives. Furthermore, because of the time required to create fairly integrated markets, these programs should be specified over a sufficiently long period of time. Given the variety of uncoordinated western approaches, it might be useful to have one technically competent international institution, perhaps in the context of the CSCE efforts, to help coordinate, monitor, and provide room for debate or at least the exchange of ideas and knowledge of the various national programs.

4. Ramifications for the global economic framework

Finally, the ongoing transformations in Eastern Europe and the unprecedented western assistance are bound to affect other countries and the global economic framework. In the first instance, there will be ramifications on the remaining CPEs and MPEs, if only because of the far-reaching reconstitution of the CMEA trade and payments regime and perhaps the thorough reconstitution of the organization as such. There will also be important changes in the east-west context, particularly in Europe, that need to be factored into the equation. In the end, the diversion of resources from west to east may constrain the financial and other forms of assistance that developed countries can sustain for the DEs. I have looked at instances of remaking Europe that may entail negative implications of this international assistance. These are likely to emerge in the first instance in the diversion of FDI and portfolio capital flows, with or without official guarantees, to the east. These may have a measurable impact on the NIEs, including the less developed countries in the EC. Inasmuch as the prospects of luring such capital flows into the least developed DEs have not been very good for a long time, the impact of a renewed east-west approach is likely on the whole to remain negligible; but individual DEs may well be markedly affected in the process. With some notable exceptions, especially the policy stance of the United States, there is thus far little evidence that ODA sums earlier earmarked by DMEs will be diverted from south to east. But some of development finance traditionally dispensed through multilateral agencies cannot but be affected by additional claims for Eastern Europe unless there were to be a sizable increase in the capital base of these multilateral agencies.

It is worth remembering that although the PETs have embarked on a difficult and protracted process of reform and adjustment, the global economy is now much stronger than when the last massive aid effort was launched after World War II; indeed, one of the latter's objectives was to strengthen the global economic framework itself. After recovering from the various shocks of the 1970s, growth in the DMEs has been sustained at relatively high rates throughout the 1980s. In Western Europe, because of buoyant expectations about the benefits of the Single Market in 1992, the underlying trend is for sustained expansion in the 1990s. If these expectations are borne out, not only should the burden of western assistance be relatively light, but so should the dismantling of protectionist barriers against imports into the MEs. At the same time, a buoyant world economy provides the PETs with the opportunity to develop outward-oriented policies and, thereby, underpin the process of their transformation into competitive economies. Taking into account the repercussions of the mutations occurring in Eastern Europe in all efforts to manage the global economy could only enhance and smooth the process of global adjustment. Is the mandate to the Fund issued by the Houston summit in July 1990 to extend a global hand also to the Soviet Union an indication of the DMEs seizing the opportunity to improve global economic management?

Bibliography

Abolikhina, Galina A., Oleg Bakovetskiy, and Boris I. Medvedev, "Sushchnost' i novye formy sotsialisticheskoy integratsii," *Voprosy ekonomiki*, 1987:1, 129-40.

Adamiec, Jolanta, "Nowe ramy współpracy EWG z krajami socjalistycznymi," *Handel Zagraniczny*, 1989:7, 16-18, 22.

Alchian, Armen A., "Property rights," *The new Palgrave - a dictionary of economics, vol. 3* (London: Macmillan, 1987), pp. 1031-34.

Amsden, Alice H., "An Asian plan for Eastern Europe, *The New York Times*, 6 April 1990, 35.

Artis, Michael and Sylvia Ostry, *International economic policy coordination* (London: Routledge & Kegan Paul, for the Royal Institute of International Affairs, 1986).

Ashdown, Paddy, "Performance, not ownership," *Private Investor*, Autumn 1989, 87-89, 150.

Assetto, Valerie J., *The Soviet bloc in the IMF and the IBRD* (Boulder, CO and London: Westview Press, 1988).

Bauer, Michel, "The politics of state-directed privatisation: the case of France, 1986-88," *West European Politics*, 1988:4, 49-60.

Bianchi, Patrizio, Sabino Cassese, and Vincent della Sala, "Privatisation in Italy: aims and constraints," *West European Politics*, 1988:4, 87-100.

Bird, Graham, "Reforming the Fund: the future role of the International Monetary Fund in the international financial system," *Three Banks Review*, 1983:4, 3-21.

Black, Stanley W., "International money and international monetary arrangements," in *Handbook of international economics, vol. II*, edited by Ronald W. Jones and Peter B. Kenen (Amsterdam: Elsevier Science Publishers, 1985), pp. 1153-93.

Bourguinat, Henri, "The European monetary system (EMS): first lessons and new challenges," in *Macroeconomic management and the enterprise in east and west*, edited by Christopher T. Saunders (London: Macmillan in association with the Vienna Institute for Comparative Economic Studies, 1988), pp. 133-53.

Brabant, Jozef M. van, "Zur Rolle Mitteleuropas im Rahmen des Rats für gegenseitige Wirtschaftshilfe," *Osteuropa-Wirtschaft*, 1976:1, 1-20.

Brabant, Jozef M. van, *Socialist economic integration - aspects of contemporary economic problems in Eastern Europe* (New York and Cambridge: Cambridge University Press, 1980).

Brabant, Jozef M. van, *Adjustment, structural change, and economic efficiency - aspects of monetary cooperation in Eastern Europe* (New York and Cambridge: Cambridge University Press, 1987a).

Brabant, Jozef M. van, *Regional price formation in Eastern Europe - on the theory and practice of trade pricing* (Dordrecht-Boston-Lancaster: Kluwer Academic Publishers, 1987b).

Brabant, Jozef M. van, "Economic adjustment and the future of socialist economic integration," *Eastern European Politics and Society*, 1987c:1, 75-112.

Brabant, Jozef M. van, "The CMEA summit and socialist economic integration - a perspective," *Jahrbuch der Wirtschaft Osteuropas - Yearbook of East-European Economics*, Vol. 12/1 (1987d), pp. 129-60.

Brabant, Jozef M. van, "Planned economies in the GATT framework - the Soviet case," *Soviet Economy*, 1988:1, 3-35.

Brabant, Jozef M. van, *Economic integration in Eastern Europe - a handbook* (Hemel Hempstead: Harvester Wheatsheaf and New York: Routledge, 1989a).

Brabant, Jozef M. van, "Economic policy aims and their implementation - summary," in *Economic reforms in the European centrally planned economies* (New York: United Nations, published by Adeco, Geneva for the United Nations, 1989b), pp. 219-25.

Brabant, Jozef M. van, "Regional integration, economic reforms, and convertibility," *Jahrbuch der Wirtschaft Osteuropas - Yearbook of East-European Economics*, Vol. 13/1 (1989c), pp. 44-81.

Brabant, Jozef M. van, "Scientific-technological cooperation - its organization," in *The status of civil science in Eastern Europe*, edited by Craig Sinclair (Dordrecht-Lancaster-Boston: Kluwer Academic Publishers, 1989d), pp. 3-40.

Brabant, Jozef M. van, "On the economics of scientific-technological cooperation," in *The status of civil science in Eastern Europe*, edited by Craig Sinclair (Dordrecht-Lancaster-Boston: Kluwer Academic Publishers, 1989e), pp. 41-72.

Brabant, Jozef M. van, "CMEA reform and the formulation of a constitutional framework" (presented at the conference on "The radical reform of the CMEA as a precondition of cooperation with the EC - theoretical and practical questions," Sopron, Hungary, 16-20 November 1989f).

Brabant, Jozef M. van, "The Soviet Union in the GATT? - a plea for reform," *International Spectator*, 1989g:2, 72-93.

Brabant, Jozef M. van, *The planned economies and international economic organizations* (Cambridge: Cambridge University Press, 1990a).

Brabant, Jozef M. van, "Trade policies in the Council for Mutual Economic Assistance," in *Handbook of national trade policies*, edited by Dominick Salvatore (Greenwich, CT: Greenwood Press, 1990b), forthcoming.

Brabant, Jozef M. van, "Is there a place for socialist integration in the 1990s?" in *CMEA in the 1990s*, edited by Vladimir Sobell (Boulder, CO: Westview Press, 1990c), forthcoming.

Brabant, Jozef M. van, "Socialist countries and development assistance," in *Alternatives to superpower competition in the third world - Latin America and beyond*, edited by John Weeks (New York: New York University Press, 1990d), forthcoming.

Brabant, Jozef M. van, "Ruble convertibility in the reform process - a sobering note," *Foreign capital and monetizing the Soviet economy*, edited by Josef C.

Brada and Michael Claudon (New York: New York University Press, 1990e), forthcoming.

Brabant, Jozef M. van, "National economic policies in the USSR," in *Comparative handbook of national economic policies*, edited by Dominick Salvatore (Westport, CO: Greenwoord Press, 1990f), forthcoming.

Brabant, Jozef M. van, "Wither the CMEA? - reconstructing socialist economic integration in the 1990s," *Osteuropa-Wirtschaft*, 1990g:2, forthcoming.

Brabant, Jozef M. van, "Property rights' reform, macroeconomic performance, and welfare" (paper prepared for the conference on "Privatization and economic reform in Eastern Europe," organized under the auspices of OECD, Paris, 20-21 June 1990h).

Brabant, Jozef M. van, "Economies in transition and privatization - the case of Eastern Europe" (paper presented to the conference on "Changing Economic Order," organized by the Studiekring Post-Keynesiaanse Economie, Antwerp, 12 October 1990i).

Brabant, Jozef M. van, "On reforming the trade and payments regimes in the CMEA," *Jahrbuch der Wirtschaft Osteuropas*, Vol. 14/2 (1990j), forthcoming.

Brabant, Jozef M. van, "Socialist economics: the disequilibrium school and the shortage economy," *Journal of Economic Perspectives*, 1990k:2, 157-75.

Brabant, Jozef M. van, "Requirements for full and equal participation of planned economies in the global trade framework," *Journal of Development Planning*, No. 20 (1990l), 163-90.

Brainard. Lawrence, "Strategies for economic transformation in Eastern Europe - the role of financial market reform" (paper prepared for the conference on "Privatization and economic reform in Eastern Europe," organized under the auspices of OECD, Paris, 20-21 June 1990).

Bruszt, Lászlő, "The dilemmas of economic transition in Hungary," *Südosteuropa*, 1989:12, 716-28.

Buckland, Roger, "The costs and returns of the privatization of nationalized industries," *Public Administration*, 1987:3, 241-57.

Campbell, Robert W., "On the theory of economic administration," in *Industrialization in two systems - essays in honor of Alexander Gerschenkron*, edited by Henry Rosovsky (New York: Wiley, 1966), pp. 186-203.

Camps, Miriam, with the collaboration of Catherine Gwin, *Collective management - the reform of global economic organizations* (New York: McGraw-Hill, for the Council on Foreign Relations/1980s Project, 1981).

Cerami, Charles A., ed., *A Marshall Plan for the 1990s - an international roundtable on world economic development* (New York: Praeger, 1989).

Cheung, Steven N.S., "Economic organization and transaction costs," *The new Palgrave - a dictionary of economics, vol. 2* (London: Macmillan, 1987), pp. 55-57.

CMEA, *Kursom nauchno-tekhnicheskogo progressa - 41-e (vneocherednoe) zasedanie sessii Soveta ekonomicheskoy vzaimopomoshchi* (Moscow: SEV Sekretariat, 1986).

Comisso, Ellen, "Property rights in focus," *Acta Oeconomica*, 1989:4, 210-16.

Cooper, Richard N., "Economic interdependence and coordination of economic policies," in *Handbook of international economics, vol. II*, edited by Ronald W. Jones and Peter B. Kenen (Amsterdam: Elsevier Science Publishers, 1985), pp. 1195-234.

Dąmbrowski, Marian, "The economic effectiveness of the self-managed enterprise - a review of the theoretical literature," *Acta Oeconomica*, 1989:1/2, 39-54.

Davidson, Ian, "Post-war history on track for a new era," *The Financial Times*, 12 February 1990, 4.

Demsetz, Harold, "Toward a theory of property rights," *The American Economic Review, Papers and Proceedings*, 1967:2, 347-59.

Diebold, William, Jr., "The Marshall Plan in retrospect: a review of recent scholarship," *Journal of International Affairs*, 1988:2, 421-35.

Dyumilen, I., "Sostoyanie mirovoy torgovli i problemy razvitiya," *Mirovaya ekonomika i mezhdunarodnye otnosheniya*, 1984:8, 94-96.

Drumaux, Anne, "Privatisation in Belgium: the national and international context," *West European Politics*, 1988:4, 74-86.

Ehlermann, Claus-Dieter, "Aid for Poland and Hungary, first assessment," *European Affairs*, 1989:4, 23-27.

Feige, Edgar L., "Perestroika and socialist privatization: 'what is to be done': and how?" (Madison, WI: The University of Wisconsin, mimeo, 1990).

Furubotn, Eirik G. and Svetozar Pejovich, "Property rights and economic theory: a survey of recent literature," *The Journal of Economic Literature*, 1972:2, 1137-62.

Garton Ash, Timothy, *The uses of adversity - on the fate of Central Europe* (New York: Random House, 1989).

Giscard d'Estaing, Valéry, "The two Europes, east and west," *International Affairs*, 1989:4, 653-8.

Goldberg, Victor P., "Public choice - property rights," *Journal of Economic Issues*, 1974:3, 555-79.

Gordon, Lincoln, "Recollections of a Marshall planner," *Journal of International Affairs*, 1988:2, 233-45.

Grinberg, Ruslan, Konstantin Ligay, and Stanislav Simanovskiy, "Mezhdunarodnyy sotsialisticheskiy kontsern," *Ekonomicheskoe sotrudnichestvo stran-chlenov SEV*, 1989:8, 16-22.

Grosfeld, Irena, "Reform economics and western economic theory: unexploited opportunities," *Economics of Planning*, 1990:1, 1-20.

Grote, Gerhard, "Einige theoretische und praktische Fragen des staatlichen Monopols auf dem Gebiet der Außenwirtschaft," *Wirtschaftswissenschaft*, 1981:2, 143-152.

Hanson, Philip, *Western economic statecraft in east-west relations - embargoes, sanctions, linkage, economic warfare, and detente* (London: Routledge & Kegan for The Royal Institute of International Affairs, 1988).

Havel, Václav, *Interrogatoire à distance - entretien avec Karel Hvížďala* (Paris:

Editions de l'Aube, 1989).

Heald, David, "The United Kingdom: privatisation and its political context," *West European Politics*, 1988:4, 31-48.

Helleiner, Gerald K., "The rise and decline of the IMF," in *Banking on poverty: the global impact of the IMF & World Bank*, edited by Jill Torrie (Toronto: Between the Lines, 1983), pp. 42-54.

Helm, Dieter and George Yarrow, "The assessment: the regulation of utilities," *Oxford Review of Economic Policy*, 1988:2, i-xxxi.

Hemming, Richard and Ali M. Mansoor, *Privatization and public enterprises* (Washington, DC: International Monetary Fund, Occasional Paper No. 56, 1988).

Hewett, Ed A., "Is Soviet socialism reformable?" (Sturc Memorial Lecture, Washington, DC: The Brookings Institution, 1989, mimeographed).

Hinds, Manuel, "Issues in the introduction of market forces in Eastern European socialist economies" (Washington, DC: The World Bank, March 1990a, mimeographed).

Hinds, Manuel, "Issues in the introduction of market forces in Eastern European socialist economies - Annex I - enterprise reform issues" (Washington, DC: The World Bank, March 1990b, mimeographed).

Hogan, Michael J., *The Marshall Plan - America, Britain, and the reconstruction of Western Europe, 1947-1952* (Cambridge: Cambridge University Press, 1987).

Hoscher, Dietmar, "Anmerkungen zur Diskussion über einen Marshallplan für Osteuropa," *Europäische Rundschau*, 1990:1, 31-38.

Hough, Jerry F., "Attack on protectionism in the Soviet Union? a comment," *International Organization*, 1986:2, 489-503.

Ickes, Barry W., "Obstacles to economic reform of socialism: an institutional-choice approach," *Annals of the American Academy of Political and Social Sciences*, 1990:1, 53-64.

Ikonnikov, Igor', "Sovershenstvovanie struktury SEV," *Ekonomicheskoe sotrudnichestvo stran-chlenov SEV*, 1988:2, 20-21.

Kaletsky, Anatole, "No to a blank cheque," *Financial Times*, 26 June 1990, 21.

Kanel, Don, "Property and economic power as issues in institutional economics," *Journal of Economic Issues*, 1974:4, 827-40.

Kay, John and John Vickers, "Regulatory reform in Britain," *Economic Policy*, no. 7 (1988), 286-351.

Kent, Calvin A., ed., *Entrepreneurship and the privatizing of government* (New York-Westport, CO: Quorum Books, 1987a).

Kent, Calvin, A., "Privatization of public functions: promises and problems," in *Entrepreneurship and the privatizing of government*, edited by Calvin A. Kent (New York-Westport, CO: Quorum Books, 1987b), pp. 3-22.

Keohane, Robert O., "Reciprocity in international relations," *International Organization*, 1986:1, 1-27.

King, Timothy, "Foreign direct investment in the East European economic transition" (Washington, DC: The World Bank, March 1990, mimeographed).

Koekkoek, K. A., "The integration of developing countries in the GATT system," *World Development*, 1988:8, 947-57.

Konrád, György, *Antipolitics - an essay* (San Diego-New York-London: Harcourt Brace Jovanovich, 1984).

Konstantinov, Yuriy A., "Valyutnaya sistema sotsialisticheskogo gosudarstva," *Finansy SSSR*, 1984:3, 28-35.

Kornai, János, *The road to a free economy - shifting from a socialist system: the example of Hungary* (New York: W.W. Norton & Company, 1990a).

Kornai, János, *The affinity between ownership and coordination mechanisms - the common experience of reform in socialist countries* (Helsinki: World Institute for Development Economics Research, 1990b).

Kostrzewa, Wojciech, Peter Nunnenkamp, and Holger Schmieding, "A Marshall Plan for Middle and Eastern Europe?" (Kiel, Institut für Weltwirtschaft, Working Paper No. 403, 1990).

Kostrzewa, Wojciech and Holger Schmieding, "An EFTA option for Eastern Europe?" *Swiss Review of World Affairs*, 1990:10, 7-8.

Kotouc, Václav, "Kolektivní koncepce mezinárodní socialistické dělby práce na léta 1991-2005," *Plánované Hospodářství*, 1988:11, 27-38.

Krenzler, Horst G., "Die Europäische Gemeinschaft und der Wandel in Mittel- und Osteuropa," *Europa-Archiv*, 1990:3, 89-96.

Lamb, Geoffrey, "Reforming Eastern European economies," *Global Economic Policy*, 1990:1, 42-47.

Lavoie, Don, "Computation, incentives, and discovery: the cognitive function of markets in market socialism," *Annals of the American Academy of Political and Social Sciences*, 1990:1, 72-79.

Lawson, Colin, "Exchange rates, tax-subsidy schemes, and the revenue from foreign trade in a centrally planned economy," *Economics of Planning*, 1988:1/2, 72-77.

Lee, Barbara and John Nellis, "Enterprise reform and privatization in market economies" (Washington, DC: The World Bank, April 1990, mimeographed).

Leipold, Helmut, "Eigentumsrechte, Öffentlichkeitsgrad und Innovationsschwäche - Lehren aus dem Systemvergleich," in *Innovationsprobleme in Ost und West*, edited by Alfred Schüller, Helmut Leipold, and Hannelore Hamel (Stuttgart: Gustav Fischer Verlag, 1983), pp. 51-64.

Leipold, Helmut, *Wirtschafts- und Gesellschaftssysteme im Vergleich* (Stuttgart: Gustav Fischer Verlag, 1988, 5th ed).

Lipton, David and Jeffrey Sachs, "Creating a market economy in Eastern Europe: the case of Poland" (paper prepared for the Brookings Panel on Economic Activity, 5-6 April 1990, mimeographed).

Ludlow, Peter M., "The future of the international trading system," *The Washington Quarterly*, 1989:4, 157-69.

MacAvoy, Paul W., W.T. Stanbury, George Yarrow, and Richard J. Zeckhauser, eds., *Privatization and state-owned enterprises - lessons from the United States, Great Britain and Canada* (Boston-Dordrecht-London: Kluwer Academic Publishers, 1989).

Mee, Charles L., Jr. *The Marshall Plan - the launching of the pax americana* (New York: Simon and Schuster, 1984).

Meier, Christian, *Die UdSSR und Osteuropa: Auf dem Wege zu einer neuen Struktur multilateraler Beziehungen?* (Cologne: Berichte des Bundesinstituts für ostwissenschaftliche und internationale Studien, 43-1989.

Milward, Alan S., *The reconstruction of Western Europe, 1945-51* (London: Methuen & Co. Ltd, 1987).

Milward, Alan S., "Was the Marshall Plan necessary?" *Diplomatic History*, 1988:2, 231-53.

Moser, Peter, "Toward an open world order: a constitutional economics approach," *The Cato Journal*, 1989:1, 133-47.

Murphy, Kevin J., "The control and performance of state-owned enterprises: comment," in *Privatization and state-owned enterprises - lessons from the United States, Great Britain and Canada*, edited by Paul W. MacAvoy, W.T. Stanbury, George Yarrow, and Richard J. Zeckhauser (Boston-Dordrecht-London: Kluwer Academic Publishers, 1989), pp. 59-68.

Nankani, Helen B., "Lessons of privatization in developing countries," *Finance & Development*, 1990:2, 43-45.

Nuti, Domenico Mario, "Stabilization and sequencing in the reform of socialist economies" (Washington, DC: The World Bank, paper for seminar on "Managing inflation in socialist economies," Laxenburg, 6-8 March 1990, mimeographed).

Olson, Mancur, *The rise and decline of nations - economic growth, stagflation and social rigidities* (New Haven, CT and London: Yale University Press, 1982).

Paszyński, Marian, "International organizations, economic security and normalization of east-west economic relations," *Development and Peace*, 1988:1, 39-51.

Pejovich, Svetozar, "Innovation and alternative property rights," in *Innovationsprobleme in Ost und West*, edited by Alfred Schüller, Helmut Leipold, and Hannelore Hamel (Stuttgart: Gustav Fischer Verlag, 1983), pp. 41-49.

Pejovich, Svetozar, "Freedom, property rights and innovation in socialism," *Kyklos*, 1987:4, 461-75.

Pejovich, Svetozar, "Liberty, property rights, and innovation in Eastern Europe," *The Cato Journal*, 1989:1, 57-71.

Pejovich, Svetozar, "A property-rights analysis of the Yugoslav miracle," *Annals of the American Academy of Political and Social Sciences*, 1990:1, 123-32.

Pera, Alberto, "Deregulation and privatisation in an economy-wide context," *OECD Economic Studies*, No. 12 (1989), 159-204.

Petrakov, Nikolay Ya., "Tsena - rychag upravleniya," *Ekonomicheskaya gazeta*, 1986:16, 10.

Petrakov, Nikolay Ya., "Planovaya tsena v sisteme upravleniya narodnym khozyaystvom," *Voprosy ekonomiki*, 1987:1, 44-55.

Pinder, John, "Economic integration versus national sovereignty: differences beween Eastern and Western Europe," *Government and Opposition*, 1989:3,

309-26.

Pommerehne, Werner W., "The empirical relevance of comparative institutional analysis," *European Economic Review*, 1990:3, 458-69.

Prowse, Michael, "How to reform eastern Europe, *Financial Times*, 22 June 1990, 21.

Ramanadham, V.V., ed., *Privatisation in the UK* (London-New York: Routledge, 1988a).

Ramanadham, V.V., "The concept and rationale of privatisation," in *Privatisation in the UK*, edited by V.V. Ramanadham (London-New York: Routledge, 1988b), pp. 3-25.

Roth, Wolfgang, "Ein Euro-Plan für Osteuropa," *Wirtschaftsdienst*, 1989:12, 590-2.

Runge, Carlisle F., "The assault on agricultural protectionism," *Foreign Affairs*, 1988:1, 133-50.

Ryan, Alan, "Property," *The new Palgrave - a dictionary of economics, vol. 3* (London: Macmillan, 1987), pp. 1029-31.

Sachs, Jeffrey, "Eastern Europe's economies - what is to be done?" *The Economist*, 13 January 1990, 19-24.

Schroeder, Gertrude E., "Property rights issues in economic reforms in socialist countries," *Studies in Comparative Communism*, 1988:2, 175-88.

Sengupta, Arjun, "The role of the IMF in the international monetary system and the developing countries," *Journal of Development Planning*, No. 17 (1987), 167-82.

Shand, Alexander H., *The capitalist alternative - an introduction to neo-Austrian economics* (New York and London: New York University Press, 1984).

Shiryaev, Yuriy S., "SEV: sovremennaya strategiya ekonomicheskogo i nauchno-tekhnicheskogo sotrudnichestva," *Izvestiya akademii nauk - seriya ekonomicheskaya*, 1988a:1, 3-17.

Shiryaev, Yuriy S., "Aktual'nye problemy internatsionalizacii sotsialisticheskogo vosproizvodstva," *Izvestiya akademii nauk - seriya ekonomicheskaya*, 1988b:6, 15-23.

Shiryaev, Yuriy S., "Sotsialisticheskiy transnatsionalizm i mirovoy rynok," *Kommunist*, 1989:5, 107-15.

Swann, Dennis, *The retreat of the state - deregulation and privatization in the UK and US* (Ann Arbor, MI: The University of Michigan Press, 1988).

Szénási, M., "A dispute on the changes in property rights," *Acta Oeconomica*, 1989:1/2, 165-72.

Tardos, Márton, "Economic organizations and ownership," *Acta Oeconomica*, 1989a:1/2, 17-37.

Tardos, Márton, "Can Hungary's monetary policy succeed," *Eastern European Economics*, 1989b:1, 64-78.

Thompson, David, "Privatisation: Introducing competition, opportunities and constraints," in *Privatisation in the UK*, edited by V.V. Ramanadham (London-New York: Routledge, 1988), pp. 39-58.

Tokareva, Praskov'ja A., ed., *Mnogostoronnee ekonomicheskoe sotrudnichestvo sotsialisticheskikh gosudarstv - sbornik dokumentov* (Moscow: Juridicheskaya literatura, 1972, 2d ed.).

Triffin, Robert, *Europe and the money muddle - from bilateralism to near-convertibility, 1947-1956* (New Haven and London: Yale University Press, 1957.

Tyson, Laura d'Andrea, Sherman Robinson, and Leyla Woods, "Conditionality and adjustment in socialist economies: Hungary and Yugoslavia," in *Economic adjustment and reform in Eastern Europe and the Soviet Union - essays in honor of Franklyn D. Holzman*, edited by Josef C. Brada, Ed A. Hewett, and Thomas A. Wolf (Durham, NC: Duke University Press, 1988), pp. 72-105.

UNECE, Economic Commission for Europe, *Economic Survey of Europe since the war* (United Nations publication No. II.53.II.E.1).

UNECE, Economic Commission for Europe, *Economic Survey of Europe, 1989-1990* (United Nations publication No. E.90.II.E.1).

Válek, Vratislav, "Rada vzájemné hospodářské pomoci: nezbytnost etapizace přestavby," *Svět Hospodářství*, 1988:101, 1.

Vaňous, Jan, "Privatization in Eastern Europe: possibilities, problems, and the role of western capital," *PlanEcon Report*, 1989:38/39.

Vickers, John and Vincent Wright, "The politics of industrial privatisation in Western Europe: an overview," *West European Politics*, 1988:4, 1-30.

Vickers, John and George Yarrow, *Privatization: an economic analysis* (Cambridge, MA: The MIT Press, 1988).

Wagner, Wolfgang, "Auf der Suche nach einer neuen Ordnung in Europa," *Europa-Archiv*, 1989:12, 693-702.

Walters, Alan Rufus, "Privatization: a viable policy option?" *Entrepreneurship and the privatizing of government*, edited by Calvin A. Kent (New York-Westport, CO: Quorum Books, 1987), pp. 35-64.

Wandycz, Piotr S., "Recent traditions of the quest for unity - attempted Polish-Czechoslovak and Yugoslav-Bulgarian confederations 1940-1948," in *The People's Democracies after Prague - Soviet hegemony, nationalism, regional integration?* (Bruges: De Tempel, 1970), pp. 35-93.

Wexler, Imanuel, *The Marshall Plan revisited - the European recovery program in economic perspective* (Westport, CT: Greenwood Press, 1983).

Williamson, John, "International monetary reform: an agenda for the 1980s," in *Towards a new Bretton Woods* (London: Commonwealth Secretariat, 1983), reprinted in *Political economy and international money - selected essays of John Williamson*, edited by Chris Milder (New York: New York University Press, 1987), pp. 212-27.

Winiecki, Jan, "A Marshall Plan for Eastern Europe?" *Swiss Review of World Affairs*, 1989:11, 28-31.

Winiecki, Jan, "Obstacles to economic reform of socialism: a property-rights approach," *Annals of the American Academy of Polical and Social Sciences*, 1990:1, 65-71.

Wolf, Thomas A., *Foreign trade in the centrally planned economy* (Chur: Harwood Academic Publishers, 1988).

Wolf, Thomas A., "Reform, inflation, and adjustment in planned economies," *Finance & Development*, 1990:2, 2-5.

Wood, Robert E., *From Marshall plan to debt crisis - foreign aid and development choices in the world economy* (Berkeley, CA: University of California Press, 1986).

Worswick, George and P.H. Ady, eds., *The British economy, 1945-1950* (Oxford: Clarendon Press, 1952).

Würzen, Dieter von, "Ein Marshall-Plan für Osteuropa?" *Wirtschaftsdienst*, 1989:12, 587-9.

Yarrow, George, "Privatization in theory and practice," *Economic Policy*, No. 2 (1986), 324-77.

Zeckhauser, Richard J. and Murray Horn, "The control and performance of state-owned enterprises," in *Privatization and state-owned enterprises - lessons from the United States, Great Britain and Canada*, edited by Paul W. MacAvoy, W.T. Stanbury, George Yarrow, and Richard J. Zeckhauser (Boston-Dordrecht-London: Kluwer Academic Publishers, 1989), pp. 7-57.

Index